War to the Death

WAR TO THE DEATH

The Sieges of Saragossa, 1808-1809

RAYMOND RUDORFF

MACMILLAN PUBLISHING CO., INC.

NEW YORK

Macmillan Publishing Co., Inc.
866 Third Avenue, New York, N.Y. 10022

Library of Congress Catalog Card Number: 73-21293
First American Edition 1974

Printed in the United States of America

PARA MI QUERIDO AMIGO JOSÉ MARÍA MARTÍN
CALLE JA, DESEANDOLE, JUNTO A SU FAMILIA Y A
SU PAIS, UN SINCERO Y FELIZ FUTURO
AND
TO TIMOTHY NORMAN FOR HIS CONSTANT
INTEREST AND ENCOURAGEMENT.

CONTENTS

*

Illustrations

Prologue

In 1808, Napoleon's armies invaded Spain to place the Emperor's brother, Joseph Bonaparte, upon the Spanish throne and make the country France's obedient satellite. After a nation-wide revolt, the French soldiers found themselves at war with an entire people.

From the beginning of Spanish resistance in May 1808 until the spring of 1809 when British armies joined the Spaniards on the battlefield, the Spanish people were alone as they fought against France's military might. During that time, the heroic resistance of the besieged city of Saragossa became a symbol to the whole country and the whole of Europe. In a country which was generally believed to be in a state of moral and material decay, in which a degenerate royal family allowed itself to be humiliated and deposed, and in which various badly led, ill-organised Spanish armies were routed by Napoleon's generals, the ancient, weakly fortified city of Saragossa endured two bloody sieges. When it was finally forced to capitulate, the French found themselves masters of a city of smoking ruins in which the dead far outnumbered the living.

The sieges and the heroic defence of the city made a tremendous impression on the French soldiers and on public opinion throughout Europe. The character of the defence, in which the entire population took part, was without precedent in the Napoleonic wars or, indeed, in all the European wars of the past century, and set the tone for the whole Spanish resistance for the next five years.

Many French officers paid tribute to the Spanish people's obstinacy and heroism in the great struggle. For General Thiébault, who had served in Spain, the quality of the resistance as shown in the siege of Saragossa meant that:

"Miracles of improvisation were achieved in this country without money, without arms or soldiers, without leaders worthy of the name, almost without fortresses, without a capital and without a government. Moreover, as it was invaded by a hundred and fifty thousand men of an army which had vanquished the whole of Europe, it seemed prostrate at our feet. An unheard-of example was thus offered to the world by a people hitherto ignored by the world and who, with one step, rose from oblivion to heroism, from disdain to the peaks of glory."

Another combatant at Saragossa remarked that:

"The great character displayed in these circumstances by the inhabitants of Saragossa is one of the finest spectacles ever found in the annals of a nation since the sieges of Saguntum and Numantia."

Most of the French soldiers in Spain had probably never heard of the epic resistance against ancient Rome by the inhabitants of the Spanish cities of Saguntum and Numantia who perished among their ruins rather than surrender. But whether they were newly enlisted conscripts or veterans of the armies which had overrun Austria, Germany and Italy, certain disturbing questions must have assailed their minds during the long, ghastly years of the Spanish war.

Who were these terrible people who opposed them so ferociously? What kind of country was this that they had been sent to as "liberators"? What inspired this wild, grim nation which had been slumbering amid its decay for so long behind the rampart of the Pyrenees, whose armies and institutions were a scandal, whose royal family had become an obscene joke, and yet whose people with their savage hatred constituted the most deadly weapons the French had ever had to face? What inspired their suicidal courage—that courage and fanaticism which, as Thiébault related, led a woman in the bombarded streets of Saragossa to drag her small son by the hand towards a smouldering bomb, crying "Come! Let me teach you how to die!"?

PART ONE

REVOLT

I

ON OCTOBER 18, 1807, Napoleon's soldiers entered Spain for the first time, crossing the narrow Bidassoa river which marks the frontier at Irun. Commanded by General Junot, their orders were to march across Spain to invade Portugal and occupy Lisbon. Their passage across Spanish territory had been agreed between the governments in Paris and Madrid although the actual convention sanctioning the troop movements was not signed until nine days later.

As the 25,000 men of the expeditionary corps emerged from the green foot-hills of the Pyrenees and the rich Basque countryside to march across the great expanse of Old Castile, they might have been stepping out of western Europe into some strange, backward, primitive world, at least a hundred and fifty years out of step with the other great nations.

Many of Junot's men were veterans who had campaigned across Europe. In Spain, they saw nothing to suggest the life, the civilised amenities, the pleasures and the compensations for the soldier's risks and hardships that were offered by Italy, Austria, Germany, Holland or Switzerland. Similarly, there was nothing in this new, harsh country to remind the conscripts of their native France. The soldiers now found themselves in a wild, rugged, under-populated, neglected, inhospitable land of great mountain barriers, stony wildernesses, wind-swept plateaux, and yellow sun-scorched plains. Only rarely was the general desolation of the landscape relieved by some huddle of poor houses or hovels, a once mighty castle, or a great church or monastery whose opulence was in striking contrast to the poverty of its surroundings. They were in a country which suffered from ferocious extremes of climate, in which the wine was often crude, and violent in its effects, in which food was often soaked in rancid oil, in which most roads were unspeakably bad and the inns often worse.

The inhabitants of this discouraging country looked no more prepossessing than the natural environment. When the soldiers made their way through the old towns and semi-deserted villages of Castile and

Leon, they found their progress being watched in solemn, unbroken silence by motionless bystanders wreathed in dark capes and clouds of cigar smoke, by peasants who looked like brigands, by ragged beggars, monks who looked like beggars, and black-costumed women who looked like nuns. The ancient towns with their narrow, ill-paved streets were as dour and unwelcoming as the grave, impassive faces of their inhabitants.

Everything the first French soldiers saw in Spain confirmed the accounts published by the few foreign travellers hardy enough to leave the main sea ports of Spain to plunge into the interior. They all agreed that after leaving the thriving and lively sea cities of Barcelona, Santander, Valencia and Cadiz, the main impression made on them by the inland regions was that of decline and decay. Not even the passage of foreign troops over their soil seemed to shake the inhabitants out of their apathy. They were still in the 17th century, unaware that they were about to be flung, without warning, into the 19th century and one of the most violent struggles of modern times.

*   *   *

In 1798, the German traveller Christian Augustus Fischer remarked that "it is not thirty years since a journey to Spain was considered an expedition to the end of the world", and he was quite right. The country had so little to offer the foreign visitor as far as amenities and pleasures were concerned that, by the dawn of the 19th century, it was the least-known country in western Europe—if indeed Spain could be considered part of Europe. Travelling in the peninsula was extremely arduous and slow, the hardships and frustrations facing the foreigner were notorious and he could expect few compensations for his sufferings. Not since the mid-17th century had the country produced one great idea, fashion, artistic or literary work to attract foreigners to its cities, its universities or its royal court. Spain was no part of the Grand Tour and no person of wealth and leisure, in search of civilised pleasures and gentlemanly education, felt the slightest need to go south of the Pyrenees. Those who did go to Spain and explore its great inland provinces were generally liable to be depressed by the experience.

Despite some recent improvements, the roads were still the worst in western Europe. The main method of travel was by horse, mule or carriage, this last pulled by mules and looking a century out of date. There was no regular stage coach system as in other countries or even posts for horse travellers. The inns of Spain were mostly atrocious and universally condemned by foreign travellers for their lack of comforts— and even of necessities—their squalor and the loathsome food served in those that did offer meals. Dirtiness was another characteristic attributed to the whole of Spain by foreigners. And as if all this were not bad enough, most of the natural scenery of the interior was distinguished by its desolation and poverty.

Writer after writer was eloquent in his description of the terrifying harshness of the treeless landscapes of Aragon, Leon, Castile or Estremadura, the deserted or depopulated villages, the great bare expanses of plain, the grim mountain ranges, the barren, stony fields and the primitive state of agriculture. Even the towns had an air of decay and neglect. After Madrid, only two cities counted more than 100,000 inhabitants. Most of Spain's formerly great inland cities seemed to be dying by the end of the 18th century and visitors spoke of their melancholy, lifeless atmosphere. One of the greatest cities of medieval Spain had been Burgos, but its population had dwindled from 40,000 in the 16th century to a mere 9,000 by 1808 and visitors remarked on the huge number of beggars in its streets. Valladolid, once the royal capital and a famous printing and commercial centre, now had a population of only 20,000 instead of its former 100,000. With the exception of the capital, a similar situation was common to every other inland city.

By the time Napoleon's troops began to discover Spain, it seemed as if the only life and vigour left in the country had fled to take refuge in Madrid. The city stood like an oasis in the centre of the peninsula and the wilderness of Castile. Visitors were constantly surprised by the contrast between the depopulation and poverty of the heart of Spain and the elegance and spacious proportions of Madrid's new streets and avenues, palaces and mansions. Much was done to embellish Madrid by Charles III and Charles IV and together with Cadiz it was accounted the cleanest city in Spain. Seen from the heights of San Isidro, as Goya depicted it in a famous work, Madrid had an undeniable air of majesty with its impressive new palace overlooking the Manzanares river, the gardens of the Campo del Moro immediately below, the great church of San Francisco el Grande with its dome, the Retiro Palace and gardens, and the wide, shady avenue of the Prado. It was a lively hodge-podge of a city with its hills, its alternation of wide and spacious streets and narrow alley-ways, its great monastic buildings and mansions side by side with houses of wood, its 17th-century Plaza Mayor, the magnificent avenue of the Alcala, and the royal viaduct leading into the Calle de Segovia. The avenue of the Prado and the square called the Puerta del Sol were famous for their liveliness and for the way in which the population would congregate there—then as now—for the evening stroll or *paseo*.

Madrid was not an important commercial city. Nor was it an intellectual and cultural centre of any great significance, although the royal court had established several institutes and learned academies in the city during the 18th century. What it did have was a population which displayed a vigour, an enjoyment of life and a spirit which were seen to be sadly lacking in the soporific towns of the provinces. The Madrilenes and, in particular, the popular, dandyish figures of the *majo* and *maja* immortalised in Goya's paintings, were reputed to be fiercely proud, quick to anger and contemptuous of foreigners and their ways. Although they were often insufferably vain, complacent and lazy, the people who regarded themselves as the true Madrilenes had a natural tough rebelliousness and courage which made them enemies to be feared. For all their faults, their attitude suggested that energy and will-power had not completely vanished together with other past glories of Castile.

But in Madrid as in the sleepiest provincial town, humblest village or liveliest sea port, foreigners were astonished by the extraordinary number of churches, monastic foundations and ecclesiastics of every condition. The whole of Spain seemed to be "one vast temple". No other Christian country, not even Italy, had so many religious institutions, monuments and shrines. A quarter of all the land which could be cultivated was Church property. Nearly 200,000 of Spain's ten million inhabitants were either members of the Church or else directly dependent upon it. There were some forty different orders of monks, nearly thirty nuns' orders, over two thousand monasteries and more than eleven hundred convents. The numbers of the clergy, the respect they obviously enjoyed at all social levels, their wealth and their influence convinced foreigners that Spain was above all a nation of monks and priests.

Spanish religious fanaticism was notorious. The extent to which Spaniards of all ranks carried religious observance and respect to the clergy never failed to astound foreigners and convinced them that the people had been made effete and servile by such excessive humility before the Church. The Frenchman Bourgoing, who wrote a highly detailed account of Spain at the end of the 18th century, declared that Spanish piety was a mixture of "strength and imbecility" and that "the Spaniards still entertain a respect for the most obscure ecclesiastics which must appear contemptible in the eyes of the most sincere Christians in any other country". Among these "obscure ecclesiastics" were vast numbers of illiterate, itinerant monks and begging friars who swarmed across the country and who were often indistinguishable from the many beggars. Abroad, they were particularly blamed for the degree to which superstition flourished throughout the country and impeded progress.

To the educated European of the Age of Reason, Spain was the stronghold of reactionary and unthinking bigotry and idolatry. Every small town and village seemed to have its precious relics and some saint to be especially venerated. Every foreign traveller had some tale to tell of Spanish superstition. French and English visitors would dwell on the horrors and fiendish tortures of the Spanish Inquisition even though the ritual burnings of the *auto da fé* had become a thing of the past. Given the power of the Inquisition, which remained strong in many ways, and the fear it had inspired, it hardly seemed surprising that so few Spaniards ever questioned the absurdity of their religious mania or ventured an original thought. The general attitude of Frenchmen in Napoleon's time as they looked towards Spain was neatly summed up by General Foy when he stated that the country had become "merely a vast convent in which the Inquisition sat in the porter's lodge to prevent truth from gaining admittance".

While monks and priests were castigated for maintaining superstition, and the Inquisition for stifling free thought and impeding progress, the Spanish Church as a whole was accused of encouraging national idleness and apathy. The laziness of Spaniards was notorious and it was noticed that there were almost as many beggars as churchmen in the country. The Spanish beggar in the streets and the gentleman-idler dreaming of past glories in his decayed mansion became as representative to travellers of the present state of the nation as the proud and warlike Don had been in the days of its greatness.

As might be expected, intellectual and cultural life—such as was known in France, Germany and England—suffered greatly. The monotony of social life and the lack of amenities in the inland cities with the exception of Madrid were deplored by foreigners. There were hardly any theatres, balls, parties, operas, concerts, debating societies, literary or artistic meeting places. Amusements were of a strictly traditional nature such as bull-fights, local songs and dances. The main culture in the country was a popular one, based on folklore and the Church. Attempts to import foreign entertainments and art were doomed to failure. The Spaniards' lack of interest in the ideas, customs and achievements of other countries was conspicuous. Mentally, the whole nation seemed to have fallen asleep.

In view of this spiritual torpor which appeared to reign throughout the country, foreign observers wondered whether the chief qualities once attributed to the Spanish people had vanished or become greatly diminished. Once, Spain had been a proud, violent and jealous nation. Spaniards had left their homes to dominate half Europe and conquer a vast empire overseas. Now, they had withdrawn into themselves, placidly contemplating their heroic past. As they lost their former martial vigour, their energy and thirst for adventure, a general relaxation of manners was noticed throughout the country by the second half of the 18th century.

The Spanish people, as Napoleon prepared to take over the peninsula, now appeared curiously pacific and mild-tempered. Despite the fierce, burning, concentrated religious fanaticism which still survived and the previous ferocity of the Inquisition, there had come about a free and easy relationship between clergy and people which surprised foreigners. Few visitors were in danger of being molested or suspected for their non-Catholic beliefs even though a Spaniard might still get into trouble with the Inquisition if suspected of heresy. Otherwise, it was noticed that Spaniards had become more tolerant and flexible. There was less violence, executions were few, tortures were no longer practised in the dungeons of the Inquisition and, although brigands still made the countryside dangerous, the cities were generally free from violent crime. Social behaviour had become freer. Foreigners remarked that the traditional fierce jealousy of the Spanish male had largely disappeared and they were often astonished by the emancipated manners of Spanish women in the towns.

According to the French traveller Laborde, who also described the state of Spain at the beginning of the 19th century in three detail-crammed volumes, the times had greatly altered in the country and "women are now freer, men more open". However, the typical image presented by the Spaniard to foreign eyes was that of "a man proudly wrapped up in his laziness". Idleness, procrastination and excessive complacency were now held to be the dominant traits in the Spanish character and those most responsible for the abject state of the nation. Only in the maritime regions, in Catalonia and the Basque country did the people seem to display any real energy and capacity for hard work.

But although they themselves were often the object of fierce Spanish prejudices and a general xenophobia which pervaded the country, the French and other foreigners still found much to admire in the Spanish character. Such things as dignity, individualism, lack of material pre-occupations and an innate, widespread democratic sense were frequently noted. General Foy wrote that "no nation, under a despotism, has preserved so well as they have done the consciousness of the dignity of man". Frenchmen who remembered the *ancien régime* and took pride in their Revolution were surprised to see the way in which Spanish beggars and noblemen, bourgeois and peasants would treat each other with such easy but always polite familiarity.

As it became obvious that Napoleon was about to include Spain in his scheme of things, the French naturally wondered whether the Spaniards could offer capable, determined resistance if the need arose. Spain had once been the most warlike nation in Europe and her soldiers had won renown for their fury and courage. But, since the War of the Spanish Succession and with the exception of a few minor conflicts such as that with England and France recently, Spain had been at peace for most of the 18th century.

General Foy was one of many Frenchmen who doubted whether the Spaniards could repeat the deeds of their ancestors since "courage is like love; it stands in need of food and stimulus; a long peace, a state of topographical insulation, and the lethargic conduct of the government, had almost extinguished the warlike spirit in a nation which had once filled the world with its renown". Moreover, the submission of the people to their bad governments and hidebound Church made a bad impression abroad. How could a people have retained their old warlike virtues and valour when they gave every sign of being passively content with their condition? Their country was in abject decline, it was the most primitive and backward in western Europe, it had hardly any competent leaders and its Church hindered all thought and progress and still there was no sign that the people were disposed to revolt against their masters who had reduced them to such a sorry state. As Foy concluded, in his history of the Peninsular War: "The soil of Spain

was not in a state calculated to receive and nourish into life the seeds of
the spirit of liberty."

What Foy and others did not point out was that, in their own way,
the Spanish people of the time *did* feel that they had the liberty which
counted the most for them. They were still free to preserve their most
prized possession: their unique and uncompromising national identity.
Were this to be threatened, then the nation which seemed the most
apathetic in Europe could prove the most violent in its reactions.

The time when Spain would be called upon to show the world what
remained of her national spirit was drawing near. But to most foreigners
and, above all, to Napoleon, conditions in Spain appeared to have
reached a state when the only hope for the country was for a more
vigorous and forward-looking race to take over its destinies. The
decline so evident in Spain's countryside and towns was equalled if not
surpassed by the appalling decadence of her monarchy, armed forces,
administration and intellectual life. As far as could be seen, there was
not one man in Spanish public life who could lead the nation back to
greatness.

*   *   *

If the general image which foreigners received of the country was a
depressing one, it was made even worse by the appearance and
behaviour of its royal family and prime minister.

The Spanish people might be complacent and blind as far as most
defects in their country were concerned, but they were aware and
resentful of the depths to which their monarchy and government had
sunk. The King, the Queen and the man to whom they had confided the
destinies of the realm were popularly known to their subjects as "the
goat", "the whore", and "the ruffian". The Bourbon King, Charles IV,
and his Queen, Maria Luisa, were the most incapable royal couple on
any European throne at the time. As if this were not bad enough, they
had made a self-seeking, corrupt nonentity into the most powerful man
in Spain. It was also widely known that the King was constantly
deceived by his wife, and made himself ridiculous by fawning upon her
lover—the royal favourite and prime minister, Manuel Godoy, Duke of
Alcudia.

Few royal families have ever looked more grotesque. One glance
was enough to show that Charles IV was completely unfit to rule. His
appearance and that of his wife and family have been recorded with

brutal honesty by Goya in the great group portrait which hangs in the Prado Museum today. It is a devastating illustration of moral and physical degeneracy.

When visitors were granted an audience with the King they saw a middle-aged man with a heavy, lumpish build, a sharply receding forehead, a nose too long, a mouth too narrow, coarse features, a turned-up chin, a look of gentle astonishment in his eyes, and a good-natured but foolish smile on his lips. He looked exactly what he was: a wellmeaning buffoon. He had good intentions always, he was naïve to the point of imbecility, ignorant, uneducated and completely unable to understand the realities of the age in which he lived.

Charles's wife, Maria Luisa, was his first cousin, the granddaughter of Louis XV of France, and had been born in Parma. Although she was aged forty-nine at the time of Goya's painting, she dressed with exaggerated coquetry which did nothing to redeem her ugliness. She might have been the model for one of Goya's witches or procuresses with her grotesque *décolleté*, her raddled features, excessively long nose, badly shaped though sensual mouth with its ill-fitting false teeth, her bird-like face and glittering wanton eyes. Together with the innocentlooking younger children, the adolescent heir to the throne, Ferdinand, the heavy-featured Don Antonio, the King's brother, and the harpy-like, grimacing Maria Josefa, the King's sister, they made an ensemble that was as pathetic as it was repulsive. With the exception of the Queen, whose face showed a certain cunning, the members of the royal family all displayed the same kind of pathetic incomprehension and naïvety that we find in photographs of the Russian Imperial family on the eve of the Revolution which destroyed them. It was Spain's misfortune to have them as rulers at a time when the most powerful warrior in Europe was busily overturning one European monarchy after another as part of the Napoleonic grand design.

Their behaviour was no better than their appearance. Charles IV's mental deficiencies seemed proof that the mental degeneracy which had afflicted the last Hapsburg Kings of Spain was repeating itself in his person. One of his brothers, Don Felipe, had been confined as a lunatic, and Don Antonio was little better than an idiot whose chief occupations were chopping down trees and preparing his own meals in the royal kitchens. Charles himself, aged fifty-two in 1800, had not one original idea in his head. He had been brought up strictly by his autocratic father, Charles III, who treated him as a fool, and when he succeeded to the throne in 1788 he knew next to nothing about affairs of state, foreign policy, his country or his people. He had never been abroad and during the whole twenty years of his reign he only made three journeys in his kingdom, twice to Badajoz near the Portuguese frontier, and once to Barcelona. Apart from these excursions, he divided his time with his family between the palace in Madrid and the royal residences near the capital at Aranjuez, the Escorial, and La Granja in the Guadarrama mountains. Like his father, he had a mania for regulating his daily life with mechanical precision and, under his reign, the court continued to be the dullest in Europe. There were no balls, no cheerful parties or galas, operas or plays. No fashions were set at the court, not an idea, not a creative innovation ever came from the royal family. Conversation was stilted, the arts were generally ignored (although Goya was made Court Painter and highly esteemed), and most of the courtiers and nobles who surrounded the King were equally ignorant and mainly preoccupied with their rank, their precedence and memories of the former glories of their families. Court life consisted of attending Mass, council meetings, stilted dinners, card games and a little music, which Charles adored. It was an enclosed, complacent society without the slightest cosmopolitan flavour. Charles IV shared his father's passion for hunting and horses when he was not playing with clockwork machinery or indulging his passion for the violin and cards. He was out in all weathers massacring game on his well-stocked estates. His simple-mindedness was legendary. One of his amusements was to display his lavish fountains and water-works in the grounds of his palace of San Ildefonso at La Granja where he never tired of playing practical jokes on his entourage and visitors by drenching them with water. Apart from such skittish behaviour, which courtiers and visitors were duty bound to witness, he was completely abstemious and always faithful to his wife, never suspecting her infidelities.

Despite his faults and failings, Charles IV was not resented by his subjects. It was the behaviour of the Queen which brought the court into disrepute. She was immoral and well-known to be such. The need to conceal, as far as possible, her amorous liaisons and intrigues created an atmosphere of dissimulation and hypocrisy to which only the King remained impervious. In 1800, the French ambassador was so appalled that he told his master, Talleyrand, that court life in Spain was "debauchery in all its ugliness; it is the most revolting scandal without any urbanity, any delicatesse, any modesty, either in private or in public.

The splendour of royalty is tarnished by this exterior of debauchery and shameless vice".

While Maria Luisa devoted herself to deceiving her husband, her eldest son, born in 1786, spent most of his time sulking, praying and plotting. Ferdinand, Prince of the Asturias, heir to the throne, was as devoid of culture and intellect as his father. He was a moral weakling and had been brought up as a narrow-minded bigot by his ecclesiastical tutor, Canon Escoiquiz, who failed to give his pupil even a minimal education. Ferdinand had no friends, he was dour and solitary, showed no interest in normal amusements and employed what energy he possessed in hating his mother for her scandalous behaviour and in an even deeper loathing for her lover, Godoy.

Manuel Godoy was Spain's real ruler. Both the King and the Queen adored him to distraction, and the cuckolded Charles depended upon him as an oracle of wisdom. Even after Godoy was found to be having an affair with the daughter of an army officer, the King showed favour to him by marrying him off to a royal cousin, the Countess of Chinchon. While Godoy continued to enjoy the royal favour and resumed his on-and-off affair with the Queen, his unfortunate wife's aversion to him grew to such an extent that the Duchesse d'Abrantès remarked that "it was beyond hatred".

Few royal favourites have been so notorious or reached so high a position in so short a time. Godoy's spectacular rise to power was unprecedented in Spanish history. He was born in the province of Estremadura and began his career as a member of the Royal Body-guard, in which his elder brother was already serving. In 1788, when he was only twenty-one, his good looks and pleasant, easy manner brought him to the attention of the amorous Queen. In a short time, he became her lover and Maria Luisa had little difficulty in persuading her husband that Godoy was suited to the highest positions in the govern-ment. By 1792, he was a grandee of Spain, Duke of Alcudia, and prime minister. After bringing to an end a two-year war between Spain and France on terms disadvantageous to his country, he was given the title of "Prince of the Peace". He was out of office for a period, but then returned to power when his adoring master piled further favours upon him. By 1808, he was commander-in-chief of the army and navy and one of the wealthiest men in Spain. He was also the most detested, nicknamed the "sausage maker" (*El Choricero*) since the main industry of his native province was the raising of pigs.

Godoy was reputed to be corrupt, greedy and sensual. His success had gone completely to his head and his casual behaviour in the royal presence astounded foreigners such as the Duchesse d'Abrantès who once found him insolently sprawling on a sofa, playing with a curtain tassel, when she was admitted into the Queen's chamber. Diplomats and ambassadors were puzzled by him. Some thought him a complete nonentity while others agreed that he had a certain amount of intelligence and ability. It was noted to his credit that some of his attitudes were positively liberal and that he encouraged the arts and sciences, as well as trying to reduce the power of the Church and abolish the Inquisition. But the fact remained that as long as Godoy was the pampered, powerful protégé of the King and Queen, the prestige of the Crown was irremediably compromised.

Despite all his faults, however, Godoy did attempt to continue a movement towards progress which had started during the reign of the previous king. Charles III had been even uglier than his son but his was an intelligent ugliness and he had been one of the ablest rulers that Spain had known for a very long time. A realist, he had been determined to halt Spain's economic decline, to modernise the country and bring it closer to the other great nations of Europe. In fact, he was one of the enlightened absolutists typical of the 18th century. Charles followed the example of Louis XIV by stripping the nobility of all political power and attracting them to his court where they were reduced to the status of puppets. In the last year of his reign, the Spanish aristocracy consisted of 119 grandees, 535 noblemen with old Castilian titles, and nearly half a million *hidalgos* or gentlemen of rank who were not supposed to work, who avoided all intellectual activities and were obsessed by their pedigrees. While the nobles vegetated at court or in the provinces, Charles III gave the most important government posts to able men of the middle classes. Only one prime minister—the Count of Aranda—was an aristocrat. Power was centralised around the court, and the ancient provincial assemblies or *Cortes*, which had once safeguarded regional rights and privileges, were no longer summoned to meet. Even the Church, though it was still extremely powerful at the end of the 18th century, had seen its influence curtailed by Charles III, and only the King's death had saved it from losing many of its territorial possessions.

As a result of Charles III's energetic efforts and the ability of some capable and progressive ministers, trade, industry and the country's decaying economy began to revive. New scientific establishments and academies of learning were founded. Madrid was given handsome new buildings, new roads and canals were built, reforms were made in the universities and foreigners with special skills were invited to settle in depressed, underpopulated areas. Had Charles III lived longer, the economic and political decline of Spain might have been halted and the structures of civil administration been overhauled. A small but growing middle class supported the King's measures and the mass of the population remained unstirred by the royal offensive against the Church's temporal power since religion itself was never challenged. Civic spirit and a sense of responsibility were encouraged by the establishment of patriotic societies called "Friends of the Country" whose members were recruited on a strictly democratic basis. By 1808, there were over sixty such societies throughout Spain and they were active in promoting agricultural and industrial improvements and innovations.

Unfortunately, although Spain's economy was beginning to show signs of growth after the many years of stagnation, much of the good that Charles III had accomplished was undone in the reign of his incompetent successor. Godoy had some sincere intentions to continue the policy of progress but he was amateurish in his methods. His high-handed manner and unpopularity repelled able men who might have helped him. By 1800, Spain's economy and administration were again in a state of chaos while the Church and the people continued to show resistance to ideas involving change and innovation.

To modernise Spain, it was necessary to overcome Spanish complacency and traditional prejudices. It was a formidable task. The majority of ecclesiastics and the common people looked upon all progressive measures and ideas as being un-Spanish and even anti-Spanish. The general, conservative attitude throughout the country was that it was more laudable, more patriotic and nobler for Spaniards to maintain their way of life than to be modern-minded. Why should Spaniards try to be like other Europeans when to be Spanish was the greatest privilege and good fortune on earth? Nonetheless, a few brave spirits in Spain did declare war on reaction and apathy in their country.

Foreigners were not alone in deploring Spanish ignorance and self-satisfaction. The Benedictine monk and university professor, Dom Benito Geronimo Feijoo, was the outstanding intellectual and scholar of 18th-century Spain. In his many books and essays he stated that science and increased knowledge did not necessarily clash with religious faith, he advocated progress, denounced bigotry and rigid adherence to past traditions. Although he became a highly controversial figure, he won royal favour and his most important works were read by the more enlightened Spaniards. Indeed, in the second half of the 18th century, intellectual life began to revive in Spain, even though it still remained extremely restricted. Charles III realised that if Spain were to prosper she would have to break out of her mental torpor and isolation and, with the support of able ministers, he encouraged the distribution of foreign scientific books throughout the country. But these foreign treatises and textbooks on the arts and sciences were inevitably accompanied by philosophical and political works which conservatives and the Church considered to be un-Spanish and dangerous to the moral health of the people.

The Inquisition continued to play a powerful part in Spanish life and in its own way reflected the xenophobia and horror of foreign innovations which travellers had found among the people. Although its burnings and tortures now belonged to the past, it remained a self-appointed police force of morals and thought, and laid down the law in art, literature and science. The Inquisition regularly banned books and, in its prohibitions, went much further than the government in exercising censorship. It had its own index of forbidden works, separate from that of the Vatican. The 1790 edition ran to 305 quarto pages printed in small type in double columns. The works of Montesquieu, Locke, Rousseau, Voltaire, Erasmus, the astronomical and physical studies of Tycho Brahe and Kepler, and the legal treatises of Grotius could all be found in its pages.

Towards the end of the 18th century, many of the better educated Spaniards were defying the Inquisition's rulings. The few Spaniards who travelled abroad brought books back with them and foreigners resident in Spain spread some of their own countries' ideas. The penalties meted out by the Inquisition were usually mild except in cases when real heresy was suspected. In 1778, a royal minister, Pedro Olavide, was sentenced by the Inquisition to be confined in a monastery for eight years for having allowed his mind to be "corrupted" through correspondence with Voltaire and Rousseau, and not even the King was able to intervene. Later, another talented minister, Jovellanos, asked the Inquisition for permission to import some foreign scientific books and was told that as there were already sufficient such books by Spanish writers, there was no need to bring in any by foreign heretics.

Ironically, he was imprisoned from 1801 to 1807 through incurring the enmity of the same Godoy who was trying to fight the influence of the Inquisition. Several of Goya's etchings reveal the repulsion it inspired in free minds at the time.

The chief and nearest source of foreign ideas was France and it was to this country that progressive Spaniards first turned. An interest in French ideas led to a limited fashion for the French way of life and culture among the small intellectual minority. In 1800, French was the only foreign language to have become even moderately popular. Private schools opened in Madrid to teach French, French fashions in dress spread among the dandies and in high society. Laborde noted that in the cities the Spanish "ridicule France, yet adopt its cookery, its dances, its fashions . . . they wish to imitate its elegance". But such Francomania remained mostly superficial. In 1805, Crusy commented that "this fashion for Frenchification which has spread throughout the whole of Europe has made only mediocre progress in Spain and despite the very great superabundance of Frenchmen who have been inundating this country since the peace of 1795, the only alterations to be seen are in clothing". In spite of protests by priests and moralists, a growing number of better educated and wealthy Spaniards preferred to discard traditional Spanish clothing for French wigs, laces, suits, hats and ruffles. In 1797, Fischer noticed how the elegant ladies in Madrid society had forsaken their traditional veils and wide petticoats for the neo-classical fashions which had been launched in Paris. When the Duchesse d'Abrantès arrived in Madrid in 1805, she found that Queen Maria Luisa had decreed that only the French style was to be worn at court receptions in the evenings and "if you arrived in a salon in a *basquina* and a *mantilla* you were looked at as though you were out of your senses".

The outbreak of the French Revolution had been a great setback to the spread of foreign ideas in Spain and to attempts at reform. The downfall of the French monarchy and the excesses of the Terror confirmed and strengthened the Inquisition and the mass of the people in in their view that French ideas in particular and foreign ideas in general were dangerous to Spain. The government, led by the energetic and progressively-minded Count Floridablanca, reacted with horror to events in France and did its best to keep the entire Spanish nation ignorant of the Revolution by imposing the severest censorship. Floridablanca was replaced by the Count of Aranda who was sympathetic towards some French rationalist ideas and philosophers. Both he and his successor, Godoy, tried to negotiate with the French revolutionaries on behalf of the French royal family, but they were unsuccessful. The execution of Louis XVI in January 1793 outraged Spanish opinion and war was declared.

The attitude of the Spanish masses and their enthusiasm for the war astonished foreigners. Spain was flooded with horror stories about the French Revolutionaries and the Terror. The clergy preached a national crusade against the French people, who were described as dangerous, blood-lusting atheists, the enemies of all religion and order in the world, who had allowed their minds to be perverted by Voltaire and the devil. Spanish xenophobia reached a peak in hatred of France and everything French. The general attitude among the mass of the people was that France was a country which had surrendered to the Devil and total insanity. Such, thundered the bishops, was the inevitable result of allowing the spread of terrible, godless, perverted ideas. The nature of these ideas was never explained to the people, but bishops, priests and monks joined in urging their congregations to fight for religion, their king and country against a people "without king, without law, without God". While monks went from village to village preaching the crusade against the godless regicides, priests and bishops whipped up anti-French hatred even further. Both ecclesiastical and secular authors poured out torrents of anti-French abuse, the champion of this form of invective being probably the Bishop of Santander who wrote a sermon over two hundred pages long. There were vicious anti-French riots in Valencia where the six-hundred-odd French colony only just escaped with their lives, and Frenchmen were murdered in Barcelona.

But popular fervour could not compensate for deficiencies in military organisation, equipment and skill. After a few early successes, the Spanish armies were defeated and driven back, and by 1795, the French had advanced as far as the river Ebro. Godoy was obliged to sue for peace.

By 1795 the Terror in France had subsided and fears of a French-inspired revolution in Spain gradually receded although the government increased its vigilance. In spite of the horrors and excesses of the Revolution, a small number of Spaniards still urged the need for reforms in their country and were sympathetic towards France. The struggle continued between the reactionaries and the reformers many of whom were known as the *afrancesados* (the "Frenchified"). Far-seeing

Spaniards, such as Jovellanos, realised that events in France in no way lessened the need for an effort to drag Spain out of her decline and isolation. New voices were raised against the abject state of Spain. A number of anonymous pamphlets began to circulate in Madrid, attributing the country's troubles to the ignorance of the people and the vices of the clergy. One of the most famous of these tracts was said to have been written by Jovellanos himself; it appeared in 1796, and was secretly circulated among Spanish intellectuals for several years. Entitled *Pan y Toros*, it was a violent attack on Spanish life and institutions. The anonymous author stated that he saw Spain in a state of depopulation, with its industry in decay, its villages in ruins, its people debased, and its administration in chaos. He attacked the Church for failing to fulfil its real mission, and the mania for bullfighting as a symbol of the people's apathy and frivolity. He mocked national complacency and scorn for foreign ideas, and stated that while Spain lulled herself to sleep the rest of the world mocked her.

In the following year, the young poet Manuel José Quintana published a well-known ode dedicated to Juan de Padilla, the heroic leader of the Castilians against royal tyranny in 1520. The people were in chains, bound by tyranny and bigotry. Quintana therefore called upon the country, "sunk in shameful dreams" and derided by the world, to rise again and make the tyrants tremble on their thrones. Godoy's rapid success and his growing unpopularity, coupled with the royal scandals, led to other anonymous libels and pamphlets which even reached the court. And, although Goya enjoyed royal protection, many of his etchings in the *Caprichos* series, published in 1797, were filled with references to the intrigues and rivalries of the time, as well as to social abuses and the corruption of power in his country.

The French Revolution and the short war had two very important consequences in Spain. First, they strengthened the already close ties between the lower ranks of the clergy and the mass of the people. The patriot priest and the village volunteer had stood together as absolute equals and as comrades in the struggle against the enemy. The Church was a tremendously powerful propaganda machine which could arouse the nation to a fervour, mobilise it against the enemy and keep its morale high. The second consequence was an unprecedented hatred for the French.

Anti-French feeling was already strong before the war. Although Charles III became popular and respected despite his French ancestry, although the two countries had been allies more than once, and although the French were by far the largest foreign contingent living in Spain (27,000 French heads of family were numbered in the 1791 census), they were also the most unpopular.

Hatred of the French was partly due to the continuous wars between the two countries in the 16th and 17th centuries. The Aragonese and Catalans blamed France for the loss of their old privileges. The Castilians accused the French of being godless, frivolous and dictatorial. In 1772, Richard Twiss observed that "there are no nations which so cordially hate each other as the French and the Spanish". Twenty years later, Gallophobia became part of the national creed. Concerning the attitude of the Spanish clergy towards France, Fischer observed that "it seems to be a part of the system adopted by the Spanish [ecclesiastical] hierarchy to oppose that formidable nation by fanaticism itself". After the war, Fischer visited Catalonia and found that "the Catalonian piques himself on a mortal hatred to the French . . . their antipathy towards the French exceeds all that can be conceived". In the Basque country, adjacent to France, "the Biscayans have in general a kind of national hatred for the French which, since the late events, has increased among this unenlightened people even to horror, and the very name of Frenchman has become a proscription or a stigma of infamy which they accompany with stones. Heretics as they are, the English are preferred". Provinces further away from the French border did not lag behind in this concentrated hatred for France and all French innovations. Other visitors confirmed Fischer's remarks. Ten years later such hatred was undiminished and ready to explode again into savage violence under the slightest provocation. But it was precisely during the twelve years which followed the end of the Franco–Spanish war that Spain's detested prime minister and despised King were seen by their subjects to be tying the destinies of their country to those of France. They were humiliating the national pride by making fawning overtures to the French tyrant and allowing him to send his armies onto Spanish soil.

*   *   *

During the reign of Charles III, Spain had been France's ally. Under Charles IV and Godoy, Spain became France's satellite. As the Spanish Bourbon Kings were of French descent, there were special ties between the two kingdoms, consecrated in what was called the Family Compact.

After the signing of the peace of Basle, Godoy resumed the traditional policy of friendship with France. He had personal reasons for doing so for he was aware of his unpopularity and was anxious to make a powerful friend abroad. After negotiations, a treaty was signed in 1796 at the royal palace of San Ildefonso. Spain agreed to give military support to France and, if necessary, to take action against Portugal who was stubbornly refusing to shut her ports to English shipping during Franco-British hostilities.

In 1798, Godoy lost favour at court, probably because of his arrogant behaviour and his affair with an officer's daughter, Josefa Tudo, which angered Maria Luisa. He was replaced by a minister who became even more unpopular because of his hostility to the Church and his determination to abolish the Inquisition. Soon Godoy returned to power and found the court filled with admiration for Napoleon Bonaparte, now First Consul of France, and regarded by the King and Queen as the restorer of religion, order and, eventually, the French monarchy.

Godoy did not delay in proclaiming his own strong attachment to Bonaparte. In 1801, he had the opportunity to prove it by making war on Portugal, who still maintained her friendship with the British. After a short and almost bloodless campaign, Godoy negotiated with Portugal instead of occupying the country as Bonaparte had wished. With the connivance of Bonaparte's younger brother, Lucien, then ambassador in Spain, Godoy signed a peace treaty. Portugal was forced to pay reparations, the two men profited handsomely from the deal, and Napoleon was furious.

Two years later, a new convention was signed in Paris by which the Spanish government agreed to pay France an annual subsidy of 72 million francs so long as the latter was at war with England. In return, Spain was supposed to be able to remain neutral if she wished. At the end of the following year, after English naval attacks on Spanish shipping, Napoleon successfully pushed Spain into open war with the hope that her fleet would help him clear the Channel for his projected invasion of England. The sole result was the defeat of the French and Spanish fleets by Nelson and Collingwood at Trafalgar in October 1805.

After the destruction of the Spanish fleet, which made him even more unpopular, Godoy began to waver in his policy towards France. Despite Spain's worsening financial position, he had paid huge subsidies to his powerful ally and he had received nothing in return. The situation at the court threatened his own position and the people were totally alienated. The royal family was split into factions. The heir to the throne, Ferdinand, detested Godoy. Ferdinand's wife, Maria Antonieta, was the daughter of the King of Naples who had been expelled by the French, was strongly pro-English and hated her mother-in-law. While Godoy, the Queen and Ferdinand intrigued against one another and Napoleon pondered how to use Spain to his best advantage, Ferdinand became increasingly popular. The people learned of his detestation of Godoy, deplored his treatment by his ignoble parents and romantically looked upon him as the future saviour of his country's honour.

While the French ambassador in Spain was sending back reports on the decadent court, Godoy was busy intriguing in Paris through his private envoy. His main aim was to obtain the highest possible price for his alliance with Napoleon, whose coronation as Emperor had been joyfully acclaimed by Charles IV and Maria Luisa. Disappointingly for Godoy, Napoleon's attitude towards Spain was that of a powerful superior. Spain was obliged to send troops to help Napoleon hold down his occupied territories in Italy. As for a plan put forward by Godoy in which he suggested the division of Portugal, with part going to him as his own principality—not a word was forthcoming from Paris.

In 1806, a new anti-French coalition was being formed on the Continent by Russia, Austria, Prussia and Sweden. No longer certain of French prospects and anxious to be on the winning side, Godoy then made a huge blunder. He whipped up a war scare in Spain, ordered conscription and the mobilisation of reserves, and asked for patriotic financial donations and horses for the cavalry—all without first obtaining the royal assent. He published a resounding proclamation which suggested that Spain was on the brink of war and urged his fellow countrymen to be prepared to cross swords "with our enemies". The identity of the "enemy" was not made clear but the French embassy in Madrid correctly reported that public opinion was convinced that it could only be France.

No sooner had Godoy made his appeal to the nation than news reached him of Napoleon's great military victory over the forces of the Coalition at Jena. Godoy panicked. He unconvincingly stated that he had only ordered mobilisation because he thought hostilities against England were imminent and sent a fulsome letter to Napoleon. It was an extraordinary document. After Godoy had congratulated Napoleon on his "unheard-of exploits", he shamelessly declared that "my sincerity, which has never been denied, authorises me to beseech your

Imperial and Royal Majesty to show me that esteem which it has always accorded to me". After complaining that hostile courtiers had spread the false rumour that he was raising an army against France, Godoy thoroughly abased himself by concluding: "I hope that your Imperial and Royal Majesty will have the goodness to see these considerations as the result of my absolute devotion to his august person and as a sincere proof of my highest consideration for the talents, so sublime in every way, with which nature has made your Imperial and Royal Majesty the most perfect example of a hero without equal in history."

Even allowing for the flowery diplomatic language of the time, this was going too far. Napoleon had already mistrusted his unreliable and conceited ally; now he despised him. His agents and ambassadors confirmed his worst suspicions. There could be no question of treating a country led by such a man as an equal partner in an alliance. While still keeping Godoy in a state of hopefulness that he might make personal profit out of the alliance, Napoleon put his grovelling protestation of loyalty to the test by demanding that he send 14,000 of Spain's best soldiers to Hamburg as reinforcements for the Imperial forces. The move also had the effect of weakening Spanish military power should Godoy ever decide once more to turn against France. If Napoleon's opinion of the Spanish monarchy and government was low after Godoy's abject behaviour in 1806, it sank even lower after Ferdinand joined his parents and Godoy in seeking favours from France. Ferdinand's wife had just died after a short, painful illness—poisoned, it was wrongly rumoured in the intrigue- and hate-ridden court. After rejecting Godoy's impudent suggestion that he should marry the favourite's sister-in-law, Ferdinand was persuaded by his supporters at court and the ambitious, intriguing French ambassador to write to Napoleon, asking him for a French princess as a bride.

On October 11, 1807, Ferdinand sent Napoleon a disgustingly obsequious letter. After briefly alluding to his unhappy position in the court, the royal heir declared that he was "full of hope of finding the most powerful protection in the magnanimous generosity of your Imperial Majesty and I am determined not only to show my heart's sentiments towards his august person but also to unburden myself in his bosom as though it were that of the tenderest of fathers". He claimed that Charles IV was being misled by wicked people and besought the honour of marriage with some princess of the French Imperial family as the best means for binding the two countries together, assuring

Napoleon that the Emperor would always find him "the most grateful and devoted of sons".

On October 27, Ferdinand, together with some of his supporters, including his scheming tutor Escoiquiz, was arrested for high treason after Godoy had set spies on him. Ferdinand's papers were searched and found to contain drafts of letters in which he begged his father to dismiss Godoy. There were furious scenes between Ferdinand and his parents and although there was no proof of real treason, Charles IV was persuaded—probably by Godoy—to issue an extraordinary public proclamation in which he accused his son of plotting to dethrone him. To the Spanish people, who knew nothing of Ferdinand's letter to Napoleon, it seemed further proof of the way in which the infamous trio —Charles, Maria Luisa, Godoy—were determined to persecute the poor Prince.

Ferdinand's subsequent despicable behaviour was also unknown to the people. He confessed that he had written to Napoleon behind his father's back, tried to throw all blame for his plotting upon his dead wife because of her known hatred for Godoy, readily supplied the names of his accomplices and begged for forgiveness. On November 5 he was pardoned and wrote a whining letter of repentance to his father. Godoy had thought it wise to intervene on the Prince's behalf and a hypocritical reconciliation took place between the two men who embraced before the royal parents. Charles IV issued another proclamation in which he stated that he had forgiven his son and would restore him to his good graces once he had shown himself to be a reformed character. Preparations for the trial of the accomplices were still going ahead when Napoleon intervened. Speaking as a master expecting immediate obedience, he formally forbade any mention to be made at the trial of himself or Ferdinand's letter or the French ambassador. Shortly afterwards, in a reply to a letter from Charles IV, he went so far as contemptuously to deny that he even knew of the existence of the Prince of the Asturias.

The "affair of the Escorial", as the incident of Ferdinand's arrest and accusation came to be known, merely completed the picture of decadence offered by the quarrelling royal family in Spain. It strengthened Napoleon's conviction that the Spanish Bourbons were worse than useless as allies. While his adviser, Talleyrand, urged him to dethrone them once and for all, Napoleon began to take other, practical measures to ensure for himself control of Spain whenever it became

necessary. In August 1807, he began to mass troops in southern France
near the border with Spain. They were to be used against Portugal if
that country would not comply with France's request that she close
her ports to British shipping and seize all British merchandise in the
country by September 1. A first expeditionary corps, under Marshal
Junot, was ordered to prepare to march on Lisbon. Naturally, it would
have to cross Spanish territory.

As Spain was such an unreliable ally, it was in Napoleon's interests
to have a large force in that country, ready to intervene as circumstances
dictated. He had already sent French spies to Spain and they reported
back to him on roads, fortresses, garrisons, the political and economic
situation and the mood of the public. Although he knew the Spanish
army to be in a very poor state, and had made Godoy weaken it still
further by sending many of the best troops to serve under France,
Napoleon still had to solve the problem of moving large masses of
troops into Spain without arousing suspicion and provoking resistance.
But Godoy helped him.

Godoy had never ceased hoping that Napoleon might prove a
generous friend to him and had been conducting secret negotiations
with the French government through his own intermediary, a man
called Izquierdo, who was director of the botanical gardens in Madrid.
The result of the talks in Paris was the Treaty of Fontainebleau. Portugal
was to be conquered and divided into three parts, one of which would
go to Godoy as his own principality. Other articles in the treaty guaran-
teed Charles IV's European possessions and gave him the title "Emperor
of the Two Americas", but the most significant article of the agreement
was a secret convention added to it. 28,000 French troops were to be
allowed to enter Spain and proceed to Portugal, together with an equal
number of Spanish troops. Another 40,000 French troops would assemble
at Bayonne near the border, ready to cross with the approval of the
Spanish government should the English land in Portugal.

Nine days before the treaty was signed, French infantry, cavalry,
artillery and baggage wagons began to pour across the Spanish frontier.
Less than a month later, after the treaty had been ratified in Spain and
Godoy had sent an obsequious letter of thanks to Napoleon, a second
French force of 25,000 men, called the "2nd Corps of Observation of
the Gironde", under the command of General Dupont marched over
the border, and began to cross the Pyrenees and occupy the chief
towns in north-west Spain. While Junot moved into Portugal, Dupont's

force began to advance southwards, into the heart of Spain, and new armies were being formed in south-west France.

At first, the hatred of Godoy was so great in the country that the French were welcomed by local dignitaries and the people of the small towns and villages as friends and liberators. Spanish and French army officers fraternised and toasted one another at dinners in garrison towns. It was widely believed that Napoleon was going to defend Ferdinand's rights to the throne and free Spain from Godoy.

Meanwhile, at court, Charles, Ferdinand and Godoy all remained convinced that Napoleon was their sincere friend who had their interests at heart in everything he did. Even while Spanish towns and villages were being systematically occupied by French forces, many of whom showed a strange reluctance to move towards Portugal, they still begged Napoleon for favours and a French princess for the royal heir.

Napoleon's tone towards Charles and Godoy hardened and became increasingly arrogant. He deprived Charles's brother of his kingdom of Etruria in Italy, declared that he could not marry any daughter of his family to a prince who had been dishonoured, and started a press campaign of denigration against Godoy in the Paris government news-paper, *Le Moniteur*. The behaviour of some French troops and officers in Spain became high-handed, popular resentment flared up and there were some violent incidents. In February 1808, another 14,000 soldiers under General Duhesme advanced down the Mediterranean coast towards Barcelona. In Paris, Godoy's secret envoy was asked: how would Spain react to the proposal that she should let France have Catalonia and part of northern Spain in exchange for a slice of central Portugal? In mid-February and March, to the great alarm of the Span-iards, French troops successfully took over the fortresses and citadels at Barcelona, Pamplona, and Figueras by the simple expedient of march-ing their troops inside when the Spanish garrisons were off guard, and then expelling them.

In the same month, Napoleon appointed his brother-in-law Murat, already Grand Duke of Berg and a cavalryman with more *panache* than brains, to be his Lieutenant in Spain and take over command of all French forces there. At first, he too was welcomed as a liberator who had come to free the Spanish from Godoy, was greeted by mayors of towns and villages and had church bells rung in his honour. Three days after crossing the frontier, Murat was in Burgos. His official excuse for his presence was that he had been sent to review the Emperor's troops, whose eventual destination he did not know. His secret orders were to advance with the armies slowly on Madrid but he was urged not to arouse any hostility, and to give the impression that a visit by Napoleon was imminent.

A few days later, another army corps of more than 30,000 men under Marshal Bessières crossed the frontier. Now that northern and part of central Spain were swarming with French troops, and Napoleon increased his demands and fulfilled none of his promises, Godoy finally saw the light. He knew that he was blamed directly for the French presence in the country and that many people expected Napoleon to sweep him from power.

His hopes in ruins, Godoy pleaded with the royal family to follow the example already set by the Portuguese rulers who had taken refuge in the New World. Ferdinand refused for he was still convinced that Napoleon was about to help him, and Charles IV wavered undecidedly. Even when Godoy and other courtiers suggested that at least the royal family should move southwards to Seville, they remained in the small town of Aranjuez near Madrid and Charles IV attempted to calm his subjects by denying all rumours of his departure. Ferdinand's supporters then spread rumours that the Prince was about to be forced to move south against his will. Crowds gathered in the town and tension rose. Ferdinand was acclaimed whenever he appeared in public and, on the night of March 17, a mob led by Ferdinand's intriguing supporters rioted, attacked and sacked Godoy's mansion and would have lynched Godoy himself had he not hidden in the attic.

Godoy's reign was over. Thirty-six hours later, he emerged from his hiding place and was arrested. Charles IV agreed to dismiss him from office and pleaded for the fallen favourite's life. When rumours spread that Godoy was to be taken to safety in the south, a mob gathered, screamed insults at Charles and Maria Luisa and wrecked their carriage. A day later, after crowds had chanted "long live King Ferdinand!" under the palace windows, the bewildered Charles signed an act of abdication, remarking as he did so, "I have never done anything with more pleasure in all my life." Ferdinand was at once recognised as lawful king by the royal ministers and nobles. Charles and Maria Luisa then wrote to Murat, begging him to help them ensure themselves a peaceful retirement, while Ferdinand sent word to Murat's headquarters informing him that he was now ruler. As soon as the news reached Madrid, there was public rejoicing and a mob invaded Godoy's palace, crying, "Death to the sausage-maker!" In the provinces, Godoy's portraits were destroyed, he was hung in effigy and messages of loyal support were sent to Ferdinand.

Four days after Charles had signed the abdication, Murat massed his troops on the northern outskirts of Madrid. It was a formidable array of power which included Dupont's carabiniers, Grouchy's hussars and dragoons, squadrons of Polish lancers who had made themselves feared on the battlefields of Europe, Egyptian Mamelukes with their turbans and curved scimitars, Moncey and his cuirassiers, infantry guns and miles of baggage trains. Murat, who loved martial display, dressed himself up in his most flamboyant uniform and made a spectacular entrance into the city.

Sitting high and straight in his saddle, Murat had the demeanour of a conqueror rather than an ally as he cantered through the streets, escorted by equally brilliantly-costumed staff officers and a hundred and fifty cavalry including a detachment of Mamelukes—the first Moors to be seen in Spain since the end of the 15th century. Onlookers were impressed by Murat's dashing appearance, in his red leather boots, his silken sash, green velvet jacket, gold braid and plumed cap. They also noted the contrast between Murat's splendour and the shabby appearance of the 20,000 infantrymen who filed after the cavalry, many of them still in their teens, their uniforms ill-fitting and their *shako* hats often too big for them. There were a few cheers and the general attitude of the Madrilenes was one of polite curiosity rather than overt hostility. After all, was not Ferdinand now king, supported by the French?

Murat's hopes were high and his confidence unbounded as he settled into his quarters in the capital. A despatch sent from Madrid and published in the French *Moniteur Universel* a week later stated that "the Grand Duke of Berg, at the head of the French army, entered our town this morning. Joy reigned on every visage and the French have been welcomed with every sign of satisfaction. The beautiful appearance of the troops after so long a march, the beauty of the regiments of Cuirassiers have been singularly remarked . . ."

Murat was at once faced with the problem of Ferdinand. He was disconcerted by Charles IV's abdication and uncertain how to proceed with regard to the royal family for he had no instructions to recognise Ferdinand as ruler even though the walls of Madrid were plastered with posters welcoming "the king's allies" and signed "Ferdinand". There was also the problem of Godoy, but that was more easily solved.

After the Queen had pleaded for the favourite's life to be spared, Murat managed to prevent him from being brought into Madrid and had him placed under guard in a small village nearby. His next move was to prevent Ferdinand's announced entry into Madrid and he sent the French ambassador, Beauharnais, to Aranjuez to request that his arrival should be postponed. He was too late.

The following day, Ferdinand entered the city to the acclaim of vast crowds, swelled by thousands of peasants from the surrounding country-side. Ferdinand's arrival was in complete contrast to that of Murat His only escort was a handful of bodyguards and he rode on a white horse followed by a closed carriage containing his brother Don Carlos and his uncle, the simple-minded Don Antonio. But his welcome was delirious. While church bells pealed out and the crowds sang and shouted "*Viva el Rey! Muera el Choricero!*" they pressed in on him so hard that his horse was practically lifted off the ground. Men, women and children kissed his hands, clothes and even the stirrups of his saddle while others laid down capes and *mantillas* in the road before his horse as it tried to move forward through a hail of flowers and scarves. But after the euphoria, it was noticed that Murat and his men had been absent from the scene. Murat was reviewing his cavalry in another part of the city in order to avoid having to meet the King. After receiving a message from Ferdinand, Murat merely sent him a note regretting that he could not pay his respects until Napoleon had recognised the new king and agreed to the succession.

After writing another pleading letter to Napoleon, assuring him of his loyalty and repeating his request for a French princess, Ferdinand began his brief "reign", still unrecognised by Murat or the ambassador. Napoleon's arrival was reported to be imminent. Murat successfully persuaded Charles IV to sign a declaration that his abdication had been forced upon him and was therefore invalid, moved the royal family under a French guard to the Escorial palace, took Godoy into his custody and sent one optimistic letter after another to Napoleon, telling him that he would come to Spain like a saviour and that the Spanish people adored him. Murat then proceeded to arouse resentment by his lofty manners and undiplomatic insistence that the famous sword that the French King François I had surrendered to the Spanish at the battle of Pavia in 1525 should be handed back in an elaborate ceremony.

While Murat strutted and paraded in Madrid and dreamed of being made King of Spain himself, Napoleon was preparing to settle the question of the Spanish monarchy. At first, he was still uncertain how to act. What should he do? he asked Murat, after ordering him to keep the Spanish in a state of expectation by saying that he would visit them from one day to the next. He warned Murat not to act precipitately or show any arrogance or violence towards the royal family and summed up his problem: "It seems difficult to me to have Charles IV reign: his government and his favourite have become so unpopular that they would not maintain themselves for three months; Ferdinand is France's enemy. That is why they have made him king. To place him on the throne would only be to serve the factions who have wanted France's ruin for the last twenty-five years."

A few days later Napoleon acted. He sent a new agent, the wily General Savary, to Madrid, to lure Ferdinand into France with hopes of his crown being confirmed and of being given a French princess. Murat had already urged Ferdinand to see Napoleon, and as the Emperor still gave no signs of visiting Spain the "King" was forced to visit him. There was little else that Ferdinand could do: he could not negotiate with anyone in Madrid, he had no armed forces behind him, and he could not flee even if he had wanted to. On April 10, he left Madrid where a Junta under the presidency of Don Antonio was set up to rule in his absence, and headed towards the frontier, expecting—as he had been told by Savary—that Napoleon would be meeting him half way. There was still no sign of the Emperor's approach by the time Ferdinand and his suite reached the town of Vitoria. Despite the misgivings of his followers and the alarm and forebodings of the local population, Ferdinand insisted on moving on to the border. Neither he nor his fellow-Spaniards knew that Napoleon had already offered the crown of Spain first to his brother Louis who was ruling Holland and refused it, then to another brother, Joseph, King of Naples, who had accepted it.

On April 19, Ferdinand was greeted politely by Napoleon at Bayonne. That same evening, he received a message telling him that the Emperor had decided that the Bourbons should no longer rule in Spain and that a French prince was to take their place. As compensation, Ferdinand could have the small Italian kingdom of Etruria. Ferdinand refused and temporised. A few days later, Charles, Maria Luisa and Godoy all arrived in Bayonne after Napoleon had sent for them, and they began to heap abuse and reproaches on Ferdinand's head to Napoleon's cynical amusement and final disgust. Eventually, they realised the harsh truth that they were powerless and that Napoleon was now in charge of Spain's destinies. It only remained to be seen how the Spanish people would react to the news. Murat continued to send optimistic reports to Napoleon, stating that "the most perfect tranquillity reigns in all parts of Spain". What he did not realise was that even the humblest Spaniard, ignorant of the complicated moves of international diplomacy and politics, could hardly fail to see that his King had been lured into a foreign country, that Spain had been humiliated, and that thousands of foreign troops were insolently camped on his native soil.

*   *   *

Murat's and Napoleon's confidence that Spain would passively accept the status of French satellite which had been forced upon her was not universally shared by the officers and men taking part in the invasion. Many French soldiers were quick to detect signs of bitterness and suspicion in the Spanish people and they sensed that these feelings could easily erupt into open hatred and violence.

In February 1808, while staying at Zamora where there was a school of artillery, Captain Charles François of Dupont's corps recorded in his *Journal* that although some officers and cadets were fraternising with the French, many other military and professional men were leaving the town. On questioning the wife of a local nobleman, François learned that large numbers of the townsfolk were said to be going south to Andalusia where a large force was gathering to oppose the French. On March 6, François heard similar rumours at a market fair. Eleven days later, at Medina del Campo, François noted that officers were reporting that soldiers straggling behind the main columns had been murdered and that a general uprising was to be feared. At the end of March, Maurice Tascher was quartered in Madrid and noted that "our existence in the middle of this capital and our relations with the Spanish authorities are as strange as could be. Each looks at the other with the greatest distrust; all we do is to look for subterfuges and intermediaries for all our requisitions and lodgings . . . the common people see us with impatience and hatred".

The situation continued to deteriorate. On April 2, a mob roamed the streets of a small town near Madrid and threatened to cut the throats of all Frenchmen. On April 3, half the French infantry and cavalry regiments stood to arms on the alert for a day and a night. On April 14, two chasseurs were badly wounded by Spaniards at Ocaña, near Aranjuez, and Tascher wrote in his diary that "people were speaking of nothing less than killing us all". On April 16, Tascher remarked: "Our relations are always the same with the Spanish. Are these people insolent and cruel then? No! They are proud and vindictive, they have a national spirit and they are oppressed." He found that the ordinary people were "easy to irritate, dangerous, cruel and capable of the greatest excesses when stirred up".

After Ferdinand's departure for Bayonne, tension increased rapidly. Each new day brought reports of some incident involving French soldiers and Spanish civilians. An officer was shot dead by a priest at a village a few miles from Madrid; a shopkeeper was shot by the French; a French soldier was killed after trying to kiss a girl on the Toledo bridge near the royal palace in Madrid. Reports reached Murat's headquarters of anti-French riots at Burgos and Toledo, and of how the large French merchant colony in Cadiz were being jeered and hissed whenever they appeared in the cafés. At the end of April, General Moncey reported that he had lost thirty-four men who had been stabbed or bludgeoned to death by civilians. But Murat still continued to write to Napoleon that Spain was quiet and he expressed full confidence that if the Madrid mob rose, he would strike them a sharp, swift blow which would forever ensure tranquillity throughout Spain.

Murat had few fears of an armed rising in Madrid. The city's military potential for effective resistance was poor. It had no militia force and only a small garrison of regular soldiers. The city was encircled by three concentric rings of French troops. Over 10,000 were quartered in the city itself. Army barracks were either taken over completely, surrounded, or simply swamped by superior numbers of French troops. The artillery park in the north of the city was occupied. Another 20,000 men with their artillery were encamped in the close neighbourhood of the capital. Additional forces were assembled in strength at Aranjuez, Toledo, Manzanares and other small towns. The Spanish forces in the city consisted only of a few companies of Royal Household troops and bodyguards, some carabiniers, fusiliers, light cavalry and palace sentries. They had no unified, tactical plan for any action, no fortified strong points from which resistance could be prolonged, and insufficient arms and ammunitions.

Madrid might be at the mercy of Murat's armies but the population were not slow to reveal their feelings towards the French. Although the *Junta* which represented the absent monarch did its best to temporise with Murat and reassure the inhabitants, clashes in the streets became more frequent. There were signs of passive resistance and non-cooperation and Murat was unable to find anyone in the capital who would print the text of Charles IV's protest against his enforced abdication at Aranjuez. On the Thursday before Easter, a monk caused an uproar in a Madrid church by announcing that a great battle was imminent between the French and the Madrilenes. Anti-Napoleonic posters and pictures of Ferdinand were prominently displayed on walls and in shop windows. Anti-French songs were sung in the streets, French soldiers were jeered and whenever they entered a church to attend Mass, members of the congregation would leave in silent protest.

The first reliable account of what was happening in Bayonne reached Madrid on the night of April 29. While Ferdinand was being pressed by Napoleon to sign away his rights, he wrote several letters to the *Junta* but they were intercepted by Napoleon's agents. Finally, a magistrate from Navarre who had been present at Bayonne managed to reach Madrid with a verbal message from Ferdinand. While the *Junta* deliberated the next day, rumours swept the city and leaflets telling the people of Ferdinand's wretched position were clandestinely printed and circulated. Crowds gathered in the Puerta del Sol to await the latest news from Bayonne and their anger grew as they realised that Napoleon was about to commit an act of premeditated treachery against the Spanish monarchy.

While Murat continued to hold parades and exchange civilities with a small number of obsequious, pro-French courtiers and churchmen, the priests and monks in the capital were preaching rebellion. On May 1, some French soldiers noticed that the city seemed to be more crowded than usual. People were saying that large numbers of peasants were entering Madrid and that the shops were selling unusually large quantities of knives, gunpowder and shot. As Captain François made his way home through the streets near the Prado that afternoon, he was struck by the number of public gatherings and was disturbed by the threatening looks cast at him and the cries of "*bandido!*" "*demonio!*" and the even more sinister "*A mañana!*" He reached his quarters safely but he was one of a number of French soldiers advised by their hosts not to leave the house the following day if possible.

*   *   *

On May 1, Murat received new orders from Napoleon. Two of the remaining members of the royal family left in Madrid were to be sent to Bayonne. They were the widowed Queen of Etruria, together with her children, and the fourteen-year-old Don Francisco de Paula, Ferdinand's brother. The only members of Charles IV's family allowed to remain were Don Antonio, the *Junta*'s president, and the Archbishop of Toledo, the King's cousin. Murat promptly communicated the order to the *Junta* but they refused. Murat threatened to impose martial law unless they obeyed and stated he would send the ex-Queen and the little Prince to France by force if necessary. There was an anguished debate in the palace. Some members of the *Junta* called for resistance. Others, led by the Spanish War Minister, O'Farrill, declared that armed resistance was impossible and would only lead to the destruction of Madrid. Late that night after a meeting with the French ambassador, O'Farrill informed the *Junta* that Murat had agreed that only the ex-Queen of Etruria and her children need leave in the morning. As her hostility to Ferdinand was well-known, it was unlikely that the public would protest at her departure. To avoid the risk of any riots, Don Francisco de Paula would not leave Madrid until the following night.

The next morning, a crowd of spectators assembled outside the royal palace to watch the ex-Queen's departure. An hour later, the capital was convulsed by the violent, popular insurrection which has made May 2 one of the most famous dates in Spanish history.

After the ex-Queen of Etruria had been driven off in her carriage, cries were heard that the *Infante*, the little Prince, was about to be taken away. Members of the crowd invaded the palace and made their way to the quarters of the *Infante*, who then appeared on a balcony. The mob roared "death to the French" and begged the Prince not to leave them. The commotion was heard in Murat's nearby headquarters, and two French officers were sent to enquire the reason for the disturbance. Amid cries of "kill them!", the officers drew their sabres and would have been attacked if a member of the Royal Guard who was on picket duty had not persuaded them to sheath their sabres and accompany him to safety. While the mob surged around the three men, a picket of twenty French guards arrived and O'Farrill came out of the palace to urge his fellow-countrymen to disperse and go home peaceably. At this critical moment, had the crowd remained undecided, the situation might have been saved, but it was reported that a French soldier had been stabbed to death on the way to his barracks and Murat was determined to punish the restive populace by using the same means already employed in the streets of Cairo, Milan and Rome. A battalion of Grenadiers of the Imperial Guard came onto the esplanade of the palace with two light cannon. There was a volley of musketry, fired in the air and then, without warning, the cannon fired grapeshot into the crowd, which dispersed in panic, leaving some ten killed and wounded in the square.

The news that French troops had opened fire spread rapidly through the city. While Don Antonio and the *Junta* remained irresolute in the palace, and the Royal Guards took up their positions, French officers sent patrols along the streets leading to the city centre. More cannon were brought out and continued to fire grapeshot at small groups of civilians as they gathered in the nearby squares and streets. As soon as the gunfire was heard, a mob in the Puerta del Sol cried "all to the Palace!" and moved off in that direction, armed with daggers, blunderbusses, kitchen knives, staves and clubs.

What might have been only a minor disturbance quickly took on the aspect of a major insurrection. Some isolated French soldiers who were found in the streets were instantly murdered, some others who were unarmed and begged for mercy were allowed by the jeering mob to run for safety while still others were murdered in their lodgings. Several of the wealthier Madrilenes sheltered the officers who were billeted in their mansions while others loaded their fowling pieces and fired upon the French from their windows.

French cavalry now began to ride into the capital from the outskirts, while the artillery in the Retiro was moved into the streets. Murat's commander-in-chief, Grouchy, deployed the French units in the city in order to block all streets leading to the centre, while sending forward the French cavalry. Fighting was vicious and desperate. After three charges, the French cavalry was still unable to move down the Calle Mayor. As a detachment of grenadiers advanced from the palace, the inhabitants of nearby houses pelted them with stones, tiles, vases, boiling water, tables and chairs. A general was killed by a flower pot hurled at him from a balcony and primitively armed crowds battled to prevent French soldiers from leaving their barracks. Some of the most ferocious resistance that the French encountered was in the working-class quarters near the ancient Toledo gate where screaming women jumped on the French cannon as they were dragged through the streets. They slashed open the bellies of the French horses with knives, sickles and carpenters' tools, dragged the cuirassiers to the ground, cut them to pieces and seized their weapons.

After the initial outburst, the main insurrection became concentrated in the heart of the city, the Puerta del Sol, which was filled by a furious, maddened mob armed with pikes, knives, and ancient blunderbusses, who proceeded to guard the mouths of avenues radiating from the square. A French platoon carrying provisions and firewood suddenly appeared. After stones were flung at them, they were overcome by the mob and massacred. Two Mamelukes escorting some French officers attempted to ride through the square. They were allowed to move on until they turned into the opening of a narrow street and fired their pistols into the crowd. While one was shot in the saddle, the other was dragged from his horse and butchered. No more mercy was shown by Murat's men. Horsemen and infantry with fixed bayonets killed every Spaniard in their path, whether he was armed or not. Cavalry swept into the centre from one side of the Puerta del Sol while infantry streamed over the Manzanares river and cuirassiers rode over the bodies of the dead women who had defended the Toledo gate.

The final phase of the unequal battle took place in the Puerta del Sol and may well have been seen by Goya who was living there and who depicted the terrible struggle in his great painting *Dos de Mayo*. As the French advanced up the Calle Mayor from the palace under a hail of missiles, a squadron of Mamelukes came charging into the square. They were among the most feared of the French forces but not even the sight of their deadly scimitars could intimidate the mob who slashed at their horses and leaped at their saddles, bringing down several riders, while snipers fired down from windows. Both the infantry and the Mamelukes exacted a terrible vengeance. Captain François described in his diary how, after shots had been fired from a ducal mansion nearby, the doors were smashed down and the inhabitants were all bayoneted in the courtyards, corridors and apartments . . . "we took no prisoners". The Mamelukes broke into a monastery and chased the terrified monks from cell to cell, cutting them down and dexterously slicing their heads from their shoulders with gleeful enthusiasm. After two hours the square was cleared, cannons were brought up and the city divided into sections.

The remainder of the resistance was scattered and sporadic. There was one last bloody, heroic episode before order was restored to the capital. Although the commander of Spanish troops in Madrid had ordered them to remain in their barracks, two officers disobeyed orders and became national heroes. One was Pedro Velarde, an artillery captain, the other his friend Captain Luis Daoiz who was in charge of

Spanish gunners at the artillery park in the north of the city. After Velarde had come to the artillery park at the head of a band of insurgents, Daoiz agreed in the name of King Ferdinand to allow them access to the guns. Although the park was guarded by a French token force, it was quickly overpowered. Arms were distributed to the men and women following Velarde, four cannon were wheeled into position and an attacking French battalion was decimated. French reinforcements arrived, a massive attack was made on the building, the defenders resisted to the end, Daoiz died on a French bayonet and Velarde was shot dead at point-blank range.

By the afternoon, the fighting had ended. A Franco-Spanish peace commission had been formed and members of the *Junta*, Spanish officers, councillors and magistrates patrolled the streets, waving white flags and urging the population to keep the peace. Murat ordered the *Junta* to calm the people and tell them that the integrity and independence of the King—Charles IV and *not* Ferdinand—would be maintained and that they should trust Napoleon. But Murat did not content himself with making promises and preaching peace. After the rising came the reprisals.

Crosses were marked on the doors of buildings from which shots had been fired. As a squadron of Mamelukes rode down the street of San Geronimo off the Puerta del Sol, they found the body of one of their comrades lying in the doorway of a noble mansion. They dismounted, knocked on the door, rushed in and proceeded to massacre every man, woman and child they found, decapitating them and throwing their heads through the windows into the street before remounting and continuing their patrol as though nothing had happened. A military tribunal was set up in the Post Office by the Puerta del Sol. Any Spaniard found bearing any kind of weapon—even a penknife—was condemned to death. Even carpenters and cobblers with the tools of their trade and a surgeon carrying a scalpel in a bag were shot. Batches of prisoners were given a summary trial in front of French officers before being sentenced to death by firing squad. Bitterly, the Spanish magistrates who had helped restore peace and promised their fellow-citizens their lives if they laid down their arms, now watched them being led away to execution. Spanish noblemen and important dignitaries were unable to stop innocent people from being shot without formality. The executions made a terrible impression upon the city. While the great mansions in the centre were deserted by their inhabitants, and corpses and dead horses lay where they had fallen, while French cannon were trained down the main avenues and the only signs of life in the streets were a few French patrols, the silence of the night was broken by the sound of continuous fusillades. Men, women, youths and priests were massacred by firing squads in the public gardens, by the banks of the Manzanares, in the grounds of the Prado, at the Puerta de Segovia, and on the nearby hill of Principe Pio. Murat forbade burials for the next two days so that the corpses might serve as a warning to the population. In the monastery of San Geronimo in the Retiro Park, the bloodstained clothing of executed victims was displayed in the cloisters by the monks, and weeping men and women filed past all night and kissed the pathetic relics of their parents, sons and friends. The story was told of how the chaplain to the nuns of the Incarnation had seized a soldier's rifle and shot a Frenchman before being taken prisoner and brought before Murat. "Priest", said Murat, "he who kills by iron dies by iron." "To die for the motherland! A beautiful death!" was the answer. It was one echoed by many thousands of Spaniards that night as they counted their martyrs.

Murat issued a ferocious proclamation on May 4. "French blood has flowed; it demands vengeance," he wrote, after saying that he knew that many "good Spaniards" lamented the disorders that had been provoked by "wretches avid for crime and pillage". A military commission was set up under General Grouchy. All Madrilenes found carrying arms without permission were to be shot; all meetings of more than eight people were to be considered seditious and dispersed by shooting; all villages where Frenchmen had been murdered were to be burned to the ground; masters were to be responsible for their servants, foremen for their workers, fathers for their children, superiors of monasteries for their monks. Anyone who wrote, distributed or sold seditious tracts was to be considered an English agent and shot. For days afterwards, Madrid was a huge armed camp. Maurice de Tascher noted in his diary that "the Spaniards are convinced that the French troops are only waiting for the signal before burning the city or sacking it and as our soldiers pass an inhabitant, they declare that they can always sense the cold steel in their backs".

Despite its ferocity and its ruthless repression, the May 2 rising probably cost less than 1,500 lives at the very most. The figures estimated by Spanish and French historians vary wildly. Murat officially estimated that 145 French had been killed and 300 Spanish but he may well have been minimising the scale of the fighting and the true numbers of Spaniards executed is not known. But even though calm returned to the city, the effects of the outbreak and the executions were immediate and far-reaching.

The news soon reached Bayonne, where Napoleon was alternately cajoling and threatening the royal family. He was not particularly surprised by the insurrection but he seized the opportunity to accuse Ferdinand of being responsible for it. There followed another unedifying family scene with Maria Luisa shrieking insults at Ferdinand and Charles accusing him of causing the deaths of his own people and the soldiers of "my great friend Napoleon". Disgusted by this sordid squabble, Napoleon ordered Ferdinand to abdicate his rights to the throne at once or be treated as a rebel. On May 6, Ferdinand yielded. On the previous day, Charles IV had signed away his rights. Napoleon informed Murat that Spain's new king would be Joseph Bonaparte and the royal family were packed off to various estates in France to live in enforced exile. Napoleon at once began to prepare a constitution for Spain and drew up a list of Spanish nobles who would be summoned to Bayonne to give some semblance of legal consent to his decisions concerning their country.

Murat was convinced that the swift crushing of the rising in Madrid had restored peace in the peninsula. He assured Napoleon that "the cannon shots of May 2nd will assure the banner of the new dynasty" and that France was now master of all Spain. What neither he nor Napoleon knew at the time was that the call for a general, national uprising had already been made.

In the late afternoon of May 2, news of events in Madrid reached the tiny town of Mostoles, a few miles to the south-west of the capital. With its church and cluster of sun-baked mud and brick houses surrounded by a few fields, it was a typical Castilian farming village. It had two mayors who exercised their functions jointly and one distinguished resident, Perez de Villamil, secretary to the Admiralty and solicitor to the Supreme War Council, who owned a manor house in the neighbourhood. As soon as they heard the news, the mayors, Andres de Torrejon and Simon Hernandez, drew up a proclamation with the help of Villamil. It was an appeal to the whole Spanish people. After stating that they had learned that Madrid was running with Spanish blood as the result of a French attack, they declared: "As Spaniards, it is necessary that we die for the King and the Fatherland, taking up arms against men of perfidy who wear the colours of friendship and alliance but wish to impose a heavy yoke upon us after having empowered themselves of the august body of the King. Let us then proceed to punish such perfidy by rushing to the help of Madrid and other towns. Let us be of good heart for there are no forces which can prevail against those who are loyal and valiant as the Spaniards are. May God guard you for many years. Mostoles, second of May, eighteen hundred and eight. Andres Torrejon. Simon Hernandez."

A postboy rode off with copies of this simple and direct appeal and reached the town of Talavera that same evening. After a halt, he went on to the town of Caceres in Estremadura, from where other copies were distributed throughout the province and in Andalusia.

The first response to the call to arms was disappointing. In Talavera, the aide to the provincial magistrate, or *corregidor*, ordered the town garrison and some regiments recently returned from Portugal to march towards Madrid but caution soon overcame him and he countermanded the order. On May 4 in Estremadura, the people of Badajoz heard the proclamation and massed before the residence of the military governor of the province to clamour for war against the French. The Captain-General was Godoy's cousin and was disinclined to risk his position by taking any action, but General Solano, commander of the Spanish divisions which Godoy had recalled from Portugal during the French advance towards Madrid, was also in the town. Solano sent appeals to his brother officers still serving under Junot in Portugal, as well as to generals in Andalusia and in Madrid, but they were not answered. A few days later, Solano submitted to Murat's orders by taking up a new command as Governor of Cadiz and Captain-General of Andalusia. On May 9, disturbances broke out in Oviedo, capital of the northern mountainous and maritime province of Asturias, the cradle of modern Spain where the crusade against the Moors had started. Students and working people ran through the streets acclaiming Ferdinand as King of Spain and shouting "death to Murat!" They invaded a building where a relic of the province's former self-government, a local *Junta* formed of leading citizens, magistrates, and officials, was sitting and demanded a general uprising. One of the *Junta*'s most respected members, the eighty-year-old Marquis of Santa Cruz, was enthusiastic for war but the assembly temporised. It was afraid of provoking stern counter-measures from the regular provincial administration which represented the government in Madrid and contented itself with forming a defence committee and despatching observers and messengers to neighbouring provinces.

As the month of May progressed, Murat continued to send Napoleon optimistic and glowing reports on the situation in Spain. Apart from the commotion in Oviedo which soon died down, the whole of the country was apparently quiet. After the resignation and departure of Don Antonio, Murat was president of what was now called the *"Junta* of Regency" in Madrid and Spain's effective—if temporary—ruler. Even though the *Junta* had received a secret message which Ferdinand had managed to smuggle out of Bayonne before his abdication and which urged them to take up arms against the French, they preferred to disregard it and obey their *de facto* superior. In spite of O'Farrill's strong protests, they handed over the command of all Spanish armed forces to Murat and continued to collaborate. To revolt would have meant the risk of arrest and of losing all their honours and positions—a dilemma which faced countless other officers and civil authorities throughout the country. Besides, the people appeared to be disposed to accept the new order of things.

Murat's exalted position went to his head. He had dreamed of being given the Spanish crown until Napoleon informed him that Joseph Bonaparte had been chosen. But there were compensations. He resided in the royal palace, he was offered the throne of Naples which he accepted, he was able to dictate to Spain's highest dignitaries and authorities, and he was ordered to persuade or bully the *Junta* and the Council of Castile officially to request Joseph as their new ruler. He had every opportunity to indulge his taste for splendid uniforms, martial display and spectacular parades. He posed as the magnanimous friend of the Spanish people and organised lavish receptions in which grandees, leading churchmen, officials and foreign diplomats came to pay their respects while awaiting the new King and a visit from Napoleon.

In a short time, Murat became disenchanted with his position. Napoleon bombarded him with orders and instructions and he made several mistakes—one of the oddest being to lift an old prohibition which forbade the people of Catalonia to wear arms. He was ordered in vain to find the royal jewels, which had disappeared, the treasury was empty, and the heat was becoming torrid. Although he was surrounded by flatterers and collaborators, all anxious for places in the new administration, an increasing number of Spanish troops and officials were deserting the capital. Provisions ran low and French officers found it hard to supply and pay their men. Murat caught a debilitating fever and then, to the consternation of his headquarters, news arrived that large parts of Spain had erupted into almost simultaneous open revolt. In a few days, it was clear that the nation was in a state of revolution.

On May 24, the sea port of Cartagena declared its loyalty to Ferdinand VII and hostility to Napoleon. On the same night, 500 miles to the north, a crowd led by a canon of the cathedral and several monks marched through the streets of Oviedo as the church bells rang the tocsin, and seized the arsenal while the officers and men in charge stood idly by. The next day, the local *Junta* declared itself to be the sovereign government in the province until the return of Ferdinand VII, elected the Marquis of Santa Cruz as its president, solemnly declared war on Napoleon, began to organise levies and sent envoys to England to ask for help. In Seville, a Catalan preacher and several monks, who had been inciting the people to revolt, led them to the arsenal. The archbishop held a meeting in the main city square, oaths of loyalty to Ferdinand were sworn and a Supreme *Junta* of resistance was formed in the name of the whole of Spain. At Zamora a cobbler, and at Logroño a stonemason, roused the population with the aid of monks, local noblemen and officers. In Santander, the bishop of the city ran through the streets, a cross round his neck and pistols in his sash, calling upon the "children of Christ" to march to victory against the godless French. In green and sea-swept Galicia, troops gathered in the hills and mountains, and *Juntas* were formed in the ports of La Coruña and El Ferrol. Within ten days, large parts of Catalonia, Aragon, Murcia, Estremadura, and Leon had joined the revolt, while regiments of regular troops and crowds of volunteers assembled in Andalusia.

After the executions of Spanish insurgents in Madrid, hatred of the French throughout Spain reached a degree of intensity unequalled even during the 1793–95 war. The country was deluged with pamphlets, poems, sermons and proclamations denouncing the French as murderers, atheists, cannibals, robbers and rapists. Poets and spontaneous versifiers composed epics and odes in which they urged fellow-Spaniards to free their soil from the invader and reminded them of the ancient wars against the Romans and the Moors. Priests and monks shared their flocks' conviction that one of Napoleon's main aims in Spain was the complete destruction of the Catholic faith. A new "catechism" circulated from village to village and became famous. It taught that

"Heaven is attained by killing the French heretical dogs"; Napoleon was anti-Christ, the "source of all evils, the focus of all vices"; Murat was "Satan's emissary". A Frenchman was no longer considered to be a human being and to kill him by any means was a Spaniard's first, sacred duty. The result of such propaganda and resentments was a mass hatred of one people for another unprecedented in modern European history.

Many of the first victims of the rising were Spaniards themselves. For three weeks after May 2, while rebellion was being preached, the masses of the working people in the towns, the peasants and artisan classes waited for their legally constituted authorities to lead them to battle. When it became plain that many high-ranking officials and army commanders were reluctant to engage themselves on the side of the people, because they were pro-French, wished to retain their posts or felt that precipitate action would only lead to disaster, thousands of normally law-abiding people rose up against them with a ferocity intensified by anti-French hysteria. Atrocious scenes took place in towns and villages. The Captain-General of Galicia who had only reluctantly accepted the presidency of the recently formed local revolutionary *Junta* was murdered by his own soldiers a few days later. In Seville, the Count of Aguila was tied to the balcony of his mansion and battered to death with rifle butts. In Jaen, the *corregidor* was shot by his own fellow-citizens. The Governor of Malaga was hacked to pieces and burned in the town square by furious peasants who had come down from the mountains. The director of the military college at Segovia was murdered in front of his wife and, in Cadiz, General Solano was beaten savagely and then stabbed to death after refusing to attack French shipping in the harbour. Some of the worst atrocities occurred in Valencia. One of the city's leading noblemen, the Count of Albalat, was murdered because he was suspected of pro-French sympathies and had his head paraded on a pike by a maddened crowd. After days of prayer and meditation, a fanatical monk emerged from his cell to preach a crusade against the French and, when public excitement was at its height, an unscrupulous agitator from Madrid, Don Baltasar Calvo, led a massacre of three hundred French residents, men, women and children, whom the *Junta* had tried to save by confining them in the citadel of the port.

The revolt against the French became more than a resistance movement: as the people swept aside or murdered the timid civil servants and officials who stood between them and the enemy, a social revolution also took place. In town after town, village after village, the inhabitants formed revolutionary committees and *Juntas* so that they might participate directly in the new, democratic structures of local administration, as they prepared to fight the French. Although they swore loyalty to King Ferdinand and often looked for some distinguished local citizen to lead them, the new *Juntas* began to issue orders in the name of their own region and in that of the entire nation.

Declarations of war against France and proclamations of defiance did not come from any government authorities officially recognised by the French. The Madrid *Junta* remained cowed and irresolute; the historic Council of Castile remained afraid and powerless. Instead, the calls to arms were made by the new, popular assemblies, by simple farmers and workmen, by men like the two mayors of Mostoles who needed to enlist the aid of a man of learning before they could begin to pen their manifesto. But whether such summons came from the citizens and nobility of the great sea ports or the peasants of remote villages, they all announced the beginning of what the Duchesse d'Abrantès was rightly to call "the murderous war of a people against a people".

The *Junta* of Seville claimed precedence over all other revolutionary bodies in Spain and gave itself the title of "Supreme *Junta* of Spain and the Indies". On June 6, 1808, it officially declared war on France on behalf of the nation and in the name of Ferdinand VII. But already, one week earlier, the city of Saragossa in Aragon had issued a resounding manifesto which circulated throughout Spain and then throughout Europe. It was signed by a hitherto unknown young army officer but it made Saragossa a spokesman and a symbol for the whole of Spain. Unlike many other centres of resistance, Saragossa was isolated in the wilderness of Aragon and practically stripped of troops. No Spanish regular force was within a hundred miles of the city; it had no access to the sea and its communications with the cities of Navarre and Castile were cut off by the French armies. Yet in the next nine months, Saragossa was to become one of the main centres of attention for all Spanish patriots and the greatest example of the Spanish people's determination to resist Napoleon's attempt to dominate the peninsula. For those Frenchmen capable of realising its significance, the revolt of such a city came as an ominous sign.

PART TWO

PALAFOX

II

AS NAPOLEON and his generals bent over their maps of Spain during the first few days of the uprising, Saragossa's defiant proclamation must have struck them as a quixotic, futile gesture. The great ports of the south and the mountainous maritime regions of the north had advantages and resources for those planning resistance to the French. Seville had particularly good reasons for considering itself to be the leader of the revolt. By the end of May, it was harbouring many important Spanish statesmen and officials who had fled from Madrid and the north. The main bulk of the Spanish army was in Andalusia; the city lay well outside the area of the French military presence; it was sheltered from the north by the mountains of the Sierra Morena and it had easy access to the sea and the ports of Cadiz and Algeciras.

The ancient kingdom of Aragon had no such comparable advantages. It was practically empty of regular armed forces and was one of the poorest regions in the peninsula. The progressive abandonment of many towns and villages, the neglect of the land and the harshness of its red, rocky landscapes and wild mountains made Aragon one of the most depressing parts in Spain for the few voyagers hardy enough to journey through it. Saragossa itself lay in a fertile part of the Ebro valley but its importance was more religious than economic. In 1808, it was one of the most isolated and least-known of Spain's formerly great cities.

Few foreign travellers found anything good to say about either Aragon or Saragossa. The main road, linking Madrid to France, by-passed the city and the secondary roads to it from Madrid and Barcelona were among the worst in the country. Laborde journeyed to Saragossa from Barcelona in 1807 and complained bitterly about the appalling travelling conditions once he had crossed the border from Catalonia. After he and his companions had passed through the dilapidated frontier town of Fraga, "once important and now reduced to three thousand souls, with ugly, ill-built houses", they passed through "naked, parched mountains" and "frightful defiles" before crossing "an immense plain,

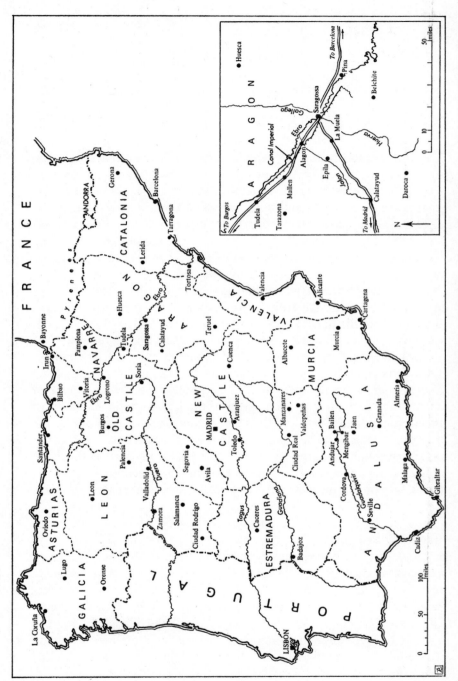

Spain in 1808; (inset) Saragossa and environs in 1808

bare, parched, and almost entirely uncultivated". Bourgoing too had journeyed to Saragossa, from Madrid by way of Alcala, and he also lamented the fact that "we have to traverse a most gloomy and wretched country". He called the roads "frightful", he was depressed by the "wretched appearance" of the whole country where "not one civilised comfort is to be found" and—this was the last straw—he warned intending travellers to beware even of "the thick black wine which they will meet with in this part of Aragon to the very gates of Saragossa, and which is the most poisonous beverage ever given to human beings".

Every visitor commented on the obvious economic decline and depopulation of Aragon. The once flourishing city of Calatayud, which lay on the main road from Madrid to Saragossa, had only 1,500 private houses by the end of the 18th century although it could still boast ten parish churches and fifteen convents and monasteries, some of which were still of great size and magnificence. Many Aragonese towns and villages had become deserted or simply disappeared. Laborde stated that when he visited the province, 189 villages were completely deserted and that 385 were reduced to only a few houses; he added that "the villages which still remain, to the number of a thousand and eighty-eight are almost all wretched, and are reduced to a very small population". Bory de Saint-Vincent declared that, after Estremadura, no other part of Spain had undergone a "more complete decadence" and also noted the number of destroyed villages of which some hundred and fifty "are only known by the name they once bore".

To the dejected traveller, the first, general impression of Saragossa and its immediate surroundings was in surprising, pleasant contrast to the poverty and desolation of the rest of the kingdom. The city was built on the south bank of the great Ebro river and for some miles it was surrounded by fertile and well-tended fields, vineyards, olive plantations, market gardens, orchards, cornfields, and meadows with grazing cattle. The river was navigable and the cultivated land was irrigated by the waters of two tributary rivers, the Gallego and the Huerva. Trade and agriculture had been given a much-needed stimulus by the digging of a canal by the Italian engineer and architect Pignatelli, encouraged by Charles III's able minister Aranda who wanted to link Santander and Tortosa by a completely navigable waterway. Despite such efforts, Saragossa had been unable to escape the general decline in population which afflicted most other Spanish cities. In the

17th century, it had a population of more than 100,000 but, by 1800, its inhabitants numbered less than 43,000. It was still the administrative centre of Aragon, which retained its title of "Kingdom", it was the seat of the *Real Audencia* which was the supreme court of the whole region, it was an important archbishopric, it had a tribunal of the Inquisition and a long and glorious history since Roman times. But after losing its importance as the capital of an independent kingdom, Saragossa owed much of its remaining prestige to the fact that it was one of the most important religious centres in Spain, since it was the home of the miraculous and fanatically revered Madonna of the Pillar which attracted pilgrims from all over the peninsula.

No other Spanish city seemed to have so many martyrs and saints. The famous Roman-Christian poet Prudentius was claimed to have been a native of the city, the Roman Saguntorum, and he had celebrated the lives of many of the Christian martyrs whose sufferings the Saragossans would describe to pilgrims with a dour relish. In 1808, the city's most famous and impressive feature was the great basilica with the shrine which housed the tiny medieval statuette of the Virgin, set upon the stone pillar which gave its name to the edifice: *El Pilar*. The basilica had been built on the banks of the Ebro between 1753 and 1765 and stood near the older cathedral of La Seo. Both churches were dark and impressive. Townsend was particularly awed by the Seo cathedral, declaring that it was "vast, gloomy and magnificent; it excites devotion, inspires awe and inclines the worshipper to fall prostrate and adore in silence the God who seems to veil his glory"; while Bourgoing curtly described El Pilar as being "a large, gloomy edifice, crowded with ornaments in a wretched taste".

The chapel of the Pilar Virgin was hung all over with images of legs and arms and other votive offerings, as well as crutches, and was constantly packed with the blind, the deaf, dumb and lame who came to prostrate themselves as they wept and prayed before the tiny image of the Virgin, in the hope of a miraculous cure. In the 17th century, a one-legged man who was employed to light the lamps in the basilica was reported to have recovered his missing limb by rubbing its stump with holy oil and the miracle was celebrated annually. In the church of the important Santa Engracia monastery by the city walls, worshippers came to pray before the ashes of the many martyrs put to death in Roman times and hear how the titular saint had walked a league, carrying her head in her hands, talking all the way and "in this manner presented herself at the gates of the convent", as Townsend learned.

In addition to her two main churches, Saragossa had twenty-five monasteries, sixteen convents for nuns, and more than seventy lesser churches, besides her seminaries and the sizeable faculty of theology in the small university which had been founded in the Middle Ages. Other important buildings included the elegant Renaissance exchange building, the *Lonja* beside El Pilar; a magnificent six-hundred-foot-long stone bridge of Roman origin; the old Moorish castle, the *Aljafería*, outside the western city gates; the palace of the provincial administration, the *Diputación*, in the centre of the city; the beautiful Renaissance House of the Infanta; and the famous, leaning, Moorish-style tower, the Torre Nueva, with its great bell and 284 steps. In the mid-18th century, Pignatelli had further enriched the city by building the municipal bull-ring, a large cavalry barracks, and a huge charitable institution, the *Casa de la Misericordia*, which had workshops, gardens, orchards and accomodation for 700 paupers.

In spite of its many historical associations, its architectural and artistic treasures and its green surroundings, foreigners found the city's general aspect a depressing one. The centre was a dark labyrinth of narrow, tortuous streets which occasionally opened into small squares, each one having its inevitable church or tower, a monumental convent or a forbidding, noble mansion with a plain façade. As there was a shortage of rock in the region, most buildings lacked stone to cover their depressing reddish brickwork with the result, said Townsend, that "all their churches, not excepting the beautiful cathedral, show cracks from top to bottom". Walking in the narrow streets was no pleasure. The French traveller Fleuriau who visited the city in 1773, had complained of them, saying that "except the street Coso, all the rest are so dark, so narrow and so dirty, that you must grope your way through them at noon-day, without knowing where to set your foot". By 1808, things were no better and Laborde repeated another complaint frequently made by foreigners, observing that the streets were mostly paved with "rough pebbles upon which it is painful to walk".

Saragossa's main and widest thoroughfare was the long Calle del Coso, its name probably derived from the Latin word, *fossa*, for a moat. It ran in a semi-circle from east to west through the centre of the city and it was here that the population would congregate for the *paseo* or evening promenade. After searching for any other amenities the city might have to offer, Laborde discovered a number of paths and avenues along the Ebro river "in front of very handsome buildings and which might be pleasant if planted with trees and kept in repair but which are bare, neglected, full of filth and obstructions".

None of the animated, pleasure-seeking social life which made Cadiz and Seville so pleasant for foreigners was to be found in Saragossa. Its artistic life was almost non-existent and its clergy were some of the most bigoted in Spain. In the middle of the 18th century, the city's theatre had burned down with loss of life and the archbishop had regarded the disaster as a sign of divine wrath. In 1805, according to the Duchesse d'Abrantès, the Inquisition Tribunal in Saragossa prosecuted a priest for having preached principles condemned by the Church. Before he was able to appear before the tribunal to answer charges which carried the death sentence, he died and the tribunal immediately suspended proceedings lest they should find him guilty and be obliged to burn his corpse.

Religious fanaticism affected everyday life. It was a sober city. Laborde stressed that "there is little luxury at Saragossa" and noted that the main attire of the inhabitants consisted of round hats and large black or brown capes for the men, and simple, plainly-coloured dresses for the women. He described the city as being "without industry and without commerce" and sadly added that "all here is serious and regular, not to say dull and monotonous: there is no society, no parties, nor any kind of entertainment. It seems quite devoid of every resource, because the inhabitants use no effort to obtain any; accustomed to this state of apathy and languour, they have not an idea of the possibility of shaking it off". Intellectual life was stagnant, "the arts and the sciences are not very flourishing in Aragon" and the city's only establishment for the arts was a drawing school which a generous private citizen had opened at his own expense. Bourgoing, on the other hand, was slightly more optimistic. He remarked on the "insignificant university" but observed that there was a "patriotic society" which "encouraged every branch of industry" and concluded that "Saragossa, in a word, is gradually awakening from her long lethargy, and is rendering herself worthy to be the capital of the fine kingdom of Aragon". The city might be a dour one but its inhabitants still had their civic pride.

That Saragossa should have revolted so readily against the French was not surprising in view of the general character attributed to the city's inhabitants and the Aragonese as a whole. Writers generally agreed that the Aragonese character was compounded of insolence, apathy, fierce obstinacy and ardent local pride. The Spanish belief that the Aragonese were exceptionally stubborn people gave rise to the well-known proverb: "Give a nail to an Aragonese, and he will use his head rather than a hammer." The harshness of the kingdom's landscape and climate were reflected in the Aragonese temperament which ranged from icy coldness to scorching fury. The people were notorious for their clan spirit, their jealous defence of their local privileges and their concentrated, inward-directed religious fervour. Travellers remarked that when the Aragonese were not being stiff and austere, they would express their chauvinism by vaunting the beauty and superiority of their capital and kingdom in the most extravagant and flowered language imaginable. But when they were not boasting about their city and saints, the Aragonese were a solemn people. Laborde declared that the typical Aragonese had "a natural asperity in voice and manners, and his address consequently is not prepossessing. His haughtiness, his dry reception, his serious air, cold manners, and abrupt tone, have something very repulsive to those who do not know him". But, like other observers, Laborde agreed that the Aragonese character was also distinguished by qualities of sound judgement, sincerity, a capacity for great endurance, and tremendous courage. Once the normally reserved Aragonese had been provoked into exploding into wrath, he became a fighter to be feared. The history of Aragon was full of examples of ferocious resistance to outside attempts to dominate the kingdom. In the Dark Ages, Saragossa had defied the armies of the French King Childebert, and the Emperor Charlemagne; it beat off the repeated attacks of the Moors, resisted Alfonso the Warrior of Castile, fought for its constitutional rights in the early 16th century and in 1710, supported the Archduke Charles who defeated Philip V's troops outside the city's walls. On the battlefields of Europe, the fury of Aragonese soldiers was famous in the 16th and 17th centuries. In 1793, the city's enthusiasm for a holy war against revolutionary France was so great that the archbishop offered to raise an army entirely composed of priests and monks. In all probability, he would have succeeded.

*   *   *

The uprising in Saragossa followed a typical pattern. As in other Spanish cities, an impatient populace swept aside the civil and military authorities who remained hesitant, afraid to compromise their positions

and incur French reprisals. As elsewhere, there were street demonstrations, meetings, spontaneous gatherings of armed groups of civilians,
and an eventual formation of a new governing body to represent the
popular will.

The first sign of agitation in the city came shortly after the population learned of the anti-Godoy riots at Aranjuez. When the news of
Charles IV's abdication in favour of Ferdinand reached the city, students
rushed to the university building, invaded the great hall where degrees
were conferred, took down the portrait of Godoy that hung there and,
after replacing it with a picture of Ferdinand, burned it in the city
centre amid public applause.

The people of Saragossa soon learned of the tragic events of May
2 in Madrid. On May 5, they were told of the formation of the Supreme
Junta in Madrid, under the presidency of the Infante Don Antonio who
was urging the country to maintain peace and order. On the following
day, the people were given first-hand, eye-witness reports of the fighting
and reprisals in Madrid by a naval engineer, Don José Mor de Fuentes,
who had just escaped from the capital. Popular fury became even more
intense after he described how some Aragonese grooms had been
massacred by the French simply because they were carrying horse
shears.

The military governor of Saragossa, the Captain-General of Aragon,
was Don Jorge Juan de Guillelmi, a Knight of the Order of Santiago
and a lieutenant-general in rank. He had held his post since 1797 and
was a veteran artillery officer who had learned gunnery techniques
under Frederick the Great. He had fought in the great siege of Gibraltar, in the Balearic Islands and against France in 1795, when he was
severely wounded in action. In 1808, he was seventy-two years old
and had been rewarded for over fifty years' service on behalf of the
Kingdom of Aragon.

Like other men in his position all over Spain, Guillelmi was too old
and cautious for heroics and mainly concerned with the need to accept
whatever new situation had been imposed on the country by the
French-dominated *Junta*. As an old soldier, he thought that armed resistance was out of the question: Aragon had no troops, it lay near the
areas under French military domination, it was cut off from the Spanish
armies of the north-west and south, and the French held Barcelona to
the east. But while he appealed for calm and the city officials temporised
in the face of popular demands for arms, local patriots began to group

together and preach revolt among the workers of the city and the peasants of the nearby countryside. As in Madrid, and other parts of Spain, the greatest, most spontaneous call for resistance came from the working people. Two of the most prominent patriots in Saragossa were Don Mariano Cerezo, a farmer who lived in the city's parish of San Pablo, near the Portillo gate, and Jorge Ibort, a short and stocky man known as "Tio Jorge" and also as *cuello corto* (short-neck) because of his build, and who was also a farmer from the suburbs of Arrabal on the other bank of the Ebro. They were soon in close agreement and began to exert great influence over the local people.

Together with other local personalities, leaders of working men's and artisans' guilds, and representatives from the city's suburbs, they sent delegations to members of the nobility, notably the Count of Sastago, whose palace was one of the finest in the city, and to provincial government officials, begging them to lead a popular insurrection. As usual, the officials and the nobles excused themselves, declaring firmly that nothing could be done without the assent of the authorities and unless it was in conformity with the law. Posters exhorting the population to take matters into their own hands went up on walls, side by side with new edicts calling for public calm. Frustrated and furious, the patriots begged the city magistrates to move on their behalf, only to be told that the *ayuntamiento*, the municipal council, had to move first. As for the *ayuntamiento*, it refused to declare itself unless given a lead by the magistrates . . .

A few days later, the Madrid *Junta* ordered the city to send its representatives to the assembly of Spanish notables which Napoleon was convening at Bayonne, to give formal assent to his plans for Spain and his choice of Joseph as king. The *ayuntamiento* met hurriedly, took advice, and decided to refuse to participate in the assembly on the grounds that it was illegal and had been brought about by violent coercion. The Count of Sastago and other leading citizens and noblemen began to hold meetings with the patriots' leaders to discuss their future line of action, while the *ayuntamiento* finally decided to ask the Captain-General for arms to resist the French who were rumoured to be on their way to the city.

The insurrection in Saragossa exploded on May 24, a few hours after the population had learned of Ferdinand's renunciation of the throne and the departure of the remaining members of the royal family for France. Several prominent citizens went down into the streets wearing red cockades, and harangued the crowds that gathered; an angry mob marched on Guillelmi's palatial residence on the Coso. There was hardly anyone to stop them for the only regular troops left in the city were a few companies of fusiliers commanded by two brothers, Colonel Antonio and Major Geronimo Torres, both of whom were to play leading parts in the city's resistance. The guards outside the Captain-General's palace gave way before the crowd, stones were hurled at the windows, the *patio* was invaded, several patriots ran up the staircase and smashed down the doors of Guillelmi's private apartments. Guillelmi was forced to appear in public and although the Torres brothers arrived and did their best to calm the crowd, they could not prevent them from taking Guillelmi under armed escort to the Aljaferia castle where the city's main supply of arms and ammunition was stored.

At the castle, a number of spokesmen for the crowd, and the mayors of the city's various wards, the *alcaldes de barrio*, argued with Guillelmi and urged him to allow weapons to be given to the population, Guillelmi vainly argued that he had written to Murat to say that all was peaceful in Saragossa, thus forestalling any French attempt at direct intervention. The crowds grew increasingly impatient outside the castle, the *alcaldes* urged the Torres brothers to open the armoury, city officials and magistrates arrived and joined in the discussions and Guillelmi finally gave way. He agreed to hand over the keys of the castle and its armoury to the Torres brothers, disclaiming responsibility for the whole affair, while his second-in-command and nephew, an Italian named Mori, and the *ayuntamiento* agreed that the arms would be distributed among the population.

Guillelmi summoned a meeting of the regional body of magistrates, the *Real Acuerdo*, but the insurgents took no chances. Much to his dismay, Guillelmi was told he was to be kept in custody in the castle "for his own safety". The peasant leader Mariano Cerezo posted guards of armed peasants around the castle; other representatives of the people argued with the artillery officers in the castle; the members of the *Real Acuerdo* waited uneasily in the Captain-General's palace until they learned of his detention and dispersed; bands of armed civilians marched through the streets, persuading the town crier to announce that every Spaniard was to proceed to the castle and there collect his arms on pain of death; Mori and the *ayuntamiento* conferred with Guillelmi and agreed that the arms would be given to the people and the armoury doors were opened. Some 25,000 muskets in good condition were found, together with some sixty-five pieces of artillery of various calibres. The cannon were taken out and the muskets loaded on to carts and driven into the town where they were handed over to the ward and guild leaders for eventual distribution.

After further deliberation, and the publication of a decree which ordered the populace to remain tranquil and submit to royal orders (although the source of the royal authority was not made clear), the city and provincial authorities dispersed. Relative calm returned although a French wine-seller resident in the city narrowly escaped a lynching after it was rumoured that he had been heard to say that he would soon be washing his hands in the Spanish blood that would run in the streets.

On May 25, Guillelmi, still detained in the castle, announced his resignation, stating that as he was indisposed and unable to continue exercising his functions, he was handing over his office to Mori. In the morning, the magistrates met again and made a number of decisions: no deputies would be sent to Bayonne; public funds in the treasury would be requisitioned; letters entering or leaving the city would be censored; the population would be armed; specially appointed commissioners would proceed to all parts of Aragon; and a *Junta* would be created to organise resistance and provide an emergency administration. The question then arose of who was to lead the people? Mori was a foreigner and unacceptable as Captain-General. The Saragossans did not only want direct participation in the preparations for armed resistance against the French—being intensely traditional and proud of their city, they wanted a leader from among their own Aragonese nobility or leading citizens. Such a man was at hand. The popular candidate for the leadership had already urged Guillelmi to resist the French and he was staying in a country house only a few miles from the city. His name was Don José Palafox y Melzi and he was an officer of the Royal Bodyguard and in imminent danger of arrest for refusing to obey the orders of the French-dominated *Junta* in Madrid.

*   *   *

José Palafox was born in Saragossa only a few hundred yards away from the Pilar basilica on October 28, 1775, during the annual feast of the Pilar Virgin, and he was baptised in the parish of the Seo cathedral. He was a true son of Saragossa and the youngest of three sons. His father was a nobleman, Don Juan Felipe Rebolledo de Palafox,

Marques de Lazan y Cãnizar, and his mother was of Flemish descent although born in Italy. The Palafox were one of the oldest lineages in Aragon. Documents mentioned a Perez Palafox as being one of a company of Aragonese knights who served under the Count of Barcelona in the late 12th century and who took an active part in the capture of Almeria from the Moors in 1201. The family had distinguished themselves ever since. Some were scholars and churchmen, others were warriors and great landowners, and they had received many honours and titles from the Crown. There was a tradition of ecclesiastical and classical scholarship in the family: one Palafox had been Bishop of Los Angeles de los Pueblos in America and José Palafox's grandfather had written a Sacred History in verse and read a dissertation on history and historic art before the Academy of Saragossa. In the second half of the 18th century, close links were established between the Palafox and the Spanish royal family which were to prove useful to the young José in his military career.

In 1759, on his way to Madrid, the new King Charles III spent a month in Saragossa because of his wife's sudden illness. Among her suite was a beautiful eleven-year-old girl of Flemish parentage, Paula Melzi de Eril. After meeting the Aragonese nobility, the King decided that Paula Melzi should be betrothed to the heir of the marquisate of Lazan y Cãnizar. The marriage took place eleven years later. Paula settled down with her husband in the family palace near the Seo in 1770 and proceeded to help her husband manage the Palafox estates very efficiently, and bore him four children. In 1772, Luis Palafox, the heir to the Lazan marquisate, was born; in 1773, Francisco was born, and then José. Later, Paula gave birth to a daughter.

While his parents lived the typical life of a provincial aristocratic family, immersing themselves in the day-to-day round of household and land administration, and joining in the monotonous social life of other local aristocrats, the tradition of learning was maintained in the family. José was tutored by Basilio Boggiero, the son of an Italian merchant who had settled in Saragossa, and a professor of rhetoric, philosophy and theology in the College of Saragossa.

The Palafox sons were all destined for royal service after being introduced at court by an aunt, and also because of their mother's connections. Luis, later the Marquis of Lazan, joined the Royal Bodyguard and rose to the rank of field-marshal by 1808; Francisco also became a royal guard and later brigadier of cavalry. In 1792, José was made a member of the Flemish company of the Royal Bodyguard, after living in Madrid with his tutor, Don Basilio, and his chaplain. Two years later Luis and Francisco saw action in the Roussillon against the French revolutionary forces during the war of 1793–1795, while José remained in Madrid, as a supernumerary cadet. Until 1808, when he was promoted brigadier in the royal armies, Palafox led an agreeable life in the pleasure-loving city where there were many opportunities to escape from the boring ritual of court life. Like many other young noblemen enjoying the royal favour and unburdened by too many responsibilities, José amused himself with bull-fights, dances, parties, and flirtations until, in 1808, he began to play his part in history.

Because of his mother's and his relatives' connections with the court, José was no stranger to royal circles. As he was a patriotic royalist, his sympathies were with Ferdinand and he must have shared the general disgust at the degradation of the court, the squalid manoeuvres of the Queen and Godoy. José also seems to have been on friendly terms with Ferdinand's tutor, Canon Escoiquiz, which was not surprising since the latter had lived in Saragossa for more than twenty years. José's eldest brother, Luis, also had close links with the pro-Ferdinand faction at court.

After the rioting at Aranjuez and the arrest of Godoy, the royal favourite was placed in the custody of José who was made responsible for his prisoner's transfer to Madrid. On the way to the capital, José received a message from Murat ordering that Godoy should not be brought to Madrid on any account but moved to a former royal palace, still in José's custody. While the French insisted that Godoy should not be put on trial, Francisco Palafox accompanied Ferdinand on his way north to Bayonne as an equerry. Murat now ordered that Godoy should be handed over to the French at once. José defiantly refused, declaring that his duty was sacred and that he would fight the whole French army rather than deliver up his prisoner unless he had orders from the Regent to do so, since he had promised Ferdinand not to allow Godoy out of his custody. But José's superiors overruled his objections and ordered him to take Godoy as far as Irun, on the border. After handing over Godoy on his arrival, José made contact with Francisco to see how they might help Ferdinand in his dangerous situation.

On May 5, news reached Irun of the May rising in Madrid. José succeeded in communicating with the Spanish consul in Bayonne, and with a number of fellow officers began to discuss how Ferdinand could be extricated from Napoleon's trap and made to accompany them to Saragossa. José then received a smuggled message from Bayonne. Ferdinand himself ordered José and his men to proceed with all available troops to the town of Tolosa and there intercept the Infante Don Antonio who was on his way to join the rest of the royal family. The Infante was to be taken to safety in Saragossa, a mass levy was to be decreed throughout Aragon and a regency was to be formed with Don Antonio as its provisional head.

Neither rescue operation was possible. French spies in Irun learned of the plot and José and a fellow officer and close friend, Gomez de Butron, only just managed to escape arrest by French *gendarmes* by taking the mountain paths through Navarre to Aragon and travelling by night. José and Butron succeeded in eluding the numerous French forces stationed in the area, disguised themselves, narrowly escaped capture by a French cavalry detachment and eventually reached Saragossa safely with the help of local peasants and officials. They found the city in turmoil.

As soon as he arrived in the city, José went to the Captain-General's residence but Guillelmi gave him a cold welcome. Although José told him of the recent developments at Bayonne, of the plans to save the Spanish monarchy, and his hopes that the name of the Palafox family would help to rouse the Aragonese on behalf of Ferdinand, the old soldier adamantly refused to take any part in what he considered to be an act of sedition. José left him without any further argument and began to discuss the formation of a revolutionary *Junta* with relatives, friends, the Count of Sastago and the Torres brothers. As they knew that Guillelmi would inform Madrid of José's arrival, Butron was sent to the capital to report on the situation there and—almost certainly—to contact the Marquis of Lazan.

While the plotters prepared for action, Murat sent a message to Guillelmi, ordering José to rejoin his Corps of Guards within twenty-four hours. José prudently withdrew to the country house of a relative at Alfranca, nine miles from the city. A few days later, Butron returned and joined José, bringing him the news that the Spanish people were ready to revolt and prepared to strike the first blow. In the meantime, Murat had decreed that all members of the Royal Bodyguard who did not return to their posts at once would lose their promotion and rank and be treated as deserters. Guillelmi followed the order by sending José an ultimatum, ordering him to present himself at his quarters within

two hours, failing which troops would be sent to Alfranca to arrest him.
José replied that he recognised Ferdinand as his King and would obey
orders from no other source, and he defiantly remained at Alfranca. The
following day, the city revolted and he no longer had to fear arrest.

The insurgents left no one in any doubt over whom they wanted as
their leader. It was José Palafox. His name was cried out at public
meetings and cheered, and José Ibort, one of the first to preach rebellion, was chosen to fetch him back from Alfranca in the name of the
entire population of Saragossa. As news of Palafox's whereabouts
spread, the nine miles of road between the country house and the city
gates were crowded with excited townspeople and peasants from nearby villages. Ibort led the way, followed by a band of armed peasants
who fired their muskets in the air with joy when they saw Palafox.
They assured him of their patriotic fervour, begged him to emerge from
his temporary retreat and lead them on behalf of their King. At the same
time, a rider came galloping from the city, bringing a message from
Mori who had surrendered to the inevitable and now begged Palafox
to come to the city at once. It was a triumphal return. By the time
Palafox's carriage had reached the square in front of the Seo cathedral,
it was impossible for it to progress any further through the cheering
crowds who fired salvoes in the air and shouted their support for Palafox and their King. Escorted by Ibort and his men, Palafox dismounted
and struggled on foot through the throng towards the Captain-General's
residence, the Palacio de las Lunas, where Mori was waiting for him. A
few minutes later, Palafox appeared on the balcony to tumultuous
applause. When he was able to speak, he assured the crowd that he had
returned to the city ready to shed his last drop of blood to restore
Spain's rightful King on his lawful throne. He begged his fellow-citizens
to return to their homes, to keep calm, to leave him alone that he might
set to work, and to trust in God and the powerful influence of the Pilar
Virgin. Several hours passed before the city returned to its customary
calm. The streets were illuminated, bands of patriots were cheering
Palafox's name on every corner, continuous salvoes were fired and the
atmosphere in the city was that of a carnival rather than that of a
revolution.

The crowds finally dispersed, except for Ibort and a few of his men
who obstinately refused to leave Palafox, as they considered themselves
to be his permanent guard of honour since they had been the first to
fetch him from Alfranca. In his own short autobiography, Palafox told

the touching story of how, as he made his way home with his escort through the deserted streets late at night, he found a group of peasants standing guard by his door with some loaded cannons and mortars which they would have fired as a salute had he not managed to dissuade them, warning them of the danger to nearby buildings.

Two urgent tasks now faced Palafox. The first was to bring the over-excited city back to some kind of order so that serious resistance against the French might be organised; the second was to have his own position legitimised. It was not enough to be chosen leader by popular acclamation and demonstrations. Mori was legally still in office as Captain-General and for his powers to pass to Palafox there would have to be some sort of official sanction by a competent body. Palafox sent a letter to Mori asking for a meeting with the regional tribunal of the kingdom of Aragon, the *Real Acuerdo*.

May 26 was Ascension Day. The city still had a festive air and large crowds again gathered in the streets while the *Acuerdo* prepared for its emergency session in the Palace of the Real Audencia in the Plaz del Seo. It was a memorable occasion. Mori told the assembly of the public desire to make Palafox commander-in-chief and Palafox was summoned to make his appearance. Wearing his brigadier's uniform which a valet had brought all the way back from Irun, he walked through the crowds to the palace and, as public tension rose, began to speak to the magistrates and councillors. He described what had happened at Bayonne, he condemned the weakness of all Spaniards who had submitted to Murat's will, and declared that the Spanish people were willing and ready to free their country and their lawful King. He then said very diplomatically that although the people were offering him the leadership, he could not accept it since such a post could only be conferred by the royal authority vested in the legitimate president of the *Real Acuerdo*. Instead, he was prepared to await the assembly's decision to submit to it and, if necessary, to serve his country as a simple private.

According to Palafox's own account of the meeting, the members of the tribunal were surprised and even somewhat embarrassed by his declaration. They were also so moved by his words and humble attitude that they promptly offered him a seat beside the president of the assembly while they debated how to reconcile public enthusiasm with the authority and dignity of the tribunal. Meanwhile, the crowds massing outside the palace doors had no such scruples and were growing increasingly impatient. There were angry cries in the square and some of Palafox's supporters began to pound on the doors of the chamber. The nervous assembly sent an usher to investigate and he returned with the news that the people wanted to be admitted. Palafox urged the tribunal not to be afraid of their enthusiastic loyal fellow-citizens and suggested that three or four spokesmen for the people should be allowed in. Three young delegates duly appeared in the chamber and, after being given permission to speak, declared that the people had sworn to remain faithful to the King, that they had no confidence in the existing authorities after they had so cravenly obeyed Murat's orders, and that they placed all their trust in their favourite son, Palafox, who was now being detained in the assembly against his will. They wanted Palafox as their leader and at once! Furthermore, they were ready to march on the prison where Bonaparte was keeping their beloved Ferdinand, and free him by force.

It was a dangerous moment. As the crowd outside grew more threatening, Palafox rose to his feet and began to say that the *Acuerdo* was the body representing the royal power and that General Mori was a legitimate authority. But he was interrupted by the delegates who angrily shouted that Mori was a foreigner, and that either Palafox would be their leader or the heads of the members of the tribunal would roll. An astonishing, melodramatic scene now took place: with a flourish, Mori offered his baton of office to Palafox, begging him to take it and declaring that he had resigned in his favour. Palafox firmly refused, stating that he would never accept a command or mandate that was not given to him by the King (the fact that the King was in no position to give any commands or mandates was conveniently ignored). No, continued Palafox, he could not accept such a position. In view of his own in-experience, his youth and lack of those qualities needed for such a post, he would rather "lose my head than appear ambitious or arrogant".

How sincere was Palafox? It is difficult to avoid the conclusion that he was making the most of the occasion. The more humble and un-assuming his attitude, the more reluctance he showed about taking any course that could be regarded as presumptuous or unconstitutional, the more likely he was to gain the support of the lawful authorities. In any case, the effect of his words was highly satisfactory. The Regent of the Council and other leading dignitaries leapt from their seats and flung themselves at Palafox's feet. They begged him, as the "liberator", to accept the mandate offered him, to save the kingdom and the King, and to accept the position that circumstances had now made undeniably legal.

The scene now changed from melodrama to grand opera. In later years, when he wrote his autobiography, Palafox looked back with a certain complacency at the attitude he had struck and the reactions he had aroused. Reading between the lines, it seems clear that he had calculated his effect carefully and with great success:

"The picture presented in the chamber of the *Real Acuerdo* was certainly one worth seeing at that moment: the tribunal in all its dignity; the portrait of Ferdinand VII under the canopy; the table covered with books of new laws; Palafox standing and leaning against the side of the table; all the ministers including the Regent and Mori on their knees around him, begging him to accept the mandate with Mori holding out the General's baton to him. On the other side [of the table], the three peoples' representatives standing in imposing and menacing attitudes; the various employees of the Tribunal scattered in corners of the chamber, filled with fear and all staring at Palafox; the porter standing by the door as though awaiting the moment to open it wide; the armed multitude outside going up the staircase of the tribunal; repeated blows on the door and cries to be heard outside; the plaza and the streets filled with a seething throng of people of every class; an impressive silence as a prelude to some terrible outburst until Palafox resolved the question with a serenity which astonished all, his first words being: 'For my king, Don Ferdinand VII of Bourbon, I offer my life, my purpose and the lives of all Aragonese. I accept the mandate so that I may hand it over with honour to the king. I do not usurp it; I shall know how to make it respected for its own worth, by the motherland.'"

For Palafox, the meeting with the tribunal took on the aspect of a solemn consecration; for the members of the assembly, Palafox represented not only a hope of salvation for their province but also for their own skins. When Palafox came out of the palace to speak to the people, he made it plain that now that he had accepted the mandate of Captain-General, he would not allow any more noisy public demonstrations. One form of legality had been replaced by another. This was to be the city's last "popular commotion". He promised the people of Saragossa that they would not be disappointed at having put their faith in him. He would march forward "with law in his hand, along the path of duty, religion, and honour". Were he to fail or in any way stray from this path, then let the people count him an enemy while he would denounce himself as a criminal! Palafox made a final appeal for quiet in the city so that plans for its defence could be made in an atmosphere of calm, and then returned home escorted by members of the tribunal and surrounded by cheering supporters. By the time he had reached the palace, his uniform was in tatters; well-wishers, many weeping with joy, had snatched and torn away pieces of the cloth as precious keepsakes.

Palafox had now become the idol and the hope of every patriot in Saragossa, indeed in the whole of Aragon. When he began his career as a leader, he was an unknown, obscure army officer who had never seen active service. In a few weeks, he would be one of the most famous men in Spain and earn himself a secure place in his nation's history of resistance to Napoleon. But although he became a national hero, we still know little of him as a person. Some of his actions have greatly puzzled historians and it is still difficult to analyse them satisfactorily in the light of his character because, in certain respects, it remains shadowy and even enigmatic to posterity.

The best-known portrait of Palafox is by Goya and hangs in the Prado. The painter depicted him in general's uniform and on horseback. He is a dashing, martial figure, with his right arm raised high, holding a sabre in a gesture of command. But of the man himself, of his inner motivations and personality, Spanish historians and biographers have written little. Palafox himself wrote a short autobiography, in which he apparently felt bound to defend himself against detractors: "As an honourable Spaniard, I have never followed nor ever will tread any path other than that of the most sincere and ardent patriotism. Such an avowal, all the more necessary at this time when atrocious calumny and poisonous envy dare with effrontery to attack me in my honour and my person, has always been permitted to every man in public life." But when we read Spanish historians' accounts of Palafox's rise to power and his subsequent actions in Saragossa, he appears as a symbolic figure, a two-dimensional character of whom only the outward appearance and deeds are known. To them he was simply a great patriot and fighter, impelled by the same straightforward motivation which inspired countless other fellow Spaniards who defied Napoleon. It is what he did that mattered—not what he was.

Despite the lack of documentary material on Palafox the man, it is nonetheless obvious that he had qualities of great energy, diplomacy, charm, stubbornness and an ability for quick organisation which bordered on genius. He was certainly not a power-hungry opportunist who forced his fellow-citizens into a desperate and futile resistance

simply in order to satisfy his own ego. He made himself available to the
people of Saragossa and they chose him, both on account of his un-
doubted patriotism and will to resist the French, and because by birth,
breeding and career they found him eminently suitable to be their
spokesman, their leader and the incarnation of the popular will.

From the very beginning, Palafox showed his talent for obtaining
the total support of the citizens of Saragossa and for reconciling their
opinions and interests. Unlike other Spanish cities, Saragossa was
spared the horrors of civil strife and massacres of officials and army
officers accused of being pro-French or reluctant to join the popular
cause. By force of character and diplomacy, Palafox succeeded in
obtaining full-hearted, legal approval for his assumption of power and
he prevented any dispersion of energies which could have been
disastrous for the city's security and public morale.

Palafox at once had to face a number of urgent tasks. The city and
the region had to be made ready for war, troops had to be raised, reinforcements found and communications established with other towns
and centres of resistance. Time was short, resources were scanty and
the treasury was almost empty.

Saragossa itself was in a deplorable condition to withstand an attack.
Although it was sheltered on the north by the wide river Ebro, spanned
by a single stone bridge, and to the south-east by the confluent river
Huerva, which was fordable, its walls were dilapidated and weak. At
no point were they higher than twelve feet; they had no proper parapets; and they were mostly made of a mixture of mud, plaster, fragments of brick, and lime. They were broken by nine unimposing gates
and a number of large buildings, the backs of which made up part of the
line of the city walls.

Within the city, there were considerable supplies of arms, cannon
and shot but very few regular soldiers. Over 20,000 muskets in good
condition had been found by the insurgents in the Aljaferia castle and,
according to the official returns of the artillery department, when the
revolt broke out, the city had 103 bronze cannon of regular calibre, 43
howitzers, although only one mortar, 51,000 round shot, 81,000 canisters
of grapeshot, and nearly seven and a half million musket balls, as well as
charged cartridges, powder, bombs, grenades and an assortment of
gun-carriages. What were lacking were men to operate the guns, defend
the city's perimeter, and hold the strong points outside the walls. The
whole of Aragon had been virtually stripped of regular army units

while Godoy was in power. As a nucleus for any new army he might raise, Palafox had only 300 cavalrymen of the King's Dragoons with only ninety horses between them, a much diminished battalion of the Volunteers of Aragon, 200 gunners and sappers, and about 500 soldiers from regiments in Madrid, Burgos and other towns, who had left their quarters to rally to the defence of Saragossa. Their sum total, according to Gomez de Arteche, the eminent Spanish historian of the Peninsular War who had access to contemporary documents and statistics, was 1,463.

Palafox immediately showed himself a quick and able organiser. After another visit to the specially illuminated chapel of the Pilar Virgin on the following day, and kissing the hand of the sacred image, he concentrated on the organisation of a defence militia and the civil and military administration of Saragossa. A *Junta* was soon formed which included aldermen, members of the *Real Acuerdo*, the dean, arch-priest and canon of the cathedral chapter, noblemen and army officers, of whom one, Don Antonio Cornel, was a general. They decided that the situation facing them was military rather than political. Their first aims were to ensure the defence of the borders of Aragon, to recover arms from the peasants so that they might be redistributed on a more rational basis, to form an efficient corps of gunners to man the cannon taken from the castle, to raise and train new fighting men and to strengthen the city's defences, since it was General Cornel's opinion that to fight the French from anywhere else than behind the city's ramparts would be disastrous. A second, purely military *Junta*, headed by General Cornel, was then convened and the city was rapidly transformed into a small, military state powerful enough to overcome any hindrance by the civil authorities.

Palafox issued a series of orders and proclamations, addressed both to the city and to the whole of Aragon. The first, dated May 28, was drafted by a member of the *Junta* and a leading nobleman, Count Cabarrus. It stated that those citizens who possessed arms should form companies of a hundred men each and observe the strictest discipline under commanders to be appointed by Palafox. These companies would present themselves every morning and afternoon in barracks organised for them in the Convalescents' Hospital in the southern part of the city. Similar companies were to assemble in the country districts and small towns and would be led by local magistrates when there were no regular officers available. The companies would be paid out of public funds and their main object would be to maintain public order and protect any Spaniard or foreigner (there was a considerable French merchant colony in Saragossa) from the danger of unjust treatment. The proclamation ended with the injunction that, although they were to continue with their usual duties, magistrates and civil servants must bear in mind that "for the moment, the government of the kingdom is a purely military one".

A second proclamation followed almost immediately: after some introductory words of praise for the courage of the Aragonese, it ordered all able-bodied men between the ages of sixteen and forty to assemble in regiments. And, on May 30, Palafox signed yet another directive stating that magistrates should draw up lists of recruits; that passports would be required by anyone leaving or entering the city; that French residents in the city should correctly declare all their possessions, on pain of huge fines; that private correspondence was to be strictly censored; that no one was to write about weapons, troop movements and defensive preparations; that the names of recipients of all letters written in the city were to be noted, and that all offences against the law were to be classed as treason and severely punished as such. In addition to these drastic measures, Palafox also announced that he was abolishing a highly unpopular wine tax.

On May 31, Palafox appointed captains to command the first two companies of citizen soldiers, who paraded to the sound of music outside his palace, and then issued a resounding manifesto which made his name ring like a trumpet call throughout Spain. It began: "Providence has preserved in Aragon an immense quantity of rifles, munitions and artillery of all calibres which have been neither handed over nor perfidiously sold to the enemies of our repose. Your patriotism, your honour and your love for the sane doctrines which you have inherited from your ancestors will make you determined to shake off the shameful slavery being prepared for you by the French government which, after modelling its conduct on a horrible Machiavellianism, aspired to deceive you, as well as the whole of Spain, and to cover with opprobrium and shame the most generous-hearted nation on earth . . ." After denouncing some of the nation's leaders who were collaborating with the enemy, Palafox exhorted the Aragonese to fear nothing since "the cause we defend is the most just that ever presented itself and we are invincible". Palafox also denounced Napoleon's intrigues at Bayonne and solemnly stated that: first, the Emperor, all members of his family, and every French general and officer were directly responsible for the safety of the King, his brothers and uncles; second, that in the case of an attempt on their precious lives, which might deprive Spain of her monarch, the nation would use its right to choose in favour of Archduke Charles, the grandson of Charles III, if the other heirs were unable to succeed to the throne; third, that any theft, pillage or killing perpetrated by the French in Madrid or elsewhere would be considered as crimes of high treason and that, in punishing them, no quarter was to be given; fourth, that all actions accomplished through French brute force at Madrid and Bayonne were null and void; fifth, that all the decisions made at Bayonne would be equally null and void and that all Spaniards crossing the frontier after the publication of the proclamation would be considered as traitors; sixth, that French deserters would be treated with "the generosity which belongs to the Spanish character" and could serve alongside Spanish troops; seventh, that other provinces still free from invasion should send deputies to Teruel or some other convenient place in order to name a lieutenant-general of the Kingdom of Aragon who would be obeyed by the heads of all other Spanish kingdoms in the country; eighth and last, the manifesto was to be printed and published in the whole of Aragon as well as in every capital and important town in every Spanish province.

Palafox's improvised army quickly grew in numbers. By the first few days of June, five regiments or *tercios* of civilian volunteers, each one a thousand strong and divided into ten companies, had been formed and were undergoing training. Where no officers were available, men distinguished either by their family name or their profession were chosen by the military *Junta* to lead the recruits. Men poured in from the provinces and even from as far away as Pamplona and Madrid. More than 10,000 Aragonese peasants came streaming into the city and were followed by fragments of regular units who had escaped the French; when Captain José Obispo and 400 veteran soldiers entered Saragossa, they were reviewed from the balcony of his palace by Palafox, who cried "Vanquish or die, my sons!" to the cheering crowds below. A particularly welcome arrival was that of Palafox's brother, the Marquis of Lazan, who had persuaded Murat to let him leave Madrid on the pretext that he would use his influence to bring the rebellious Saragossans back to submission.

While the numbers of the army swelled, and the citizen soldiers drilled in the meadows outside the Portillo gate and marched with bands playing beneath his windows, Palafox continued to appoint men he could trust to key positions, to issue orders and organise the defence of Aragon's frontiers. A highly-respected business man, Don Lorenzo Calvo de Rozas, who had returned to Saragossa from Madrid after May 2, was made chief intendant for the army; two other prominent citizens were given charge of the hospitals and the treasury; the garrison of the Aljaferia castle was increased and placed under the command of Manuel Cerezo, the farmer who had played such an important role during the uprising of May 24.

As donations of money and weapons came in from patriotic citizens, arrangements were made for their administration and distribution; a magistrate was sent on a mission to Majorca to ask for help from the English who were on the island; a captain of engineers surveyed the region on both sides of the Imperial Canal to find the best defensive points; and various companies were despatched to the nearby towns of La Lamunia, Calatayud and Daroca—the last feared reprisals from the French after it had refused to hand over gunpowder from the local factory.

There was no way of concealing Aragonese war preparations from the French and in a few days rumours reached Saragossa that enemy forces were marching towards Aragon. They were right: throughout Spain the French armies were indeed on the move. The war had begun.

*   *   *

When hostilities broke out, Napoleon regarded the whole Iberian peninsula as a secondary field of operations, and Spain as a disorganised, weak and inefficient nation that would soon be forced into submission. He had shared Murat's optimism that Spain would remain tranquil after the May 2 insurrection, and even after serious and wide-scale revolts had occurred, he and Murat were still convinced that a few punitive expeditions would suffice to restore peace. His attitude to the country and his lack of interest in the circumstances behind the revolt, coupled with the physical nature of the country and the mood of the people, dismayed several of his advisers. The Duchesse d'Abrantès was among those near to him who witnessed his over-confidence at the start of the Spanish revolution: "Napoleon seemed struck by a kind of vertigo. He would listen neither to Junot, to Duroc, to Beurnonville,* nor to anyone who knew the state of the country."

* Ambassador to Spain, 1802–1806.

Napoleon was convinced of one apparently unassailable fact. Indeed his spies and ambassadors had inundated him with reports of Spain's military incapacity. At the time of the French invasion, Spain could only put a total of 86,000 regular soldiers in the field and of these more than one sixth were Swiss and other foreign mercenaries. 15,000 of Spain's best soldiers, under their general, the Marquis de la Romana had been sent by Godoy to northern Europe at Napoleon's request—or rather, his order. The army which remained was short of money, supplies and equipment and had been scandalously neglected under Godoy's administration. As far as logistics were concerned, "the Spanish army was still in the Middle Ages", as Sir Charles Oman wrote in his great history of the war. It lacked any kind of organised commissariat, it had few engineers, and, by 1808, there remained only one small military college for the training of cadets in the entire country. Many regiments and battalions were greatly under strength, there were too few officers, too many cavalrymen without horses and too few mules and horses to pull the cannon. The administration was cumbersome and chaotic, morale was often low, and many high-ranking officers owed their promotion to corruption and favouritism instead of to any military talent. Only the Spanish artillery, traditionally one of the best in Europe, remained an efficient force—when there were enough trained gunners. The infantry were badly drilled, badly uniformed, and badly disciplined. But they could still fight bravely if led by capable commanders. The cavalry were reputed the worst in Europe.

The quality of the armies which Napoleon sent into Spain between October 1807 and May 1808 showed the low opinion he had of the Spanish forces. He had the world's finest war machine at his disposal but he felt inclined to spare only a small part of it for operations in Spain. In the peninsula as a whole, the best army, with the highest proportion of veteran troops, was that operating in Portugal under the command of Junot. The armies of Dupont, Bessières and Moncey were mostly composed of conscripts, many of whom had been called to arms before their time. Many regiments had been hastily formed, were classified as "provisional" and were composed of a medley of Swiss, Italian, Portuguese, German, Neapolitan and Irish auxiliaries. Although the cavalry were equally heterogeneous, they did, admittedly, include a small number of the terrifying Mamelukes who had so impressed the Madrilenes, and several squadrons of the murderously effective Polish lancers who had proved their worth on the battlefields of Europe. But although the French far exceeded the meagre Spanish forces in numbers, it was the French artillery and engineering corps which had the most experienced, reliable soldiers.

When the revolt exploded throughout Spain, Junot's army had already captured Lisbon and conquered Portugal after her royal family had fled to Brazil. He and his troops remained in the country as an occupying force. The other French armies were positioned like a great arrow pointing at the heart of the peninsula. In the east, General Duhesme held Barcelona with his 14,000 men; in the north, Irun, Pamplona, Vitoria, and Burgos were occupied by strong French contingents; in the centre, Madrid was encircled, occupied and subdued, while a further sizeable force was stationed at Toledo, ready to strike to the south or south-east if necessary. The whole country was therefore cut in two between Irun and Toledo, and the road to France was constantly swarming with French regiments, couriers, supply trains, artillery detachments and cavalry patrols—which made communication between Aragon and central Spain, and between central Spain and the northern provinces, extremely difficult.

Towards the end of May 1808, the main bodies of the Spanish regular forces were in the north-west and in Andalusia, where many thousands of peasants were joining the army commanded by General Xavier Castaños since the murder of Solano. As the risings developed, Napoleon and Murat had to decide where to strike first in order to subdue what they considered to be only a series of minor and disconnected revolts. That they would subdue them quickly, they had no doubt. The only serious threat they acknowledged was that of an attack from the maritime provinces of Galicia and the Asturias where two Spanish generals, Blake (he was of Irish descent) and Cuesta, had assembled considerable regular forces and might attempt to cut the long French lines of communication between Madrid and France. Otherwise, the main effect of the revolt was that the French were prevented access to the important southern ports of Valencia, Cartagena, Seville, and Cadiz. In Castile and Aragon, the risings were considered to be of little importance since the rebel forces consisted in the main of poorly armed peasants and volunteers.

The first French army of repression moved off from Toledo on May 24. It was led by General Dupont and its orders were to march southwards through Andalusia, taking Cordova, Seville and, finally, Cadiz. Ten days later, another army under Moncey advanced towards

Valencia, while at the same time Duhesme's army in Catalonia began to move southwards from Barcelona. In the north, Bessières's army was ordered to guard communications, keep watch on the north-west and send a force into Aragon.

Operations in northern and central Spain began at the end of May. On June 2, the French occupied the rebellious city of Logroño, where they killed several hundred poorly armed peasants and hanged and shot several prisoners as an example to the population. Ten days later, some miles north-east of Valladolid, on the road to Burgos, they completely routed a force of volunteers and a few regular cavalry under General Cuesta, and then occupied Valladolid.

So far as Aragon was concerned, the French had no military threat to fear; nevertheless Saragossa not only provided the focus for revolt in the old kingdom, but remained, since the circulation of Palafox's manifesto throughout Spain and even in England, an irritating example of unsubdued rebellion. Napoleon consequently turned his attention from more important operations in the south and ordered Bessières to detach a force to march on Saragossa, writing on June 4 that "it is indispensable that an example should be made of Saragossa between the 10th and the 15th of June. Send howitzers and twelve-pounders; when it is a matter of marching against houses and cities, a great deal of artillery is needed". Four days later, Napoleon again wrote to Murat about Saragossa, stressing that "it is a very important centre to be pacified". Palafox could not have received a better compliment.

*   *   *

On June 7, Marshal Bessières's chief-of-staff, Brigadier-General Charles Lefebvre-Desnouettes, marched out of Pamplona with a small force of 3,500 infantry, 950 cavalry and a battery of six four-pounder guns. Lefebvre was thirty-five years old, and a brave, dashing, experienced warrior who had seen active service since the beginning of the Revolutionary Wars in 1792. He had fought in Germany, the Low Countries, Poland and Italy, had distinguished himself at Marengo and Austerlitz and had been made a Count of the Empire by Napoleon, whose aide-de-camp he had once been. The little army under his command consisted of the 2nd Regiment of the Supplementary Reserve and three battalions of regiments of the line. Unlike most other commanders in Spain at the time, he was fortunate enough to have a fair proportion of veteran soldiers among his infantry. In addition, he had three squadrons of the redoubtable Polish lancers.

Lefebvre's plan of operation was straightforward. He was to march southwards from Pamplona and through the mountains of Navarre to the town of Tudela which commanded a bridge across the Ebro. Tudela, which had a population of 12,000, was the most important town on the river between Logroño and Saragossa and for centuries it had been known as the "key to Aragon". Napoleon had been quick to see its importance as he studied the map of northern Spain. It was situated at the entry to the Imperial Canal leading to Saragossa and, as it was only three days' march from the city, it provided an ideal base and supply depot for an army operating deep within Aragon. Furthermore, Tudela commanded the right bank of the Ebro which boasted the only good roads, the navigable canal along which heavy supplies and artillery could be brought if necessary, plentiful natural resources for the feeding of the troops, a covered left flank, and the flat plains where the river valley widened near Saragossa and infantry and cavalry could manoeuvre easily.

The inhabitants of Tudela soon realised the threat from the French and sent messages to Palafox and the *Junta*. On June 6, Colonel José Obispo and his 400 fusiliers were sent to the town of Tarazona, a few miles to the south-west of Tudela in the mountains. At midnight on the 7th, Palafox's brother, the Marquis of Lazan, left Saragossa with one thousand men of the 1st Aragonese *tercio* and four cannon and hurried to the aid of Tudela; with the assistance of the local armed peasants, they would also defend the passage over the Ebro.

As Lazan's and Obispo's forces advanced, they found the inhabitants unsure of French movements. It was rumoured that the French had entered Logroño, sacked the town and massacred many of the inhabitants. Some people, however, claimed that they had never been near the town. When Lazan entered the village of El Bocal, his men captured a courier carrying letters from Bayonne together with a pamphlet addressed to the inhabitants of Saragossa and the Kingdom of Aragon. The pamphlet was signed by twenty-seven of the Spanish nobles who had gathered at Bayonne on Napoleon's orders, was dated June 4, and called for an end to the rebellion since the signatories had heard "with sadness that some ill-advised inhabitants had captured their Captain-General [Guillelmi]". The "Lieutenant-General of the Kingdom of Spain" was determined to appoint another Captain-General for Aragon and was therefore marching on the city to disperse the rebels. The twenty-seven collaborators urged the Aragonese to submit, to return to "their duties and obedience" and "contribute to the regeneration of Spain".

Lazan's answer was to send a request to his brother for another four guns and additional muskets. As he waited for the expected reinforcements from the outlying villages and Obispo's troops, his ill-trained men became increasingly nervous, fired wildly at the slightest alarm and eagerly listened to every latest rumour. What they did not know was that Lefebvre was already on the right bank of the Ebro.

As Lefebvre advanced southwards without meeting opposition, he learned that the Spaniards were waiting for him at Tudela and had broken the bridge. Instead of proceeding as planned, he made a diversion towards a former ferry point further up the river at Valtierra, and brought his army across on commandeered boats. On the morning of June 8, he marched his troops to within sight of Tudela, to the great surprise of the defenders. After a brief, futile parley with the insurgents, Lefebvre launched a vigorous attack and swept aside Obispo's men as they came down from the hills and tried to prevent the French from reaching the town. In Tudela, Lazan had gathered together a total of some 5,000 fighting men but, despite his efforts, the town was in disorder. The French fired their field pieces and stormed the town. The Polish lancers charged, routed the peasants and relentlessly hunted them down, spearing them as they fled through surrounding olive groves and fields. Lazan rallied his remaining thousand men as best as he could, spiked his four cannon, and withdrew.

Instead of pursuing the fleeing Spaniards, Lefebvre halted a few days at Tudela in order to disarm the region, make sure of his communications, rebuild the bridge and shoot some inhabitants who had been found under arms. On June 12, he was reinforced by the Polish troops of the 1st Regiment of the Vistula, a *bataillon de marche* and an artillery convoy of eight guns, bringing the total of his forces to over 6,000. On the following day, he moved his army forward again, to meet Lazan in a second battle.

The Marquis, with a force composed of some 4,000 armed peasants, a battalion of Tarragona volunteers who had deserted from Pamplona some time previously, 200 fusiliers from Saragossa and less than a hundred horsemen, had taken up a position on the heights near the small village of Mallen by the Ebro. On the evening of the 12th, the

French army came into sight, after having occupied Tarazona without resistance. Although the heights on which Lazan had stationed his forces were accessible to the French cavalry and field artillery, he was sheltered on his left by thick olive groves. The Spaniards had regained their morale and were confident of reconquering Tudela. At dawn on the 13th, the French attacked and Lazan's army withdrew towards Mallen in disorder. The Spaniards were soon outflanked and routed; the thin line of peasant soldiers stood only two deep and was quickly broken by the French cavalry. Lazan and his fusiliers were forced back between the Ebro river and the canal, the guns were abandoned, the peasants scattered and again hunted down by the Polish lancers, and Lazan only saved himself by taking a boat across the Ebro. For Lefebvre, the way to Saragossa was now clear.

*   *   *

Troops continued to arrive in Saragossa after Lazan's departure for Tudela. A regiment of the King's Dragoons rode into the city on June 7 and on the following day, while volunteers continued to pour in from small towns and villages of the province, Palafox was joined by his second brother, Francisco, who had escaped from Bayonne in disguise. Palafox was now showing the utmost energy in keeping public morale high and in tackling the problems of administration which increased from day to day. On June 7, another proclamation bearing his signature and designed to whip up the enthusiasm of the peasants and townspeople was published. On June 8, he decreed that all men holding muskets and other firearms should hand them over for the army's use; horses were to be commandeered and paid for in order to form cavalry regiments; carts and carriages were to be requisitioned; lists would have to be submitted of the amounts of cloth and grain held by private individuals; all French goods and possessions were to be surrendered to the authorities; the amount of public funds was to be declared; the sale of goods belonging to the Church was to be suspended and anyone committing a public disturbance would be severely punished.

Palafox was determined to sweep away all obstacles which might impede the efficiency of his operations and preparations for the town's defence. Preachers in the city were warned not to interfere in the affairs of government and to confine their activities to praying for the aid and protection of God. Continuous efforts were made to form the most effective governing body and, with this aim in mind, Palafox summoned a meeting of the ancient Aragonese *Cortes* or regional parliament, formed of delegates from the Aragonese nobility, the clergy, and the nine cities of the ancient kingdom. Another object in convoking the *Cortes* was to ensure the full legitimacy of Palafox's position and to make it appoint a committee from among its members, to act as a permanent advisory body to Palafox and his *Junta*.

At ten o'clock on the morning of June 9, the *Cortes* met under a portrait of Ferdinand VII in the historic *Sala de las Juntas*, next to the elegant Renaissance building of *La Lonja* by the Pilar basilica. A few minutes later, Palafox, preceded by dragoons and foot soldiers, made his way through the crowds which had gathered in the Plaza del Seo and entered the building. He received the greetings of the deputies from the various towns, high-ranking Church dignitaries and noblemen, then the assembly solemnly declared its allegiance to Ferdinand VII, and finally Palafox made a long speech in which he outlined the general situation and described the measures he had taken so far.

In response to Palafox's invitation, the strategically important cities of Tortosa and Lerida had rallied to the Aragonese cause. Following a petition he had received from the civic authorities at Lerida, Palafox had appointed a governor for the town and sent it both arms and men. The city of Tortosa was equally desirous of "sharing in our triumphs" and it had already obeyed Palafox's orders to liaise with the British by giving them a copy of his manifesto of May 31 so that it might be circulated throughout Europe. Palafox had also negotiated an attempt to bring over the Spanish troops stationed in Majorca and Minorca and he was preparing to establish regular correspondence with the Austrian government. As Logroño and Tudela had also asked for military leaders and help in preventing the French from invading Aragon, Palafox had named his brother as plenipotentiary officer and commander of an armed force for this very purpose. He had received deputies from many towns in Navarre and the city and province of Soria, he had established contact with Santander and set up posts along the road to Valencia. He had asked the Valencian *Junta* to send him arms and artillery and he had issued manifestoes to that city with orders that they were to be circulated throughout Andalusia, La Mancha, Estremadura, Galicia and the Asturias, calling on the local resistance leaders to act jointly with Aragon against the French. To administrate public wealth and finances in Saragossa, Palafox had appointed the well-known and incorruptibly honest Don Lorenzo Calvo de Rozas.

Finally, Palafox asked the *Cortes* to appoint some of their members as a permanent *Junta*, each deputy to correspond with his own region. This *Junta* was to devise plans for the aid of the city, advise him, help circulate orders and messages throughout Spain, proclaim Ferdinand VII as King, and decide whether deputies from outside the Kingdom of Aragon should be allowed to participate in their own councils for the public good of the whole nation.

The members of the *Cortes* decided by acclamation that Ferdinand VII should be solemnly proclaimed King and that Palafox should be Captain-General and political and military governor of Aragon, thus giving the fullest legal and constitutional confirmation to his appointment by the *Real Acuerdo* on May 26. They also agreed that a permanent *Junta* of six members should be formed and headed by Palafox. But Palafox graciously declined the honour of being appointed Captain-General of the army in the name of the Kingdom of Aragon, declaring that he was only a brigadier and that he could only accept the proposed title if it were conferred upon him by the King. Moreover, in the present circumstances, he needed neither honour nor title but only "valour, rectitude, integrity and sincerity for the great task of saving the King and nation". The real authority, Palafox diplomatically insisted, lay with the *Cortes* until such time as the King returned to Spain. After Palafox had spoken, the members of the assembly, deeply moved, declared that they admired Palafox's delicacy but resolved that they would still give him the proposed title on another occasion when he was not present. Before they dispersed, it was agreed that the next meeting of the *Junta* would be held in five days' time.

During the afternoon and evening of June 9, the French residents in the city (there were several hundred—an astonishingly high proportion for a city of less than 50,000 souls) were arrested and placed in custody in the cells of the castle and prison for their own safety as much as for any reasons of security. Morale was high in the city but war fever made it dangerous for anyone of French nationality, or even descent, to venture into the streets which were filled with volunteer battalions with flags flying and drums beating, excited peasants, preaching monks and onlookers.

On June 10, while the monks of the city's Dominican, Franciscan and Capuchin monasteries were busy making cartridges in the Misericordia building, nearly 10,000 volunteers assembled by Colonel Geronimo Torres gathered in an open space known as the Campo del

Sepulcro outside the Portillo gate. They had been given muskets from stocks found in the castle and then filed three abreast into the city, marching through the Carmen gate and along the Coso avenue to the Plaza de la Magdalena and thence to the front of Palafox's palace. A simultaneous order was issued that all officers should form their regiments during the next twenty-four hours—any lapse would be considered unpatriotic. Indeed order followed order at such a pace that many households were in a state of confusion, and Palafox was forced to make the concession that all married men in the city were allowed to go home until summoned to return to their units. That evening, a small number of soldiers who had escaped from Barcelona arrived to swell the already considerable forces which had accumulated in the past few days.

On the following morning, Palafox issued a proclamation stating that as the French residents were not in prison on his orders, and as they had always proved themselves to be loyal and useful citizens, it was unjust to keep them detained any longer and they should therefore be allowed to return home on condition they swear before a judge an oath of fidelity to the monarchy and the Catholic faith. It was an ill-timed proposal. Rumours of a French advance were already circulating. They were said to have reached Tudela (which was true enough) and a battle was believed to be imminent. Angry crowds of citizens protested at the proclamation and urged Palafox to revoke the order—which he did, sending his brother Francisco and two aides-de-camp into the streets to calm the people. On the following day, more French and other suspects, including the Italian director of the Canal company's hydraulic machinery, were imprisoned.

Soldiers and peasants continued to arrive; these included a company of 250 volunteers of the first regiment of Aragon who had escaped from Madrid with their regimental drums and marched past Palafox's residence to the cheers of the populace. Morale was still high and it was generally believed that Lazan's army would expel the French from the region near Tudela. Rumour followed rumour: it was said that the French had been routed in Catalonia, that Lefebvre's force had been encircled at Tudela and, then, that Lazan was preparing to give battle at Mallen. By the evening, rumours of victory had changed to those of defeat. Several citizens panicked and asked the authorities for their passports so that they might leave the city. As the night wore on, rumours became reality as the first retreating survivors of Lazan's force came straggling through the gates with reports that the French were advancing on the city. Palafox at once cancelled the forthcoming session of the *Cortes*, ordered the church bells to ring the alarm and preparations to be made for a mass sortie against the enemy. For a moment, public morale sank and, in the words of the eye-witness and historian of the siege, Alcaide Ibieca, "the lugubrious silence of the night, broken by the anxious voices of the peasants and artisans, the din of horses and carriages, the idea of an imminent danger—everything wrought in our souls an impression of overwhelming sadness".

Soon the streets were filled with crowds of men, followed by their wives, children and relations, making their way outside the city walls to the Campo del Sepulcro, or *Eras del Rey* as it was also called, where Palafox had ordered all fighting men to assemble at two in the morning. Wagons were laden with provisions, peasants and townsmen rushed to collect muskets, blunderbusses, swords and pistols, while the great bell of the Mudejar-style Torre Nueva boomed throughout the night. As some 7,000 to 8,000 men gathered in the Campo del Sepulcro, companies and battalions were hastily formed on a makeshift basis as many of the men had still not been allocated to any of the previously formed regiments and *tercios*. They joined whichever company they knew best. They banded together according to friendship, common acquaintance or the fact that they came from the same city or provincial district; and they selected their officers from among relatives and friends.

A vanguard force left first and reached Alagon at seven in the morning, surprising and capturing eleven French soldiers who had been sleeping in the local *posada*. At dawn Palafox and the main force moved off. His army was largely undisciplined and untrained. Many men had never handled a gun before in their lives and the heavy baggage and ammunition trains moved slowly as the sun rose and announced a day of scorching heat. As the first shots were being exchanged with Lefebvre's forward skirmishers who were drawing near the village, the fourteen miles of road between Saragossa and Alagon were still swarming with men, horses and women carrying provisions. When they did reach their destination, some men prepared an ambush among the thick olive groves by the village while others flung themselves down, exhausted after the speed of the march and the heat of the sun. By mid-morning, the main body of the enthusiastic people's army entered Alagon and took up position. On the left of the line drawn up to oppose the French advance was Palafox with some 500 regular infantry and

200 horsemen; several thousand men with shotguns and muskets made up the centre; and a further mass of peasant soldiers and volunteers formed the right flank among the olive groves and fields as far as the Ebro.

The battle was an unequal contest. Lefebvre had fewer men but at least even his conscripts were better trained than the Spanish and he knew how to manoeuvre. He sent forward two columns towards Alagon by the road from Mallen and from the direction of a farm to the south of the road, ordering them to open fire from a distance as though they were about to attempt to break through the Spanish lines in a frontal attack. Meanwhile, the third French column, advancing from the south, crossed the Imperial Canal in order to surround Alagon and drive the Spaniards towards the river.

Palafox's regulars exchanged fire with the French and stood their ground firmly for a few hours but as the French attacked from the south and their cavalry charged, the lines of peasants and townsfolk, seeing themselves outflanked, wavered and broke. Palafox himself led two desperate charges with his tiny force of cavalry, but he was slightly wounded in one arm and unable to prevent a general rout. Once more the French cavalry, and the Polish lancers in particular, charged, spearing and trampling the demoralised peasants and citizen volunteers. All that Palafox could do was to try to rally his remaining forces and fall back along the heavily encumbered road towards Saragossa.

In the city, the anxious inhabitants held their breath and waited for news of the battle. Ibieca graphically described the tense atmosphere of that morning and early afternoon: "Saragossa presented the most lugubrious aspect. The gates were shut; there was a silence as profound as it was extraordinary after the tumult and confusion of the previous night. A few decrepit old men who patrolled the streets, their trembling hands armed with swords and pikes, preparing to make their last effort, pale-faced, silent wives and mothers who did not know if they would ever see their husbands and sons again—such was the scene to be beheld on all sides." Their worst fears were confirmed towards four o'clock when the first dust-covered and bedraggled fugitives from the battle-field staggered, gasping from thirst, through the Portillo gate. Many others who had escaped the lances and sabres of the French cavalry fell dead or lay in various states of collapse along the road; others still had been taken prisoner. Palafox himself returned later in the evening and immediately ordered the whole city to be placed on an alert. Nothing could now stop the French from advancing to the city's gates, but it was essential to barricade the gates, sandbag a few walls, place the city's cannon at strategic points and prepare to make one last, desperate effort.

But Lefebvre did not follow up his victory at once or make any attempt to pursue his routed enemy as far as the city. Instead, he ordered the Spaniards taken prisoner to be freed and sent to Saragossa to encourage a surrender. One prisoner was given a note to deliver to Palafox, saying that if he did not agree to negotiate, the city would be reduced to a heap of ruins, and its people killed or else treated with all the rigour of martial law. Resistance would be useless: Lefebvre stated his firm intention to enter the city "in spite of the thirty thousand idiots who wished to oppose his war-experienced troops".

Saragossa's citizens and leaders had been so confident of repelling the French outside the city that defensive preparations had been lagging. Throughout the night of June 14, men, women and children toiled to make up for lost time. Many of the city's plentiful cannon were still in the squares and market places. Now, led by their priests, officers and local magistrates, the people hurriedly moved them to the city's walls and gates, placing them behind flimsy ramparts of timber and sandbags. Embrasures were pierced in the walls of the convents, gardens and cavalry barracks, and ammunition was brought up. Colonel Geronimo Torres, with a force of 450 men including some of Mariano Cerezo's volunteers, and two guns, stationed himself a few miles from the town, by the bridge over the canal near the village of Muela, to impede a French advance in that direction. In the suburb of Casa Blanca, another peasant volunteer force, under the command of Colonel José Obispo and the other Torres brother, Antonio, and with two cannon, took up its stand.

The French resumed their advance in the morning, with one force continuing to advance on the city along the road from Alagon while another moved towards Muela and the canal. At nine o'clock, a squadron of French cavalry appeared along the canal but was driven back by Spanish cannon fire. A few minutes later, the defenders saw the French infantry, supported by cavalry and field artillery, advancing along the edge of the canal, along the Muela road, and through the vineyards and open ground. After a short exchange of fire, the Spaniards realised that they were about to be outflanked at the bridge and fell back to Casa Blanca where Obispo and Antonio Torres had drawn up their battalion in line. The French guns opened fire, one Spanish cannon

exploded, and the other broke its gun-carriage. There was nothing else
the Spanish could do but continue their withdrawal towards the city as
the French began to stream across the Muela bridge. It was obvious
that the Spaniards were no match for the French in the open.

News of the French approach led to a general alarm being sounded
in Saragossa. Masses for the city's salvation were said in the Pilar and
Seo churches while the nuns of the three convents nearest the Alagon
road were evacuated to other religious establishments inside the city
walls. Palafox rode up and down the streets, holding a white banner
embroidered with the Pilar Virgin, and then sent a messenger to the
officer holding the post of King's Lieutenant for Saragossa, Don
Vicente Bustamente, saying that he now entrusted him with the military
command; he had decided that the city's fate was sealed and that the
best hope of opposing the French lay in setting up a new headquarters
elsewhere and in raising a fresh army in the province. After kissing the
hand of the sacred Pilar Virgin, he quietly rode out of the city with a
few officers and headed for the small town of Belchite to the south-east.
Two hours later, before news of his departure had spread, and while the
disconcerted Bustamente was conferring with the city magistrates on
the apparently hopeless situation, the citizens lining the walls glimpsed
the distant flash of bayonets in the shimmering sunlight as Lefebvre's
columns continued their inexorable progress towards Saragossa.

PART THREE

THE FIRST SIEGE

III

AFTER THE demoralising defeat at Alagon, Palafox came to the conclusion that his disorganised, amateur soldiers were incapable of preventing the capture of Saragossa. Lefebvre-Desnouettes fully shared his conviction but also realised that, with the few troops at his own disposal, there could be no question of laying conventional siege to the city. Instead, he would deliver strong attacks at various points along the walls, burst through the weakly defended gates and then bring the rebellious population back to their senses with a few executions and whiffs of grapeshot.

Preparations for defence were still far from complete when the French came within sight of the city. An experienced sergeant-major of engineers, Don Antonio San Genis, was reconnoitring the city's perimeter to plan new defensive works when he was arrested by an excited crowd accusing him of treason and espionage. Outside the walls, from east to west, there lay four important monastic buildings: that of a barefoot order of Augustine monks, the *Agustinos Descalzos*; the monastery of the Trinitarian fathers; and that of the Capuchin friars, all three in a line between the Aljaferia castle and the bend of the Huerva river; and, towards the Ebro on the eastern side of the city, the monastery of San José, which commanded a bridge across the Huerva and access to the Quemada gate. If a small number of defenders had been placed in each of these solidly built structures, they could have enfiladed the French as they advanced and protected the city's main gates. But the buildings remained vacant except for the handful of monks who simply shut the doors and, in Ibieca's words, "waited for the moment when the enemy would batter them down". Apart from the Aljaferia castle with its few guns, ancient walls and volunteer garrison, the only other outlying point of strategic importance was the hill of Monte Torrero by the canal, a mile to the south of the city.

Otherwise, the defenders contented themselves with taking up their positions along the line of the walls and converting a number of substantial buildings into strongpoints where snipers could be posted at the

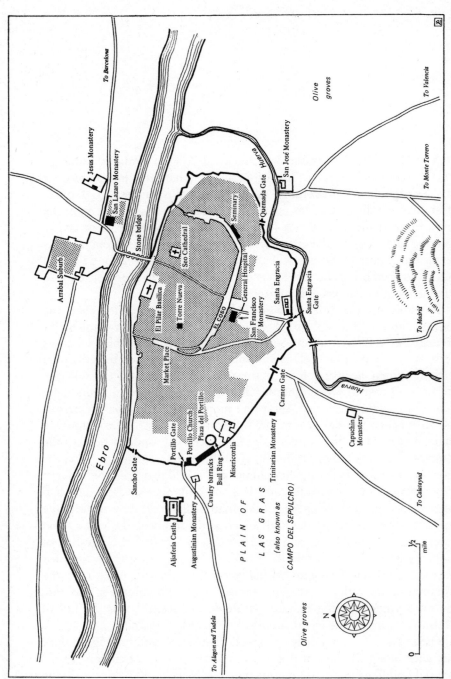

To Barcelona

Jesus Monastery

San Lazaro Monastery

San José Monastery

Olive groves

To Valencia

Stone bridge

Huerva

Quemada Gate

To Monte Torrero

Arrabal Suburb

Ebro

Seo Cathedral

Seminary

El Pilar Basilica

Torre Nueva

EL COSO

General Hospital

San Francisco Monastery

Santa Engracia

Santa Engracia Gate

To Madrid

Market Place

Carmen Gate

Huerva

Portillo Gate

Portillo Church

Plaza del Portillo

Misericordia

Bull Ring

Trinitarian Monastery

Capuchin Monastery

To Calatayud

Sancho Gate

Cavalry barracks

Augustinian Monastery

Aljaferia Castle

PLAIN OF

LAS GRAS

(also known as

CAMPO DEL SEPULCRO)

To Alagon and Tudela

Olive groves

N

0

½

mile

Saragossa at the beginning of the first siege in June 1808 windows and on the roof-tops and supplies of ammunition could be stored. From east to west, these buildings were: the convents of San Agustín and Santa Monica; the historic and massive monastery of Santa Engracia with its great church, many relics and art treasures; the Torre del Pino, a large house with garden enclosed in a salient between Santa Engracia and the Carmen gate; the convent of the Incarnation; the Misericordia hospital and workhouse, and the long, two-storey cavalry barracks near the Portillo gate. The two small bridges over the Huerva river, which ran parallel to the walls before curving away to the south towards Monte Torrero, were covered by artillery although there was no time to protect the guns by digging a ditch or raising a parapet in front of them. Cannon and rough barricades were set up in the gate-ways, on the banks of the Ebro and on the great stone bridge which linked the city with the Arrabal suburb on the left bank.

After Palafox's sudden departure, soon followed by that of Lazan, Vicente Bustamente summoned the magistrates, district mayors and other officials and dignitaries. Now thoroughly despondent, Bustamente told them of their leader's decision to leave Saragossa and of the French advance. The situation could not be worse: Saragossa only had fifty regular gunners and a small supply of munitions; the French were masters of the surrounding country and were sending out columns on all sides to attack the city. But, before a full session of the authorities could get under way, armed civilians broke up the meeting, urging members to occupy windows and balconies and to prepare to shoot at the enemy. The assembly promptly dispersed, and civilians and *tercios* began to line the walls of the Misericordia, the gardens of the convents north of the Portillo, the Incarnation, the Torre del Pino, the Carmen gate and the walls of the gardens of Santa Engracia. Every window had its defender, and even the roofs were covered with armed men and spectators who came to watch the fighting and take part whenever a weapon became available.

While Saragossa's gunners stood by their pieces, Lefebvre's forces continued to manoeuvre. After advancing along the road from Alagon towards the Portillo gate and along another smaller road from Muela, and after forcing the Spaniards to withdraw from the suburb of Casa Blanca, the French forces moved out of range of the castle and avoided Monte Torrero. Progress was slow in the torrid midday heat, as they deployed over a difficult, bumpy terrain covered with olive trees, orchards, vegetable patches, and small country houses with enclosed gardens. The ground was criss-crossed by low stone walls behind which the Spaniards might have posted men to delay the French advance, but after the clashes at La Muela and Casa Blanca, they encountered no further serious resistance. About two thirds of a mile from the walls, Lefebvre ordered the main body of his army to halt near the country estate of Torre de Escartin while he prepared three columns for attack.

After a brief reconnaissance, Lefebvre decided to storm the city at three points: on the left, the Portillo gate, with the weak walls of the convent gardens on its right; in the centre, the Carmen gate; and to the right, the Santa Engracia gate which gave the quickest and most direct access to the city's centre. As his columns moved forward again, three or four hundred Spaniards, who had heard of the capture of Casa Blanca, made a sortie and clashed with a party of French hussars at a fork in the Casa Blanca road. A few shots were exchanged, a French field piece fired a charge of grapeshot and the Spaniards hastily retreated into the town. A few moments later, the Spanish guns opened fire as the attackers came over the little plain of Las Eras and through the olive groves facing Santa Engracia.

As soon as the first shots were fired, there was excitement and confusion in the city but no lack of enthusiasm for the fight. Most of the defenders were virtually leaderless, there was no overall plan of defence and Palafox had gone, but a number of brave and resolute men took a series of initiatives where and whenever they were most needed. While the Spanish cannon began to thunder back at the French, the streets leading to the walls became packed with shouting crowds of civilians, some carrying arms, others praying, and still others bearing provisions and ammunition. A well-known priest in the Portillo quarter of the city, Santiago Sas, appeared with a quantity of arms and soon persuaded his followers to join him in support of the battery at the thinly-defended Portillo gate. Mariano Cerezo had been to Casa Blanca and then to Monte Torrero but, finding that the hill position was not being attacked, hurried back to the city to reinforce the castle garrison. A few minutes later, he reappeared at the Portillo gate with an improvised force of volunteers and was joined by his brother with another armed band. The engineer San Genis escaped from his cell with another wrongly arrested suspect, a retired lieutenant called Luciano Tornos. They were joined by a drummer and raised a force of local men, women and priests to defend the walls, rooftops and balconies of the nearby houses.

As the Spanish cannon opened fire from the Portillo gate, the French column attacking on the left halted and then made for the shelter of the walls of the Augustinian monastery outside the city perimeter, where they would also be sheltered from the guns of the Aljaferia castle. Mariano Cerezo attempted a sortie at this point and was only dissuaded with difficulty after his son and a number of his men had been killed by the French artillery.

When the central French column neared the Carmen gate, it found itself faced by a line of townsfolk, standing two deep in a file which stretched as far as the Portillo. The Spaniards began to fire at the on-coming infantry but as the French field guns opened up they fled for the safety of the Misericordia while the gunners at the Carmen gate rein-forced by the peasants fired back. This was the signal for the waiting townsfolk to come rushing forward to defend the gate; at the same time, the defenders at the Portillo waited for the enemy's next move and the French column of the right consolidated in the thick olive groves by the bridge over the Huerva. Alcaide Ibieca was one of those present: "It is impossible to give an idea of every detail of that scene: what is certain is that the Calle de la Puerta del Carmen was covered with people, the major part of them armed, that in that mass there were women, old men and boys, that now a platoon would detach itself to go towards the Plaza del Portillo, now towards the Puerta de Santa Engracia, that some were carrying the wounded on their shoulders, that others, especially the womenfolk, were rushing towards the cannon to give drink to the gunners, that spirit reigned in every countenance, that they looked calmly or even enviously at the in-animate or dead citizens . . . that priests and monks came to give them the last comfort and that there were quarrels because the de-fenders would not let them go to the gate."

After halting by the Augustinian monastery, the French column of the left charged forward to attack the cavalry barracks and so outflank the Portillo gate. There were no guns in the gateway to enfilade them, and when the musketeers posted there saw the direction of the French attack, they came running towards the barracks. While their field guns thundered away at the Portillo, the French infantry stumbled through the dust and smoke and began to pour into the great building, through windows, and over the low walls; the defenders clustered in the corridors in scattered groups to await them. The fighting was vicious and often hand to hand. Some French troops were protected and hidden from the Spanish by the thick walls of the building and slipped unseen into the stables, while others charged up the stairs and then wandered aimlessly through the rooms until discovered, pursued and shot down by the defenders. As other French soldiers ran through the maze of corridors, they would suddenly collide with groups of Spaniards; fighting was with the knife, the pistol and the bayonet. The few Frenchmen who managed to emerge from the deadly building into the city were killed at once, and in a short time, the surviving attackers were forced to abandon the barracks and to retreat over the plain which was being swept by volleys from the Portillo battery. All this time, Cerezo, a lieutenant of dragoons and the priest Santiago Sas whipped up morale and directed the defenders as they dragged artillery up to the gate.

In the centre sector, the French column, backed by artillery, came to within three hundred paces of the Carmen gate. Then, after an advance party of *chasseurs* had rushed forward and almost reached the guns before being shot down, the main force formed into line and moved forward in parade ground formation, firing rapidly. The artillery continued to hammer the gate and walls and several Spanish gunners fell by their pieces, but they were at once replaced by civilian volunteers who reloaded and aimed the guns as the French cannon balls whistled harmlessly over their heads. The French charged to within a few yards of the gate and were then forced because of heavy casualties to withdraw. The Spaniards were now firing at such a furious rate that they even killed a number of fellow-defenders from Santa Engracia who had come to their aid outside the walls.

While French corpses piled up within pistol shot of the Carmen gate, and the hitherto inexperienced civilians learned to man the cannon, the French column of the right moved into the thick olive grove facing the Torre del Pino and sent a cavalry detachment forward to reconnoitre the ground under fire from the monastery. Seeing that they were in imminent danger, the Spanish gunners hurriedly pulled their two cannon back from the Huerva bridge to the gate. As the French infantry emerged from the olive grove and charged forward, supported by cavalry, a cry went up that the Santa Engracia gate had been left unprotected while its defenders rushed to the Torre del Pino. The infantry moved on quickly, silenced the guns, and then stood aside as Lefebvre unleashed a cavalry charge. Following the progress of the fight, he had decided that the already disordered crowd of civilians and volunteers behind the Santa Engracia gate would flee, thus giving his infantry access to the city's centre, if he sent in his Polish cavalry against them. A moment later, a full squadron of lancers, pennants streaming from their lances, careered up to the gate, jumped over the pitiful remains of the battery, the silenced guns and dead gunners, and rode furiously into the city.

After they had thundered through the gateway, sweeping aside the few men who tried to stop them, they turned left down the widest of the streets facing them, which led to the Plaza del Carmen and then on to the cavalry barracks and bull-ring near the Portillo gate. Within a few minutes, the impetus of their charge had brought them into the Plaza del Portillo, but several riders already lay dead or wounded on the uneven, cobbled streets after civilians, alerted by cries that the enemy were within the gates, had shot and stoned them from houses along their path. In the Plaza, the squadron lost direction. Horsemen galloped wildly around the great square while the inhabitants poured out of their houses and rushed at them with knives, sticks and hatchets. Rider after rider was pulled down by screaming women and youths, hacked, stabbed and bludgeoned to death as their fellow-soldiers had been in Madrid's Puerto del Sol six weeks previously. A few minutes later, the survivors and a few maddened, riderless horses galloped back the way they had come while the battle continued to rage around the Santa Engracia gate and the Torre del Pino. The French infantry had been unable to follow the cavalry and, after enduring a heavy, continuous fusillade from the walls and windows of the Santa Engracia monastery, they abandoned their perilous position and withdrew in confusion to the shelter of the olive trees.

To the west of the city, the French were faring no better. The Spanish had brought another cannon by boat along the Ebro to an embrasure overlooking the Campo del Sepulcro and its line of trajectory crossed with that of the Portillo battery and the musket fire from the convents near the gate. Despite serious losses, the French charged again and succeeded in entering the cavalry barracks for the second time. But once more there was desperate hand-to-hand fighting inside the dormitories and corridors and the grim massacre was repeated; the few attackers who emerged into the square near the bull-ring were immediately shot down.

In the centre, the French continued to suffer as the Spanish fired into the olive groves from the Torre del Pino and the convent buildings.

They now moved away from the buildings along the open but narrow
paseo or promenade between the walls and the Huerva which led to the
Santa Engracia gate and charged with such desperate impetuosity that
they almost succeeded in recapturing it. But this time they did not
succeed in reaching the guns. At first, seeing the French onrush, the
gunners fled but a moment later a farmer called Zamoray arrived with
a company of militia and restored order. Meanwhile, one of Saragossa's
few regular veterans, the cavalry officer Mariano Renovales, left the
Angel gate near the Ebro at the head of 150 townspeople, advanced to
the San José bridge and poured fire into the French attackers for two
hours until, threatened by cavalry, he withdrew to the Santa Engracia
gate.

The French brought up a field gun and further cavalry but the
Spanish gunners by the gate stood firm. Renovales then launched a
counter-attack: his men rushed forward with such fury that they dislodged the French from their positions, took five prisoners and, joining
forces with the defenders of the Carmen gate, fell upon the right flank
of the French column, who hastily retreated to the shelter of the
Capuchin monastery after losing four colours, a drum and five guns.

As the fighting raged on until late in the hot afternoon and into the
evening, Lefebvre kept up the pressure of his attacks despite his now
very considerable losses. To such an experienced professional soldier,
it must have seemed inconceivable that a force composed mostly of
untrained civilians and unorganised peasants could have kept his
infantry and lancers for so long out of a weakly protected town with
crumbling, ancient walls; but the hideous piles of corpses in the cavalry
barracks, on the plain by the Portillo gate, in the olive groves, along the
banks of the Huerva, and under the very muzzles of the Spanish cannon,
proved that they had done so successfully.

Still grimly determined Lefebvre prepared to order a final charge on
all three fronts. How long could the citizens maintain such a desperate
resistance? Their losses—particularly at the Santa Engracia and Carmen
gates—had been heavy and their ammunition was running short although they still appeared to have plenty of powder. After the first
clashes the supplies of bullets in the city had run short. At great risk
from the French skirmishers and sharp-shooters, Mariano Cerezo had
made a dash from the Portillo gate to the castle and returned with a
case of cartridges. But these could not last long. Now everything was
used to make rough and ready cartridges—strips of cloth or linen,

nails, glass, pieces of scrap metal from blacksmiths. Doña Josefa, Cerezo's wife, brought iron for use as grapeshot as well as food and drink to her husband and his men, and even offered to sacrifice all the much-prized Aragonese iron-work in her house; a scrap-seller handed over his entire stock and was followed in his example by a locksmith who hired workmen to turn the material into bullets. Women and children ceaselessly brought provisions and ammunition to the walls and gates. The whole city had been mobilised and, with the setting of the sun, morale rose even higher as the inhabitants realised that they were succeeding in keeping their formidable enemy at bay.

The French made one more resolute charge. For the first time, the Aljaferia castle was attacked but, after its garrison had replied with volleys of grapeshot which tore holes in the lines of advancing infantry, the French withdrew. A new attack was launched against the Portillo gate, where the defenders were almost driven back; and, for the third time, French infantry scaled the walls of the cavalry barracks and resumed the hideous struggle there as they slipped and stumbled in their comrades' blood in the corpse-filled patios, staircases, and corridors, only to be once again driven out or to succumb to the smoke from the numerous fires caused by exploding grenades.

While the Spaniards reinforced the Portillo gate, French cavalry and infantry renewed their attack on the Santa Engracia gate and the Polish soldiers once more penetrated the walls. At the Carmen gate, a French battalion of the 70th of the Line temporarily took possession and forced the defenders back into the city. But the attack could not be sustained for long. While the Spaniards returned fire from nearby houses, roofs and the openings of the narrow streets, reinforcements suddenly arrived. A Spanish colonel, Don Francisco del Pont, rode down into Arrabal from the heights of San Gregorio with a force of 1,100 Catalan volunteers, local recruits, and a light cannon, crossed the bridge into the city, and dispersed his men among the various threatened points. Two French guns were captured near the Portillo gate; Renovales stood firm at Santa Engracia and drove the Polish lancers back to the Capuchin monastery; the battalion of the 70th was forced to abandon the position it had taken up just inside the Carmen gate; the Spaniards began to make a series of counter-attacks and sorties in the olive groves while crowds within the city collected tiles and stones for the defence of their houses and prepared street barricades. After a few last skirmishes in the Campo del Sepulcro and in the olive groves near the Carmen and

Santa Engracia gates, the whole French force withdrew and moved towards the heights of Santa Barbara, south of the city and beyond the range of the Spanish artillery. 700 French soldiers had been killed, thirty had been taken prisoner and six guns lost as they could not be dragged away under the defenders' heavy fire. Spanish losses were estimated at about 300.

The city burst into wild rejoicing when news of the French withdrawal was confirmed. Crowds poured into the Plaza del Pilar to see the horses and weapons of the Polish lancers who had been killed inside the walls. Peasants and citizens scoured the area outside the city and brought back muskets, sabres, pouches, haversacks and the shakos of the French and Polish infantry who had fallen. Fresh guards were posted at the gates, groups were formed to fight the fires which were burning near the Portillo gate and in the cavalry barracks, the streets were patrolled, and all private households were ordered to leave their doors and windows open and fully illuminated in case of any French surprise attack during the night. But it soon became clear that the French were not returning. As Lefebvre's men lit their bivouac fires in the hills, they could hear singing in the city. All this, wrote Alcaide Ibieca, took place at exactly the same time as the shameful assembly of Spanish collaborators who were meeting at the bishop's palace in Bayonne to hear Napoleon's decisions . . .

*   *   *

While Lefebvre and his men pondered the lessons of their defeat, and on the way in which untrained civilians had driven them back from the gates of a poorly fortified city, French soldiers in another part of Spain were experiencing a similar popular resistance and the first of those horrors which were to make the Spanish war so different from the others fought by Napoleon in Europe. A week before the attack on Saragossa, the French had also given the Spanish an example of what one of their cities might expect if it had the temerity to resist.

On May 24, General Pierre Dupont de l'Etang left Toledo with a force of 13,000 men to begin a 300-mile march south to Cadiz. He was a brave, dashing officer who had distinguished himself at the battles of Ulm and Friedland and, at the age of forty-three, had been given his first independent command when he was placed at the head of the expeditionary force misleadingly called the "2nd Corps of Observation of the Gironde". He was now ordered to invade Andalusia with only the first division of his corps and two cavalry brigades, to occupy Cadiz after passing through Cordova and Seville, and to prevent any British squadron from using the port as a base for an attack on the French ships there. Napoleon and Murat were confident that one division would be enough to pacify Andalusia and a despatch had been sent from Madrid to the War Ministry in Paris predicting that Dupont's "last column will enter Cadiz on June 21". The fact that most of the soldiers were young recruits with little training and no battle experience and that 1,800 men were Swiss who had formerly served in the Spanish army did not seem to worry Dupont's superiors in Madrid and Bayonne.

The army crossed the vast, yellow-brown, empty plains of La Mancha without trouble, and headed for the mountain passes of the Sierra Morena, passing through the pleasant little towns of Manzanares and Valdepeñas. Although the local inhabitants looked sullenly at them, the soldiers encountered no resistance or signs of overt hostility. They were well supplied with food, they were accompanied by a herd of cattle, they had ten days' supply of biscuit, and their officers were confident of being able to obtain provisions from the towns of Andalusia. At the end of May, the army began to make its way through the steep defiles and rugged passes of the Sierra Morena range which divides New Castile from Andalusia. As the men followed the winding road, they were pleasantly surprised by the pretty little town of La Carolina with its well laid-out streets, gardens, promenades and orchards. The town had been built in the middle of the 18th century as a colony for foreign settlers but was later taken over mainly by Spaniards after the attempt to encourage large numbers of foreign farmers to live there had failed. Now, La Carolina was almost empty since most of the inhabitants—like those of nearby villages—had fled to the mountains, fearing French reprisals for the rising in Seville.

Dupont's army bivouacked at Baylen, at the foot of the mountains in pleasant, well-cultivated country where many of the French soldiers saw their first palm trees. Dupont now received reports that the whole province was in a state of rebellion and that sizeable armed contingents were gathering under General Xavier Castaños near Seville. The following day, after passing ominously deserted houses and villages, the French reached the town of Andujar with its fine Roman bridge spanning the Guadalquivir river. Further reports reached Dupont of the rising in Andalusia, the reserve of the remaining townspeople turned into obvious hostility, and several of the Swiss troops deserted. Dupont also learned that, two days previously, a rebel leader had threatened the town with reprisals if it did not provide him with two hundred young men to join his bands. The town had complied.

Dupont began to realise the dangers of his position. His supplies were running low, the local population were fleeing after destroying any foodstuffs they might have left behind them, the remainder of his Swiss troops were of doubtful loyalty, armed bands were gathering in the vicinity, and his lines of communications with Madrid were under constant threat. Dupont therefore wrote to Murat asking for the second division of his corps, commanded by General Vedel, to join him. In the meantime, he decided to press on towards Cordova as soon as possible, before the rebels there had time to organise themselves.

After following the Guadalquivir for forty miles through a wide, fertile valley, Dupont's force reached a long, handsome, black marble bridge at Alcolea, and met with Spanish armed resistance for the first time during the expedition. Six miles beyond the river lay Cordova. Several hundred armed peasants led by an army colonel had come from the city and were barring access to the bridge. Dupont brought up his field guns, opened fire on the insurgents and then sent his troops forward to storm the bridge. It was captured at once and, after fierce but brief fighting in the village of Alcolea on the far bank, the rebels were routed and fled back in disorder towards Cordova.

By half past two in the afternoon, the French were outside the gates of Cordova—once one of the glories of Moorish Spain and now just another decayed, sleepy Spanish town with a much reduced population. As Dupont had expected to find an open city, he was surprised to see that the heavy wooden doors of the main gate were shut. While one of his aides-de-camp went forward to demand entry for the French, a shot rang out from a house near the gate and a few Spanish grenadiers appeared on top of the crumbling walls. Without attempting to continue negotiations, Dupont ordered a cannon to be brought up and to open fire on the gate. It was soon blasted open and the French infantry charged through with fixed bayonets. What happened next shocked even the most war-hardened of Dupont's officers.

Most of Dupont's soldiers were young conscripts in their teens, with no battle experience. They were new to war and the experience of campaigning in a foreign country; after the rigours of a hasty training, camp discipline, and the long march through the blazing sunshine of La Mancha and Andalusia, they were tired, hungry, thirsty and, no doubt, thoroughly homesick. But once they burst into a largely unarmed and defenceless city, they immediately became possessed by a madness and a fever of lust which has so often, in the history of war, transformed normally law-abiding and essentially decent men into murderers and rapists. From the moment Dupont's men became masters of Cordova, they proceeded to kill, pillage and rape on a scale and with a frenzy which defied all their officers' attempts to control them.

After smashing their way into the house from which the shot had been fired and massacring all but one of its inhabitants, the maddened conscripts rushed down the deserted streets ahead of them, shooting wildly at the windows, breaking down doors and shooting and bayoneting every human being in their path. Wholesale killing of unarmed men and women was followed by an orgy of pillage and rape. The cathedral was stormed and ransacked; the precious gold- and jewel-encrusted crowns of the sacred images of the Virgin and Child were stolen; pictures and hangings were slashed, trampled upon or carried off; women and even nuns were assaulted in their houses and convents and dragged into the churches to be raped in turn by groups of jeering soldiers while their sergeants and officers, by now fired with the same frenzy, invaded the deserted houses in search of plunder. For twenty-four hours, the normally sleepy atmosphere of the city was made hideous with the screams of raped women and dying men, the crash of musketry, the smashing of doors and windows and the roars of drunken soldiery. Some men serving under Dupont, like Jean-Baptiste Chevillard, an *inspecteur aux revues*, were too horrified to venture into the town during the first night of its occupation, but they were honest enough to record the atrocities committed by their fellow-soldiers: "The town was deserted, the inhabitants were terrified and abandoned children and old people, blood was running in rivers and all the houses were broken into as the most horrible and also the longest of all pillages began . . ."

After killing and rape came drunkenness as the soldiers invaded the wine cellars of houses and taverns; and then systematic extortion, with even high-ranking officers demanding huge sums from the owners of the houses in which they had quartered themselves. While the rank and file filled their haversacks, Dupont and his staff officers emptied the treasury and the church coffers. Privates, sergeants and officers were seen staggering out of houses and churches carrying gilt crucifixes, silver plate, musical instruments, chairs, tables, clothes and other booty. Nine days later, after order had been restored and Dupont had cele-

brated a celebratory Mass in the cathedral, the army moved out of
Cordova, followed by an enormous procession of carts filled with
plunder.

News of the savage sack of Cordova spread throughout Andalusia,
and terrible retribution for French atrocities followed quickly. Dupont
now realised that without strong reinforcements he could not hope to
reach Cadiz. The whole region was swarming with insurgents, thirsting
for vengeance, and it was rumoured that General Castaños was approaching fast. On June 16, the French army began to withdraw to
Andujar where Dupont decided to wait for reinforcements and guard
the bridge over the Guadalquivir. As he retreated, his lines of communication were continually harassed, French messengers and patrols
were attacked, men disappeared, and others would be found dead and
horridly mutilated along the road; all the time, threatening bands of
peasant marauders kept watch on the French columns from the nearby
hills. Very soon, every member of the expedition realised the grim truth
that the French were at war with a people and that, in such a conflict,
human savagery knew no bounds.

A similar conclusion on the nature of the war which had begun was
quickly reached by some of the soldiers on their way to reinforce
Dupont. Early in June, young Maurice de Tascher was riding with just
such a cavalry force. At Manzanares, he observed that "the mood of
the peasants is not a good one: they are very haughty, they have a very
insolent air and are ready, at the least signal, to run to arms". Next day,
Tascher was at Valdepeñas where a line of well-armed peasants were
drawn up in battle formation across the road leading to the town.
During a parley, the representatives of the local *Junta* of defence announced that they would only give food to the French on condition
that they did not enter the town and laid down their arms. The French
general, Ligier Belair, with his detachment of a thousand cavalry,
promptly mounted an attack. But as soon as they reached the outskirts
of Valdepeñas, the dragoons were forced to turn back by the barricades
which had been placed in every street. A squadron of *chasseurs* broke
into the town from another direction only to find nails and pieces of
sharp scrap iron embedded in the ground, and cords stretched between
carts to trip up the horses; everywhere, the defenders had posted themselves in windows and on roof-tops. Tascher was one of those who found
themselves fighting a new kind of war: "The riders were pierced by a
hail of fire from all the houses while paving stones, pots, and furniture

came raining down on their heads from every side without their being able to resist or defend themselves. As soon as one *chasseur* was wounded or dismounted, the peasants would drag him into a house where they would despatch him by mutilating him with frightful ferocity and refinements . . ." Women and children joined in the fight with hatchets, daggers, scissors and cooking implements. Women hurled boiling olive oil or vinegar and even their stews at the French. Juana Galán became a local heroine by standing at her kitchen door and smashing in the heads of dismounted French cavalrymen with her heavy cast-iron stew-pan.

The fighting in Valdepeñas lasted from morning until evening. All the houses broken into by the French were set on fire and their inhabitants massacred, while the fleeing Spaniards were sabred by the cavalry. The following day, Tascher returned to the scene of the battle: "When poetry and the arts celebrate victory with so much pomp and brilliance, they hide the real side of the picture: victory is a goddess avid for carnage . . . I saw with horror the houses in ashes, slaughtered women, children, and animals under the wreckage; peasants, soldiers, horses strewn in the streets . . ." But there were worse horrors to come.

As Tascher proceeded towards the Sierra Morena, he heard rumours that the inhabitants of neighbouring villages had attacked the hospital of Manzanares in the rear, and massacred the invalid French soldiers. Bands of guerrillas were everywhere, all communications were cut and a soldier's life was in danger if he moved more than a hundred paces away from his comrades. The scene of desolation which met the French troops as they arrived at a village at the mouth of the mountain pass horrified Tascher: "Few spectacles have struck me with as much horror as our arrival in this town! . . . It was entirely deserted! The most terrible uproar would have inspired less fear in me than this frightful solitude and calm!" After a search, the only remaining inhabitants, who normally numbered three or four thousand souls, proved to be three very old women and their eighty-four-year-old brother. Naturally, the town was pillaged: "It was necessary to break down all the doors to penetrate into the houses and soon the need to find food, impatience to begin pillaging and the thirst for gold effaced the impression of horror and painful reflections which no one had been able to avoid. As for myself, every step I take, every object I glimpse fills me with fear and sadness! How they must execrate us! Great God! What curses they must call down upon our heads! What a scene must that have been of the departure of this people, what a scene of desolation, and as for our soldiers who share the remaining effects in their greed . . . it is the invasion of Rome by the Gauls!"

A few miles further on, the French found an abandoned Spanish battery and, behind it, missals, chalices, the Host and sacred vessels— all of which led Tascher, like many other French soldiers, to reflect: "Love of religion and motherland combine with every effort to fight against ambition. Certainly, the finest rôle is not for us! But what will the *dénouement* be ?"

The result of this new type of war, in which Napoleon's armies found themselves faced by an entire people, was not to be decided for six years; but, from the very beginning, its horrors outstripped all those of other campaigns. As at Saragossa, the French armies found themselves faced more often by armed civilians than by regular troops, but they also met with something even more demoralising: a popular ferocity and cruelty intensified by the hatred the French were arousing every-where throughout Spain.

At Manzanares, the sick French soldiers had been butchered with revolting cruelty by bands of peasants and monks. A young French conscript, Louis Gille, who survived to write his journal, visited the hospital after the massacre: he saw dismembered corpses and the re-mains of others which had been thrust into cauldrons of burning oil after suffering terrible mutilation. Captain Charles François observed the same appalling scene and heard how the Spaniards had cut off the eyelids and torn out the nails of one French officer before sawing him into bits and throwing his remains to the pigs. Some soldiers had been stoned to death and flung on to refuse dumps; another had escaped with the loss of only his ears but, by the time François saw him, the man had gone mad and was running around the fields in agony . . .

With every day that passed, the horrors of the war escalated. François saw dismembered limbs strewn along the tops of walls and hedges as his column marched to join Dupont's army. Gille reported that the guerrillas were cutting notches in their lead musket balls so that, like the dum-dum bullets of a later age, they would inflict more serious wounds; and he found a number of French soldiers near Baylen who had been buried alive up to their chests and with the ends of their fingers cut off so that they could not dig themselves out. Not even the atrocities François had seen during the Egyptian campaign could rival those he witnessed in Spain: "I have seen . . . officers and men, even women, cut open from the groin to the stomach and the breasts cut off, men sawn in half, others with their private parts cut off and placed in the mouth, others buried alive up to their shoulders, their parts in their mouths, others hanging from the feet in chimneys, their heads burned; finally, at Valdepeñas, I have seen fifty-three men buried up to the shoulders around a house serving as a hospital where 400 men were massacred, cut into pieces and thrown into the streets and court-yards . . . Brave General René . . . who came to join General Dupont's army with his wife and child was captured in the gorges of the Sierra Morena and when he came to a farm half a league from La Carolina, named Ceñaperos, escorted by his executioners, he was sawn in half in front of his wife after seeing her dishonoured, after which the child was cut in two before its mother who was then sawn in half like her husband."

Such reports were not exaggerated. They were confirmed by many other soldiers and illustrated in Goya's horrific etchings of the *Disasters of War*. Their effect on the morale of the French troops was shattering and led to ferocious reprisals. Spanish cruelty surpassed anything that could be imagined: as the French soldier, be he a battle-scarred veteran or fresh conscript, saw the hacked, mutilated, charred or scalded rem-nants of some unfortunate comrade in the blinding light of the harsh Spanish sun, he was encouraged to react with equal fury and hatred. Many French soldiers realised that, in this dreadful war of "a people against a people" which had just begun, there was no foreseeable military solution, no glory to be won and no mercy to be shown. If the French were to win, they would have to exterminate a whole race.

*   *   *

That the war in Spain promised to be different from any he had previ-ously experienced must also have occurred to General Lefebvre-Desnouettes after he saw his troops beaten back from the gates of Saragossa. On June 12, only three days earlier, a Spanish regular force had been routed near Valladolid, which was then reoccupied by the French. It was all the more surprising, therefore, that a band of poorly armed volunteers could fight with such fierceness and tenacity. Napo-leon had certainly never imagined that a city with practically no regular garrison or fortifications could offer serious resistance. He had written to Murat on June 8, referring to Saragossa: "It is a very important point to be pacified." And, on the 16th, after news of Lazan's rout at Mallen, he expressed his conviction to Murat that "Lefebvre . . . must have entered Saragossa on the 15th". Two days later, Napoleon wrote, in a note to Berthier, his chief of staff with the Grande Armée at Bayonne, that Lefebvre must be instructed to disarm the inhabitants of Saragossa, fortify the castle, recover the money taken from the royal treasury, take hostages, sequestrate Palafox's possessions, and have his own proclamations and the declarations by the *Juntas* at Bayonne and Madrid posted up in the city. Meanwhile, Lefebvre decided against any fresh attack on Saragossa and waited for troop reinforcements and guns from Pamplona so that he could begin a regular siege. Two weeks previously, a French force in Catalonia, which was to have pushed into Aragon towards Saragossa, had been beaten back at Bruch by Catalan levies and local militia, and no immediate help could be expected from that quarter.

In the city itself, the people were jubilant as they realised the extent of their victory. The *Junta* issued a proclamation: "Aragonese, your heroic valour in defence of the justest cause which history can present was made manifest yesterday by the triumph we won. The 15th of June will make your exploits known to all Europe and history will record them with admiration . . . Seven hundred dead, a considerable number of wounded, thirty prisoners and many deserters who have passed over to our flags are the fruit of the enemy's temerity. We have taken six field guns, a drum, some horses, equipment and weapons . . ."

Bustamente, Calvo de Rozas and other members of the *Junta* realised the urgent necessity of communicating with Palafox and of organising the city's defence as quickly as possible in expectation of an imminent siege. While the locksmiths worked desperately to forge grapeshot and round shot for the cannons, Bustamente issued a stream of orders and made several promotions. After seeing how Colonel Renovales had distinguished himself in the defence of the Santa Engracia gate, Bustamente appointed him commander of that sector; Calvo de Rozas was given command of the Portillo gate. At other points of likely danger, the lack of regular officers and men had to be compensated for by the citizens themselves. A prominent role had been played during the fighting at the Portillo gate by the parish priest of the San Pablo district, Don Santiago Sas. He now formed two companies of men, armed with shotguns and known as the volunteer *escopeteros* of San Pablo, and himself assumed command. At Santa Engracia, the farmer Zamoray raised a force to defend the gate down to the last man; while the city's mayor, Don Miguel Abad, enlisted 300 men for the defence of the Quemada gate and the line running between it and the vegetable garden of Santa Engracia.

June 16 was the feast day of the Holy Sacrament but public rejoicings were forbidden; all the churches shut their doors, except for the Pilar which only allowed admittance to women. And, while the French dead were being buried in a large crater near the Campo del Sepulcro, reports reached the city that Lefebvre's army had spent the night in the neighbourhood of Casa Blanca and had sacrilegiously broken into the monastery of Santa Fé, robbed it of its silver plate and killed the abbot, three monks and four servants.

Thousands of citizens were now involved in maximum defence preparations. More cannon were brought from the castle, and orders given for the construction of batteries; gunpowder was taken from stores; cartridges were being busily manufactured in the Casa de Misericordia; an armoury and arms factory were set up in the Plaza del Portillo; the University building was transformed into an arsenal; wheat, tools and other supplies were brought from Monte Torrero and often carried by hand since many draught mules had been lost at the battle of Alagon; and arrangements were made for the feeding of families and the defenders on the walls once the attack began. While many of the townspeople constructed rudimentary street barricades out of church benches, cupboards, tables and shop counters, to impede the French cavalry should they again break into the city, a force of workers directed by the engineer San Genis helped to place cannons in position, fill sandbags and throw up parapets. Volunteer guard patrols were posted in all public buildings and squares, and special working parties went out to block the roads and paths leading to the gates with tree trunks and branches.

On June 17, while bands of youths were digging ditches in front of the gates and batteries were being fortified with sandbags, planks and sacks of wool in order to deaden the impact of enemy cannon balls, a Spanish dragoon captured by the French rode in bearing a message from Lefebvre ordering the *Junta* to surrender and also copies of proclamations signed by Murat and Napoleon. Lefebvre's letter was sent on to Palafox and a counter-proclamation was drawn up by Calvo. In it, he declared that there was no kind of infamy which the enemy had not perpetrated, since "they have battered churches with artillery, they have profaned their altars, robbed the sacred vessels and, when they have encountered villagers, have shot some of them so as to inspire terror"; and ended with a call to the people to stand firm and not "imitate the conduct of these porfidious men".

Palafox, who was no more than a day's ride from Saragossa, was greatly heartened by the news of the victorious battle of June 15, but he still had no intention of returning until he had raised his new army and attempted to defeat the French in open country. On the 18th, he invested Lazan with full power in his continuing absence and sent him back to the city with a letter to be relayed to Lefebvre's messenger. The war of words continued: Palafox told Lefebvre that "my sword guards the gates of the city and my honour answers for their safety . . . Far from being extinguished, the fire started by Spanish indignation burns ever higher at the sight of the atrocities committed by your soldiers". After informing Lefebvre that a large part of Catalonia had placed itself under Saragossa's orders, and accusing him of pillage, murder and sacrilege, Palafox concluded: "Does your excellency believe that such behaviour can soothe the anger of a valiant people? . . . Your Excellency may do as he wills; I do that which is my duty."

The news of the June 15 battle had by now spread through Aragon and gave fresh encouragement to all patriots, notably in Lerida. Colonel San Clemente, on arrival in that town, found only a few soldiers and gunners. He was promptly recognised by the *ayuntamiento* and *Junta* as military governor, and a message was sent to Palafox asking for reinforcements. On June 19, the town decreed the immediate levy of 40,000 men. Back in Saragossa, troops continued to arrive to swell the small defence force. Eighty Portuguese soldiers from Bayonne were followed by contingents from Madrid and Barcelona; and, on the 19th, a reduced battalion of 300 men from the regiment of Estremadura marched through the Angel gate and were billeted in the monastery of San Francisco.

While Lefebvre's army explored the terrain around the city and started to build a battery on the Bernardona heights, the Spanish countered by placing guns on the Buena Vista hill, south of the city, in order to defend the approaches to Monte Torrero; and a further three guns were added to the two already in position by the Puente de America bridge over the Imperial Canal. The defence of the Monte Torrero strongpoint was entrusted to an artillery officer, Lieutenant-Colonel Vicente Falco, with a garrison composed of some sixty men of the 1st regiment of Aragonese volunteers and nearly 200 Saragossans; while yet another force kept watch over the Ebro.

On the French side, limited reinforcements brought the total of besiegers to almost 5,000 infantry, over 1,100 cavalry and twelve pieces of artillery. More guns were expected from Pamplona and one of Napoleon's former aides-de-camp and a highly esteemed military engineer, Colonel Lacoste, began to prepare a new attack on the city. On June 21, General Grandjean arrived with two battalions of Polish soldiers from the 2nd Regiment of the Vistula. Meanwhile, Lefebvre learned that Palafox had succeeded in raising some companies of volunteers and a few veteran soldiers in the region of Belchite where he had set up his headquarters; and had joined up with his brother Francisco and an Aragonese nobleman from Calatayud, Baron de Versage, combining their forces with his in order to march on the small town of Epila and cut French communications along the main road to Madrid.

The Palafox brothers had a total force of between 2,000 and 3,000 infantry and only 300 cavalry but the threat they represented to the French lines was a real one. But, although he had no more than 6,000 men at his disposal, Lefebvre decided to divide his force in half, sending a Polish colonel, Chlopiski, with the 1st Regiment of the Vistula, one French battalion, fifty cavalry and a four-pounder to intercept Palafox at Epila, and keeping the remainder of his small army within striking distance of Saragossa.

Lefebvre's gamble was completely successful. At nine o'clock in the evening, after the Spanish had arrived at Epila, and had taken up a position with their left flank protected by the river Jalon, the advancing French opened fire. Many of the Spaniards were short of ammunition and some even lacked flints for their muskets. Disorder spread and the inhabitants of Epila evacuated their homes during the early part of the night. Before dawn, Chlopiski launched a full-scale attack. Palafox's cavalry and guns managed to delay the Polish infantry for a while but Epila was soon captured and the Spanish forces—now cut off from Saragossa—retreated towards Calatayud. According to the Spanish historians, when the French entered Epila the only remaining inhabitants were the parish priest, a few peasants and children, a surgeon and sixteen patients in the hospital. The French and Polish soldiers shot the priest and several peasants, broke into the houses and sacked them. The pillage lasted for five hours and it was only after using his cavalry to bring some order to the scene, and arresting two drunken soldiers who were shooting wildly in the town's main street, that Chlopiski persuaded his force to leave the unfortunate town.

On the same day as the battle of Epila, the Spanish made a small sortie from Saragossa and there was a skirmish with the French near Casa Blanca. Another monastery and the Colegio del Carmen were convented into additional barracks and new, deeper trenches were dug in front of the gates. When night fell, the defenders in their look-out posts and towers could judge from the lights of the French camp fires how close the enemy had approached to the walls. The next day, there was another skirmish, and two French cannon managed to fire a few shots at the city before the answering guns in the Aljaferia castle forced the gunners to withdraw their pieces. The Spaniards now expected a full-scale attack at any moment and rapidly completed fortifying the gates with mounds of earth, bales of wool, fascines, pits and ditches. Some of the citizens suggested such additional methods for discouraging a French cavalry attack as the placing of beams with nails and spikes in covered ditches, and even the shooting of flaming *banderillas* at the horses.

At this juncture, the Marquis of Lazan summoned a meeting of the city's military leaders, together with the most important civil and religious officials, and decided to send a message to Lerida asking for the men and heavy artillery that had been gathering there to come without delay. He too expected an imminent attack by Lefebvre's army.

Meanwhile in Madrid, the new French ambassador, La Forest, was sending reports in which he emphasised the importance of a speedy surrender of Saragossa. On June 20, he declared: "The submission of Aragon will not only be a very important event because of the influence it will have on the minds of the Catalans and on the kingdom of Valencia's return to obedience; it will also be [important] through the effect it will produce in the Castiles where the Aragonese are regarded as the heroes of Spain, and in the southern provinces which are relying on this bulwark." Two days later, he wrote that the Council of Castile were waiting for Aragon and Saragossa to submit before they encouraged obedience to Spain's new King; and he added, in his letter to Napoleon's foreign minister Talleyrand: "Now, your Excellency knows that, at this moment, Aragon means everything to the Spanish public." On the 25th, La Forest again stressed that "our attention, like that of all Spain, is above all fixed on Aragon; we are longing for the rebellion to be severely chastised in Saragossa".

On that same day, the French made further efforts to persuade the city to surrender peaceably. While some workmen were fortifying the Portillo battery, they saw five French soldiers signalling to them from behind the walls of a cemetery by the road to Alagon. They were allowed to come forward and were met by a Spanish delegation which included the priest Sas, the governor of the castle and Calvo de Rozas. While a French officer stepped forward and dilated on the city's folly in continuing to resist Napoleon's might, crowds lined the walls and fortifications and cheerfully cried, "*Viva España!*" The following morning, the Marquis of Lazan sent an aide-de-camp to the French with a defiant message. After informing Lefebvre-Desnouettes that he had just learned from Calvo de Rozas of the summons to surrender and of the French claim that they had only come to Spain in order to assure the happiness of the populace, Lazan scornfully remarked: "What you have done in Austria, in Italy, in Holland, in Poland, in Sweden, in Denmark, in Portugal and, lastly, in Spain gives us an idea of how much trust we should put in you." There would be no surrender: "The valiant soldiers besieged in Saragossa have sworn to die rather than submit to the yoke of France . . . Know then that a powerful nation which has not forgotten the crimes of your soldiers is invincible when it defends the most righteous of causes."

Lazan held another meeting of the *Junta* and the city's officials. They agreed that, in view of reports that French reinforcements of men and heavy guns were on the way from Pamplona, a heavy bombardment was imminent. Additional members of the *Junta* were elected and it was decided that officers, soldiers and volunteer recruits should assemble in the Plazuela del Carmen and at the gates of the city in order to swear a solemn oath of resistance to the French. In the presence of Saragossa's leading churchmen, who stood beneath a banner embroidered with the image of the Pilar Virgin, and to the accompaniment of martial music, a sergeant-major of the regiment of Estremadura inspected the lines of troops and citizen-soldiers and shouted: "Do you swear, valiant and loyal soldiers of Aragon, to defend your sacred religion, your King and your fatherland, without ever accepting the yoke of the infamous French government, nor abandoning your leaders and this banner under the protection of the very holy Virgin of the Pilar, your patron saint?" There was only one answer: "*Sí, juramos!*"

A remarkable gazette was published to raise morale even higher. After a glowing account of the enthusiasm with which the population had sworn their oath, it went on to give details of imaginary Spanish successes, saying that the French army in Andalusia had been routed, Marshal Moncey had been taken prisoner, and a great army was marching to relieve Saragossa. All this time, work continued on the batteries and fortifications. Then, on June 27, General Jean-Antoine Verdier, a veteran who had served in the French army since 1785 and fought bravely in Egypt with Bonaparte, arrived with nearly 3,500 men and a mixed train of artillery. He at once took over command from General Lefebvre-Desnouettes who was his junior. A new phase in the siege had begun.

Verdier at once sent advance posts closer towards the city, reconnoitred the region and concluded that the key to Saragossa was Monte Torrero. As he began to draw up plans for its attack, a devastating explosion shook Saragossa and the surrounding countryside at three o'clock in the afternoon of the 27th, and the sky was covered by a huge dark cloud. Some enormous barrels of gunpowder, which were being taken from storage in a priests' seminary on the Coso, had exploded and destroyed the seminary and a number of adjacent houses. The disaster was apparently caused by a spark from a workman's cigar. The explosion was so great that it was heard thirty miles away.

The catastrophe threw the city into a temporary panic. Stunned inhabitants rushed into the streets which were so thick with dust and smoke that they could hardly breathe. Cries were heard of "treachery!" as men, women, children, priests and nuns dug for survivors among mountains of smoking rubble and burning wooden beams; but Calvo de Rozas's efficient organisation of rescue work soon restored order. Outside the city walls, the French sent patrols forward to see whether the gates were deserted following the explosion, but they were soon disappointed. Saragossa had suffered a severe blow but the defenders stood fast at their posts and drove back the French with musket and cannon fire. Instead of attempting a sudden surprise attack, Verdier adhered to his plan for an attack on Monte Torrero as a preliminary to further offensive operations.

Early in the morning of June 28, the French guns on the Bernardona heights opened fire on the castle, the Santa Engracia and Carmen gates, while General Lefebvre, supported by Colonel Lacoste of the engineers, began the attack on Monte Torrero. The commander of the strongpoint, Colonel Vicente Falco, had a defending force of 500 men, a battery of four guns on the plateau of Buena Vista behind the canal,

and another two guns to cover the Puente de America which spanned
the canal near the main warehouse of the canal company. The main
approach paths were cut by ditches. Four French battalions, some
Polish lancers and four field guns made up the attacking force. One
column advanced alongside the canal to attack the Buena Vista battery,
a second outflanked the hill, and a third moved through the olive groves
on the left bank of the Huerva to cut off an eventual Spanish retreat.
To prevent help being sent from the city, Verdier sent sharpshooters
up towards the gates to engage the defenders.

The battle was a short one. To begin with, the Spaniards stood firm
against Lefebvre's first two battalions but, as the third threatened to cut
them off from the bridge on the Huerva which led to the Santa Engracia
gate, they fled back into the city where Falco was promptly arrested
for cowardice and desertion of his post. The French were able to place
heavy guns on the hill, and had captured four four-pounders, a howitzer,
two large barges, and stocks of timber, wheat and wine. They now
dominated the whole right bank of the Ebro. Saragossa could only maintain its contacts with the outside world via the far side of the river.
There was a solitary compensation for the defeat: the arrival of two
twenty-four-pound cannons, two mortars, two howitzers and a supply
of powder, bombs and shot which the governor of Lerida had sent in
answer to Lazan's plea. The guns were at once placed in the vegetable
garden of Santa Engracia and at the Portillo battery from where they
could cover the castle and nearby buildings.

The French also received more guns and ammunition. From Bayonne,
Napoleon had ordered a heavy assault to be made on the city on the
29th, after a preliminary bombardment, but Verdier was reluctant. In a
letter to the general staff, he expressed his view that such an attack would
be too costly: the inhabitants were still full of confidence, they had a
formidable amount of artillery along the walls and other guns within
the city, so that even if the French entered it they would still face some
sixty to eighty guns, many manned by experienced gunners who had
deserted from Pamplona and other garrisons. Verdier preferred to postpone the attack until he had set up more batteries. To the right of the
great Bernardona battery, which now consisted of nine guns of various
calibres, he installed another battery of four cannons and howitzers
to cover the castle and the Portillo gate; a further battery was brought
up to within 500 yards of the Carmen gate; and yet another was set on
the slopes of Monte Torrero.

While the French prepared a bombardment, the Saragossans hanged a Spanish stage hand. He had come from Madrid carrying notices of French triumphs and had been found guilty of treason. They also reinforced their own batteries. More embrasures were made in the walls of houses and gardens, open spaces through which the enemy might attack were cleared to give an unimpeded field of fire, and gunpowder stocks were moved to the safety of the crypt of the church of Don Juan de los Panetes in the centre of the city. The outer doors of the Misericordia were filled with earthworks, embrasures were pierced for muskets, and three cannon were brought in to cover approaches to the building. Two more cannon were posted in the artillery barracks; the castle had seven cannon distributed on three of its four sides; the garden of the monastery of the Barefoot Augustines beyond the walls was given five guns and a garrison of 200 men; the parapet of the Portillo redoubt was raised to a height of four and a half feet and defended by two huge twenty-four-pounders which had just arrived from Lerida, together with one twelve-pounder and additional lighter guns on each side to cross the fire from the Sancho gate near the river. A five-gun battery was established at the Santa Engracia gate and ditches were dug in the streets behind it. Two more cannon were placed in the gardens of the Torre del Pino, another five on a small elevation overlooking the river, and four guns were set behind two ditches at the Carmen gate. On the other side of the Ebro, the streets leading into the Arrabal suburb were barricaded and defended by batteries behind sandbag parapets.

The total number of armed defenders in Saragossa now amounted to some 8,000 men. They included 250 gunners helped by civilian auxiliaries, 700 regular soldiers and 170 cavalry. The *Junta* sent a message to Palafox asking him to bring his men to reinforce the city, and also despatched an officer to find the Spanish army which was said to be on its way from Valencia. On June 29, Calvo de Rozas published a new decree: all old people, women and children were ordered to stay in their houses and not go out into the streets in case of bombardment or a general alarm; all doors of houses were to be kept shut and defended; windows of houses were to be used for firing at the enemy and for hurling stones at them should they break into the city; the people were to be resolute, morale was to be kept high, and the name would be taken of anyone who left his post during an attack or a sortie.

On June 30, the French batteries were completed. Additional siege material, as well as a column of more than 2,000 men of the 3rd regiment of the Vistula and a battalion of grenadiers, led by Colonel Piré, one of Napoleon's aides-de-camp, arrived from Pamplona. Verdier by now had over twenty cannon, mortars and howitzers as well as light field pieces, abundant munitions, nearly 14,000 infantry and over 1,000 cavalry. While they made ready for action, the Supreme *Junta* in the city prepared to sit all night in Palafox's palace, and the *ayuntamiento* assembled in its consistorial chamber. On the same day, Napoleon wrote to Berthier, stressing the importance of establishing a bridgehead on the left bank of the Ebro in order to complete the blockade of the city: "It is certainly to be desired that Saragossa should surrender promptly; it appears that this event will have a very great influence on the submission of the whole of Spain." The following day, La Forest in Madrid described how people there were anxiously awaiting the news that Saragossa had fallen, since "it is of great political utility that this event should bear the character of a severe chastisement and be an impressive example."

An hour after midnight on June 30, while the night-watchmen in Saragossa were calling out "*La una, sereno, dormid, zaragozanos!*" ("One o'clock and all clear; sleep, Saragossans!"), the silence in the sleeping city was broken by the noise of a huge shell whistling through the air and exploding on the banks of the Ebro after nearly grazing the main cupola of the Pilar basilica. The long-expected bombardment had begun. As the great bell of the Torre Nueva started to sound the alarm, the first bombs screamed over the city and exploded harmlessly in the river and on the far bank. Despite the *Junta*'s orders to stay in their homes, many inhabitants rushed out for fear of being buried in the ruins. Men and women ran wildly and aimlessly about the streets, candles were lit in the churches, the Pilar Virgin's shrine was crowded to capacity, and armed men raced to the walls in the expectation of an attack. While the French gunners adjusted their trajectory, some of the more frightened inhabitants and peasants from outside the city fled through the streets to the stone bridge, making their way to the Arrabal and then towards the villages in the hills; many others took refuge in cellars.

After their first panic-stricken reaction, the Saragossans regained their composure. It might sound terrifying, but the bombardment was not razing the city to the ground as had been feared, although damage was soon becoming extensive. The brick buildings stood up well to the shelling and the French noticed that many cannon balls simply embedded themselves in the brickwork leaving the walls standing. The look-outs posted in the Torre Nueva kept the French batteries under observation, ringing the bell once to announce that a bomb was being fired from the battery on Monte Torrero, and twice when they saw the Bernardona battery taking aim. Most of the grenades fired into the city tended to explode on the second or third floors of the solidly built buildings without causing excessive damage, and few of the inhabitants were killed. At dawn, the whole city was still under fire. The bombardment continued with greater intensity as the twenty French guns battered the castle, the Portillo, the monastery of the Barefoot Augustines, the Sancho, Carmen and Santa Engracia gates, and the Misericordia, while the defenders did their best to close the gaps in the parapets and plug the holes in the walls with sandbags.

In the first light of day, it was possible to see that the castle and the Portillo, in particular, had been badly damaged. In the castle, the west parapet, the courtyard, barracks, roof and turrets had all suffered badly, but the walls, though crumbling in places, were still an effective barrier against attacking infantry. In the Portillo sector, the buildings adjacent to the gate were reduced to ruins and the guns were left virtually unprotected except by a few weak earthen parapets and sandbags.

At nine o'clock, the French advanced on the Sancho and Portillo gates and sent skirmishers towards the cavalry barracks, but the defenders received them with a steady fire and forced them back. The main bombardment was now concentrated on the Sancho, Portillo Carmen and Santa Engracia gates. Most of the gunners were killed at Santa Engracia but their places were quickly taken by new defenders who braved the fire to bring more sandbags and build a second line of defence in case the first should be stormed or have to be abandoned. At the Portillo, cases of munitions were blown up by a grenade, causing great havoc and confusion. Mariano Renovales hurried to the threatened spot and, in the words of Ibieca, found that "the battery presented a lugubrious aspect: sacks on the ground, cannons without artillerymen, various scattered corpses, explosions following ceaselessly, and the watchful enemy ever ready to launch an audacious attack". Renovales ordered the remaining, demoralised gunners back to their posts, threatening to shoot anyone who ran away. Some of the men wanted to spike the guns, but he quickly brought reinforcements to the battery while women carried food, drink and cartridges to the defenders behind the adjacent parapets.

Throughout the day and into the night, the French continued to bombard the city and to send out small groups of skirmishers to probe the defences, while the batteries at the Portillo, Carmen and Santa Engracia gates fired back resolutely. It was a day of confusion and constant threats of an all-out attack. Ibieca described it vividly: "It is impossible to describe the haste with which we worked and the variety of scenes which took place. As shooting died down in one spot, it broke out with even greater violence in another. Soldiers and civilians came running through the streets towards the batteries, bringing carts and munitions; some others went to Lazan to complain of the disorder and ask for reinforcements. The citizens were awed by the continuous crash of bombs and grenades. The horror of it all was accentuated by the tolling of the great bell and the quivering of the ground under each explosion. It seemed that there was not one single place in which one might hide from death."

Even at this critical time, Spanish troops continued to enter Saragossa from outside, by crossing over the stone bridge. Two artillery lieutenants arrived, one going straight to the Carmen, the other to the Portillo battery. Two regular army officers, Del Pont who had come to the aid of the city on June 15, and a lieutenant-colonel of the regiment of Estremadura, Domingo Larripa, were respectively appointed commanders of the Portillo and Carmen gates, while Renovales took over at the Sancho gate. That same evening, Palafox at last returned to the city. He had been at his headquarters at Belchite after the defeat at Epila and had managed to rally a force of 1,300 men and sixty cavalry. He set up his headquarters in the great monastery of San Francisco in the Coso, within quick and easy reach of any one of the threatened gates.

The bombardment now reached a crescendo. At two o'clock in the morning of July 2, all the French guns were fired in unison, with two mortars, three howitzers and four cannon concentrating on the castle. An hour later, they fell silent. The bombardment had lasted almost without pause for twenty-seven hours and, according to the Spanish look-outs, over 1,400 shells, bombs, grenades and cannon-balls had fallen in the city. The batteries on the French right consisted mainly of mortars. Their rate of fire remained comparatively low, but the heavy-calibre cannon on the left fired with great rapidity at the castle and the eastern walls and outworks in order to widen the breaches and gave the defenders no respite in which to fill them. By dawn, the French soldiers could see that great holes had been torn in the castle walls; breaches had been opened in the Augustinian monastery, allowing a storming force easy access into its vegetable garden and workshops; there were wide gaps in the walls of the cavalry barracks and Misericordia; and many of the parapets in the gate openings were almost razed to ground level.

Verdier decided that the time had come to launch a general assault on the city. While the rest of the army was held in reserve, two simultaneous attacks were prepared. One of the main objectives was to capture the Sancho gate and the cavalry barracks. If they succeeded, the French could then fall upon the Portillo gate from the rear since any frontal assault would expose them to cross-fire from the castle and the Augustinian monastery. A determined effort would also be made to take the castle by storm.

Six columns, each of 500 to 600 men, were assembled and moved up during the night. On the left, three were to attack the Sancho gate, the castle and cavalry barracks; the three on the right would proceed against the Carmen and Santa Engracia gates and the monastery of San José outside the walls. In the words of Jean Belmas, an officer in the engineers and historian of the siege, "when the signal was given, our troops rushed forward with intrepidity under a frightful musket and artillery fire which came from embrasures pierced in every house and from every opening giving access into the city". The infantrymen, as they moved forward, were preceded by companies of sappers with axes, picks and bundles of tarred wood to fill in the ditches in front of the walls and gates.

The assault on the Sancho gate was intended to take the defenders by surprise. Before the first light of dawn, at about half past three, the attacking force made its way along the sunken San Lamberto road which ran parallel to the Ebro. Taking advantage of the darkness, the French came within pistol shot of the gate but their movements were heard by the ever-watchful defenders commanded by Renovales, who ordered them to open fire at once. As the flashes from Spanish muskets and cannon lit up the scene, and the mass of French soldiers stumbling and running towards the gate became clearly visible, a further volley tore through their ranks and made them falter. There was another fierce exchange of fire and the French column fell back in some confusion, many soldiers tripping over their dead and wounded comrades and fallen weapons in the semi-light of early dawn. At the same time, a French column rushed towards the battered castle, braving its artillery. The attackers had been so confident of climbing through its gaping breaches that they had not brought scaling ladders, which might have slowed their impetus. But when they came up to the castle they found the breaches were too high and were driven back before they could even reach the walls.

The attacks on the Sancho gate and castle served as a general alarm for the whole city. Firing increased in intensity as civilians of both sexes recharged the defenders' muskets, returning them so rapidly that Ibieca remarked that as dawn broke, the rattle of musketry fire was like a sustained counterpoint to the continuous low roar of the cannon.

Despite the French reverse at the castle and Sancho gate, the city's position as a whole soon began to look critical. The French returned to the attack and advanced towards the battered Augustinian monastery where Sas and his San Pablo volunteers waited for them behind the garden walls; the third column hurled itself against the cavalry barracks and Misericordia. Sas's men stood firm: some French soldiers reached the gate of the monastery, less than twenty yards from its battery, only to die at the foot of the shell-swept walls. Not a single man entered the breaches.

At the Portillo gate, more than fifty of the defenders had been killed or wounded, and grenades and cannon balls had destroyed the feeble earthworks protecting the battery. The few remaining gunners, supported by sharpshooters in the nearby buildings, were working frantically to reload and set the giant twenty-four-pound cannon when through the smoke they saw the line of French infantry with fixed bayonets quickly moving forward over the small plain of Las Eras. As the French began to break into a run, a band of civilians who had come to reinforce the battery, hearing a rumour that the French had entered the city, rushed back to the market square. There they met Calvo de Rozas who urged them to return to the Portillo. But, meanwhile, the last gunners remaining on their feet had decided that their position was hopeless and had fled.

It seemed that nothing could prevent the French from capturing the now-silent battery and advancing over its scattered sandbags and corpses into the city. Suddenly, to their amazement, they saw a dark-haired girl emerge through the haze of smoke and dust and run towards the battery. As she reached one of the twenty-four-pounders, she snatched the still-smouldering linstock from the hand of a dying gunner, fired the cannon and stood on its carriage shouting encouragement to the civilian volunteers who were hurrying back to the position. The cannon was loaded with grapeshot and, discharged at almost point-blank range, its effect on the closely bunched French column was devastating. A moment later, the defenders had rallied and poured a volley of musketry fire into the French who wavered and then retreated.

The girl, Agustina Zaragoza, had saved the gate from certain capture. Her action seized the imagination of all Spain, and then of all Europe. The popular heroic image of a slender young girl, leaping forward to take the place of the dying gunner said to have been her fiancé, and then firing the great cannon single-handed and remaining by it to defy the oncoming French and put heart into her fellow-countrymen, was both romantic and inspiring. Agustina symbolised the heroism and determination of every Spaniard who took up arms to face Napoleon's might, heedless of the odds. For the public, she was the incarnation of embattled Spain. She was young, she was pretty, and the image of her female grace combined with amazon-like fervour in battle was poetic and immensely striking. Goya rendered the essence of the situation— the slight girl and the huge gun—in an etching in the *Disasters of War* series and he entitled it quite simply: *Que valor!* Four years later in 1812, when Byron published his *Childe Harolde's Pilgrimage*, he needed no long explanatory footnote for the stanzas in which he referred to Agustina's gallant action:

> Yet who shall marvel when you hear her tale?
> Oh! had you known her in her softer hour,—
> Mark'd her black eye that mocks her coal-black veil,—
> Heard her light lively tones in lady's bower,—
> Seen her long looks that foil the painter's power,—
> Her fairy form, with more than female grace;
> Scarce would you deem that Saragossa's tower
> Beheld her smile in danger's Gorgon face,
> Thins the closed ranks, and leads in glory's fearful chase.
>
> Her lover sinks—she sheds no ill-timed tear;
> Her chief is slain—she fills his fatal post;
> Her fellows flee—she checks their base career;
> The foe retires—she heads the sallying host.
> Who can appease like her a lover's ghost?
> Who can avenge so well a leader's fall?
> What maid retrieve when man's flushed hope is lost?
> Who hang so fiercely on the flying Gaul?
> Foil'd by a woman's hand, before a batter'd wall?

*   *   *

Marshal Lannes, Duke of Montebello. Painting by Perrin.

"El Tio Jorge," one of the
popular leaders of the
insurrection in Saragossa.
Etching from the series
Las Ruinas de Zaragoza
by Galvez-Brambila, 1814.

British Museum;
Photo John Freeman

Agustina Aragon.
Etching from the series
Las Ruinas de Zaragoza
by Galvez-Brambila, 1814.

British Museum;
Photo John Freeman

Que Valor! Etching by Goya from *The Disasters of War.*

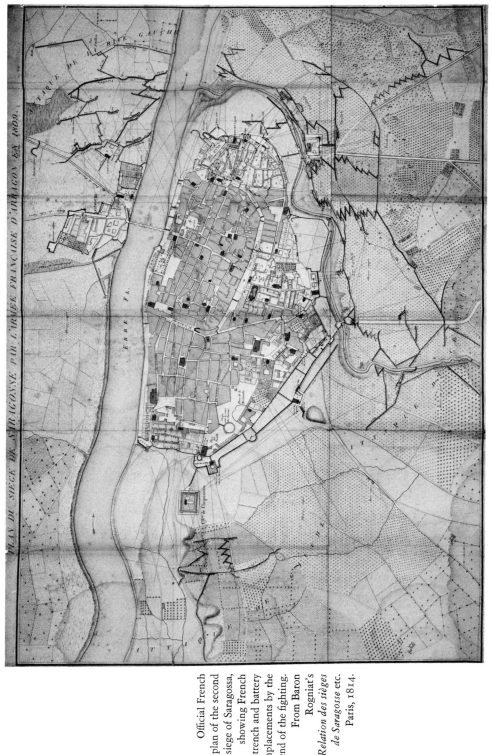

PLAN DU SIÈGE DE SARAGOSSE PAR L'ARMÉE FRANÇAISE D'ARRAGON EN 1809.

Official French
plan of the second
siege of Saragossa,
showing French
trench and battery
emplacements by the
end of the fighting.
From Baron
Rogniat's
*Relation des sièges
de Saragosse* etc.
Paris, 1814.

The ruins of the Seminary after the explosion of June 27,
1808. Etching from the series *Las Ruinas de Zaragoza,* by
Galvez-Brambila, 1814.

Interior view of the ruined church of the General Hospital
after the first siege. Etching from *Las Ruinas de Zaragoza,*
by Galvez-Brambila, 1814.

The French assault on the city on January 27, 1809. Lithograph by Victor Adam.

The fighting at the Artillery Park during the May 2 insurrection in
Madrid. From a contemporary Spanish print.

The Third of May, 1808. Printing by Goya.

General José Palafox. Painting by Goya.

While Agustina's fellow-citizens manned the Portillo battery, and a company of musketeers arrived to reinforce them, messengers ran to fetch further aid; one wounded Spaniard even clambered on to a horse, rode off to fetch an experienced gunner and returned carrying him on his saddle. The French column was now caught in the cross-fire between the castle and the garden of the Augustinian monastery, and was also under fire from the battery. Despite the urging of their officers, the French soldiers broke ranks and ran, some of them leaving their haversacks, muskets and cartridge cases behind on the ground.

The French column advancing across the Las Eras plain was also in serious difficulties. Its target was the cavalry barracks where the only artillery consisted of two light field pieces posted in the gateway. The upper floors, corridors, windows and roofs, together with those of the adjacent Misericordia building, however, were filled with men armed with muskets whose running fire stopped the French from advancing any further.

Another obstacle in the way of the French was the Capuchin monastery by the road which ran in a straight line to the Carmen gate. Its defenders were meant to prevent them from attacking the irregular line of parapets and trenches protecting the battery at the gate; but as the Spaniards there possessed no guns to cover either flank, the French succeeded in advancing with one field piece under cover of the olive trees which grew on both sides of the road, until the fierce firing from the battery eventually brought them to a halt.

At about the same time, a look-out in the tower of Santa Engracia sighted a new French column on its way from Monte Torrero to the bridge across the Huerva. As it drew near the French forward column rushed towards the ancient, half-ruined Torre del Pino in the salient overlooking the walls between the Carmen and Santa Engracia gates. Once again, intensive fire from the defenders forced the troops to retreat to the shelter of the olive groves, after they had suffered heavy losses from the fusillade poured into their flank from the Santa Engracia defenders.

The new column from Monte Torrero reached the walls of the San José monastery forced its way into the building and then attacked the Huerva bridge. Although it was defended by two light cannon, the Spaniards were unable to prevent the French from sustaining a steady fire from the windows of the monastery. The defenders spiked their guns and retreated to the Quemada gate and to an old olive oil press

water by them. The letting off of rockets or fireworks in the city was prohibited because of the danger to the stores of powder.

While the Saragossans continued to sally forth from the city to cut down trees and clear the ground with relative impunity, Verdier resigned himself to the prospect of a protracted, conventional siege according to all the rules. Sieges were usually monotonous affairs: they consumed valuable time, supplies and men. They involved days and even weeks of digging systems of parallel trenches linked by short, diagonal and zig-zag trenches to bring the attackers as close as possible to the city walls while all the time protected from the enemy's crossfire; heavy pieces of siege artillery had to be dragged up and placed in specially-dug batteries, from where, often with the aid of mines, they could attempt to make a breach in the walls; and even when a large enough breach had been made and infantry could be sent to storm it, there was no guarantee that they would not suffer heavy casualties and even be repelled. If Saragossa were not to be taken by storm, it had to be starved into submission, which meant that the besiegers had to maintain a successful blockade and still scour the countryside for sufficient food for themselves. Unfortunately, Verdier did not have enough troops for this type of operation. In the meantime, Napoleon and the French general staff were becoming impatient. Verdier therefore had no other alternative but to make preparations for the blowing of a breach wide enough to assure the success of a massive storming party. But even then, he knew that his troops would have to face the determined opposition of the entire civilian population and that they could expect armed resistance or at best passive non-cooperation from the inhabitants of the whole region. La Forest in Madrid also realised the nature of the war that had begun for, in a further letter to Talleyrand, he observed pessimistically: "There is, Monseigneur, a great difference between what the Spanish people were in the middle of May and what they are now. An ignorant people, unable to endure uncertainty, have thrown themselves *en masse* into opposition."

*   *   *

On July 3, Verdier sent his superiors a request for more men, guns and ammunition. The bombs, shells and round shot which had been brought all the way from Pamplona had been exhausted in the intensive bombardment and no attempt to batter breaches in the walls could be made until a system of siege trenches enabled the French to position heavy

guns closer to the city. Verdier was also afraid that a continuing failure
to take Saragossa would encourage more armed uprisings throughout
Aragon, and that bands of insurgents would threaten his communication and supply lines. He badly needed reinforcements so that he could
make the blockade of the city complete, protect his sappers against
sorties, control the left bank of the Ebro and deal with the rebels in the
surrounding countryside. Verdier had already been obliged to reduce his
siege army by sending Lefebvre to Calatayud with five battalions and a
detachment of Polish lancers in order to disperse the armed bands
gathering there, and he had also despatched a smaller force in the
direction of Tudela to protect his communications with his base there.

On the same day, Verdier and the chief of his engineering corps,
Colonel Lacoste, drew up siege plans and reconnoitred the terrain to
decide where to begin digging the first long line of siege trenches or
"parallels". They agreed that one trench should be dug against the
castle and another against the Carmen gate. Their plan was forwarded
to Bayonne, but Napoleon had other ideas. As he studied maps of
Saragossa, he was surprised to see that Verdier was contemplating
attacks on what were obviously some of the strongest points along the
city's perimeter. He ordered Verdier to concentrate instead on the most
vulnerable points: the area around the Torre del Pino and the walls of
Santa Engracia which, being salients, were free from defensive flanking
fire.

Napoleon's plan had further advantage: if the French could make a
breach and storm the city at these points, they could advance towards
the rear of the Carmen gate through the gardens and grounds of the
Torre del Pino and of the Santa Engracia monastery instead of having
to fight their way through dangerous narrow streets.

Verdier and Lacoste were at first reluctant to follow their master's
orders and continued to attract the enemy's attention by digging in
front of the castle. But, after further reconnaissances, they realised that,
although Napoleon only knew the city's lay-out from maps, he was
correct. The right bank of the Huerva in front of Santa Engracia was
higher than the left so that, if batteries were placed there, they would
dominate the walls and buildings, as guns on the lower ground in front
of the Carmen gate would not. Also, it was both easier and safer to
construct approach works and battery emplacements in the Santa
Engracia sector since the Huerva with its sunken bed would serve as a
ditch to protect them from sorties.

stationed at the Angel gate to inspect parcels being brought out of the city, arrested an old woman who was found to be carrying some cartridges and papers. Although the unfortunate suspect claimed that she had taken them from a French haversack she had found in the market place, she was accused of treachery and so roughly handled by the hostile crowd which gathered and threatened to lynch her that she died before the authorities could intervene. According to the *alguazil*, or secretary to the Audiencia, Faustino Casamayor, who kept a diary of the siege, several women were discovered to have been taking powder and cartridges to the French and were arrested. Public punishment of other offenders became harsher. A beggar was given two hundred lashes for threatening passers-by who refused him charity. On July 18, two murderers' bodies were publicly displayed, hanging from tall gibbets, after they had been garrotted in their cells during the night. Palafox issued a decree stating that unless all inhabitants who had left the city since May 31 did not return within a week, their entire possessions would be requisitioned.

Although they were seldom successful, the civilian volunteers' enthusiasm for sorties remained undiminished and led to several clashes with the more experienced veteran and regular soldiers whom they often accused of cowardice. The *Junta* declared that much of the disorder in the city was being caused by excessive patriotism and that several worthy citizens were being unjustly imprisoned; and ordered that, unless people were found in the act of committing an act of treason, no action was to be taken against them without the prior consent of the courts. After encouraging civilians and troops by promising that financial compensation would be paid to the widows and children of men killed during sorties, Palafox was forced to deal with the increasing number of quarrels which arose between hot-headed civilians and regular soldiers. Some of Sas's San Pablo volunteers were particularly bad offenders in this respect, being inclined to disregard their superiors' rulings on the grounds that valour and a will to fight justified any indiscipline. A decree forbade the use of "indecorous" expressions during arguments, and priests were asked to use their influence so that no word of such disputes should reach the ears of the French. In another decree, Palafox referred to the "disunity which some troublemakers have tried to sow between troops and citizens" and thundered that "any officer or soldier who insults any inhabitant with any odious comment" would at once suffer "all the rigour of military law"; while any civilian, regardless of age or sex, who insulted the military with "indecorous expressions or those not appropriate to such an honoured profession would be taken and punished according to martial law with the greatest rigour".

Palafox was not the only commander who faced increasing problems. He might have been heartened had he been able to read certain passages in the reports which Verdier was sending to the general staff. On July 16, he wrote that "the terrain over which we are moving is extremely difficult, being covered with gardens and country houses; we conquer it only foot by foot from the enemy who defends it with incredible fury. This warfare—the only kind which allows us to advance close enough to the walls of the town to see where we must open a breach—is very favourable to the enemy. He knows it well and makes us pay dearly for every bit of ground we conquer from him, day by day: every wall, every house offers the rebels a shelter which they defend vigorously. Apart from this defence, which truly is conducted with all possible energy, nearly every day the enemy makes sorties though these—to tell the truth—are less successful for him. They are always repelled; when we move forward at the charge we overcome him but never without some loss on our side." On the next day, Verdier explained why it was still not possible to say when the breaching batteries would be ready or to give details of the proposed attack, since "the terrain is so cut, wooded and traversed in every direction by walls that we can only see ahead four paces at a time, and every time we cover those four paces we have to entrench ourselves anew in order to save the soldiers' lives".

On the day he penned this despatch, Verdier launched a further attack to distract the attention of the besieged while his zig-zag trenches moved relentlessly closer to the walls and to prevent another sortie. On the 13th, the Spanish had counter-attacked so fiercely in the afternoon that they had driven the French back temporarily from the Santa Engracia area towards Monte Torrero and even expelled them from the Capuchin monastery. But it was a short-lived triumph for, that evening, the French re-occupied the smouldering ruins. Nonetheless, Verdier could not allow the Spaniards to harass his siege operations with repeated sorties. He therefore continued to launch limited attacks in anticipation of the day when he could order an all-out assault on the city.

The July 17 attack was repelled after three hours of vicious fighting

the peasant leader Jorge Ibort, with troops, peasants, women and children bringing up the rear. Only two things were missing from the ceremony: the giant wooden figures of Christ, the Virgin and saints usually carried in such processions, and the customary sermon after the Mass, in case the French made a surprise attack.

While Palafox did his best to keep spirits high in Saragossa and hoped for the expected army of relief said to be on its way from Catalonia, the military situation remained static in the rest of Spain. Marshal Moncey's force which had been sent to take Valencia had been too weak for the purpose and, after being driven back from the well-garrisoned port, it had wisely withdrawn into Castile. In Andalusia, General Dupont's army waited for reinforcements at Andujar on the Guadalquivir before resuming the attempt to take Seville and Cadiz; and in Catalonia, Duhesme's army was engaged in a prolonged struggle with the local militia and scattered regular Spanish army units. Then, in mid-July, a decisive blow by Marshal Bessières's army in Castile removed the threat to the long French lines of communication and any possibility of help reaching Saragossa from the direction of Castile or Navarre.

On July 14, General Cuesta of the army of Castile, who had already been defeated near Valladolid on June 12, and General Blake of the army of Galicia had moved their combined forces into Castile and offered battle against the French outside the small town of Medina de Rio Seco. Bessières hurried a French force northwards to meet the threat to the French lines, and although his infantry were outnumbered nearly two to one by the Spanish, he swept them from the field. Once again, the battle displayed the incapacity of many of the Spanish generals and officers and the failure of Spanish regular soldiers to stand up to the French on an open battlefield. Cuesta and Blake were on bad personal terms, each jealous and suspicious of the other, and made the terrible blunder of dividing their forces in such a way that neither could help the other when necessary. As their armies streamed from the field in utter confusion, and they bitterly began their mutual recriminations, the French troops stormed into Medina de Rio Seco. The horrors of Cordova were repeated. Normally well-disciplined veteran soldiers and young conscripts broke into houses and churches to rape, pillage and murder without restraint and with a ferocity which horrified their superiors and aroused even greater anti-French hatred throughout the country—if that were possible.

The victory at Medina de Rio Seco made it possible and safe for Spain's new King, Joseph Bonaparte, to proceed to Madrid for the first time. His brother Napoleon temporarily forgot about Saragossa. Already, on July 13, he had written that, like Valencia, Saragossa was of "little importance" since "Saragossa is useful for finishing the work of pacification but counts for nothing in the offensive system". On July 17, after news of Bessières's victory, he wrote exultantly to Joseph: "This event is the most important of the Spanish war and gives a decided colour to all affairs there." Joseph, however, was less optimistic as he made his royal progress towards Madrid. On July 13, he wrote despondently to Napoleon: "No one, so far, has told your Majesty the whole truth. The fact is that there is not one Spaniard who shows himself to be for me except the small number of persons travelling with me. I repeat to your Majesty that we will not be able to make sufficient efforts to pacify Spain: we need troops and money." On the 18th, far from being heartened by the battle of Rio Seco, he remarked that "my position is unique in history: I have not a single supporter".

King Joseph's entry into Madrid was to have been a triumph but it turned into an abject fiasco. As he rode through the deserted streets to the royal palace, the only cheers along his route came from the French troops. Windows were shuttered, the populace stayed at home, and although they had been ordered to hang out carpets and tapestries as the traditional sign of rejoicing, most had not done so or else had displayed tattered rags as a sign of derision. Balls, firework displays and festivals were held for the Madrilenes who obediently put in an appearance, and pieces of money were flung to the crowd. The French army pharmacist Blaze remarked that the coins bore the head of the Bourbon Kings of Spain—a bad omen for Joseph, said the people.

Napoleon continued to write encouraging letters to his well-intentioned, pleasure-loving but weak eldest brother. The fact that many Spaniards were hostile and continued to show signs of resistance was of no importance, he told the depressed Joseph: "You should not find it too extraordinary that you should have to conquer your kingdom. Philip V and Henry IV were obliged to conquer theirs. Be gay, do not let yourself be affected and do not for a moment doubt that things will end better and more promptly than you think." As for Saragossa, wrote Napoleon, "everything is going very well". On July 21, he sounded a more cautious note: "Saragossa has not been taken. Today, it is surrounded and a town of forty to fifty thousand souls defended by a

As Castaños's force approached, the number of rebels in the nearby hills increased and more French soldiers' bodies were found hacked to pieces and rotting in the fierce sun. But Chevillard, the *inspecteur aux revues* who accompanied the expedition, noted that "in the midst of all this, our young officers kept the French character. Each evening, the camp was lit up. Elegant hutments were built and the richest furniture was moved into them. Here, someone was playing the piano, a little further on, someone was playing the violin; elsewhere, a kind of comedy was being performed and everywhere, men were thinking little of the future". However not even amateur theatricals and impromptu camp concerts could make the soldiers forget the heat and their increasing distress. Tascher was alarmed at the way in which the French troops seemed bent on doing everything possible to inflame the people against them. On July 2, he was particularly dismayed to hear that the town of Cuenca in Castile had also been sacked and that a solemn *Te Deum* had then been sung by the French after they had killed more than a thousand inhabitants. Each day brought new rumours that reinforcements were on their way and more reports that messengers had been killed. Dupont's expeditionary army was now all too obviously isolated in the midst of hostile country. It could only retreat or wait for the Spaniards to attack; but Castaños seemed content to let the French suffer for as long as possible before engaging them in battle.

As each long day dragged by, the inactive French soldiers grew increasingly despondent as they wearily waited near the banks of the Guadalquivir and gasped for breath in the furnace-hot air. On July 11, Tascher noted how "as we lie night and day on the burning sand, breathing the scorching air, we are suffering all that it is possible to suffer. Men and horses, all perish. We have only half the regiments on their feet and about a thousand men in hospital. Everyone has diarrhoea, fever and dysentery. One loaf of bread for eight men—sometimes for thirty-two; every dwelling, every house, all are abandoned. We are reduced to having to go and cut the wheat for ourselves and our horses. If only our cause were just, I would not complain of privations or of the frightful heat!"

Dupont again asked Madrid for reinforcements but his messengers were captured. His pleas for help were read, translated and circulated among the Spanish troops by their commanders who were only too delighted to learn of his plight. Meanwhile, Savary had sent a third force to Dupont's aid on July 3, General Gobert leaving Madrid with most of

Moncey's second corps, amounting to some 5,000 or 6,000 men. In order to cover any eventual retreat that Dupont might be obliged to make, Gobert garrisoned several battalions at small towns along his route as he proceeded southwards. He had orders to remain north of the Sierra Morena, but a few days later, in response to Dupont's pleas, Gobert and about half his force came over the mountains and moved towards Baylen. The French now had a total of some 20,000 men in Andalusia.

General Xavier Castaños slowly advanced to the attack. He was an experienced, cool-headed officer, fifty years old and a veteran of the Franco–Spanish siege of Gibraltar in 1779–83 and the Spanish–French war of 1793–95. His army, by the beginning of July, totalled more than 30,000 men, both veterans and recruits, and was divided into four divisions; as he neared Andujar, he received further reinforcements from Granada. The men were well armed since Seville was the most important centre in Spain for the manufacture of weapons, and their morale was high. Unlike other Spanish armies, Castaños's included a large force of cavalry of which one contingent had attracted particular attention as it paraded in Seville: a squadron of 200 horsemen in Andalusian costume known as *garrochistas* because they were armed with *garrochas*, heavy goad lances, which they used with great skill for the purpose of knocking down young fighting bulls during training.

By mid-July, Castaños had re-entered the martyred city of Cordova and his main force was facing Dupont across the river at Andujar. It was intended that one of his divisions, under the Swiss general Coupigny, would try to cross the river to the east, while another division under General Reding was to attack and capture the ferry point at Mengibar, advance to Baylen and then fall upon the French from the rear. What the Spaniards did not know was that Vedel and his 7,000 men were between Baylen and the river and that Gobert's force was also within easy striking distance.

The French at once began to make a series of disastrous mistakes. Instead of ordering Vedel's men to join him in a combined attack across the river against Castaños, Dupont came to the conclusion that Savary wished him to refrain from any offensive operations and remain inactive until Valencia and Saragossa had surrendered. He therefore decided to keep all the French forces strung along the north bank of the Guadalquivir in a defensive line between Andujar and the mountains.

On July 14, Reding's vanguard skirmishers clashed with the French

mob led by armed monks, and when the remaining prisoners reached
Cadiz, with cries of "Cordova!" ringing in their ears, it was only to
find that the *Junta* of Seville had refused to repatriate them and that,
officers excepted, they were to be sent to the dreaded prison hulks in
the harbour. Many prisoners were later transferred to the rocky, barren
prison island of Cabrera in the Balearics where half died before the
final release of the survivors in 1814. Dupont with his generals and
officers reached France only to suffer the full blast of Napoleon's fury.

The news of the Spanish victory electrified Europe. Even more
sensational than the fact that a Spanish army had won a victory in the
field was that, for the first time since the Revolution, a French army had
been forced to capitulate. That many of Dupont's and Vedel's men were
raw conscripts was overlooked. In Spain, the victory was hailed as a
triumph over the victors of Austerlitz and Iena, and Castaños was fêted
in Seville. Spain and the rest of Europe had been shown that Napoleon's
armies were no longer invincible.

The immediate effect of the capitulation at Baylen was that King
Joseph and Savary were forced to evacuate Madrid and central Spain.
News of the disaster was confirmed in the capital on July 28 and soon
followed by alarming rumours that Castaños and a huge Spanish army
were rapidly approaching. A council of war was held and, despite
Savary's pleas to stand and fight, it was decided that the French armies
should pull back to form a line along the left bank of the Ebro. On
August 1, Joseph and his court, a crowd of Spanish collaborators, a
small army of officials and 20,000 soldiers began their retreat to the
north. Joseph did not have a friend left in Madrid. In a letter to Napoleon, he wrote that, when it was time for him to leave the palace, his
men had been unable to find one postillion in the royal stables to bring
out his coach and horses, although 2,000 men were normally employed
there . . .

*   *   *

While Joseph and his army were evacuating Madrid as quickly as
possible, Verdier devoted all his efforts to the speedy capture of
Saragossa. Unaware of Dupont's defeat in Andalusia, his troops dug
battery emplacements less than 200 yards from the walls, so that the
heavy siege guns recently arrived from Pamplona could blast the
necessary breaches for the final assault.

By July 27, the trenches and batteries were almost completed. The siting of the guns had been decided by Napoleon himself after studying maps of the city. The four main batteries were set in a line extending, on the right, from the vicinity of San José, facing the church of San Miguel, to the sector facing the Santa Engracia gate and the Torre del Pino. They were all protected by the Huerva ravine—six to eight feet deep—where the attacking columns, after moving up from the trenches, could re-form before storming the breaches. The main targets for the batteries were the weak walls confining the patch of open ground with vegetable gardens known as the Huerta de Campo Real to the right of the monastery of Santa Engracia; the walls of the enclosure of Santa Engracia; the monastic building itself; the gate and the walls of the Torre del Pino. In the third and main breaching battery, the French had placed their heaviest-calibre cannon: six sixteen-pounders and four eight-inch howitzers. Other batteries were placed to the right of the Capuchin monastery, to bombard the Santa Engracia monastery, the *plaza* of the same name and the Carmen gate. In view of the decrepit state of the walls, and the poor protection for the Spanish guns, it was a formidable concentration of fire power. The city's small southern salient, formed by the Santa Engracia monastery and the adjoining walls on both sides, was to serve as the target for thirty-eight guns of heavy calibre as well as a number of small pieces. At such close range, the effect could only be devastating.

While Verdier waited for still more supplies and men to reach him, the Spaniards continued to make forays on the left bank of the Ebro in order to maintain as far as possible their communications with the rest of Aragon. On July 29, a cavalry sortie led by Francisco Palafox and Fernando Butron pushed back a French detachment away from the Arrabal suburb towards the hills to the north-west, inflicting a number of casualties and returning to the city with some French muskets, haversacks and cartridges. On the following day, another larger-scale action was fought near the suburb. As Butron was holding back a French infantry column supported by cavalry which had crossed the French engineers' bridge on the Ebro, he was assailed by two strong columns advancing from the nearby heights and threatening to turn his left flank. Butron rallied his men and with the aid of a company of regulars from the regiment of Estremadura, who had hurried across the stone bridge to the Arrabal, finally withdrew unscathed. The action was hailed as a victory with the French being routed, although the truth was probably that they had decided to break off the engagement after seeing

those who could walk leaped through the windows into the street, often breaking their limbs. Part of the hospital was used as a madhouse and the lunatics' demented screams could be heard mingling with the cries from the sick and wounded who begged their comrades to carry them from their beds to safety. As men and women volunteers rushed to the hospital to evacuate the inmates, there were stampedes to the doors. Patients and wounded of both sexes were seen staggering through the streets in their bandages, splints and hospital nightdresses. Many fell as they ran, some were hit by bomb splinters and falling masonry, others were blown to bits by falling projectiles. Soon, dismembered limbs, even severed heads, crutches and blood-stained bandages littered the streets in hideous profusion. Several lunatics escaped and intensified the horror of the scene by singing, crying and laughing wildly as they ran through the streets and even among the ruins of collapsing, blazing buildings. Several madmen, as they tried to escape, even reached the walls of the city. Some were still locked in their wooden cages and cells howling like beasts in agony, their cries rising above the roar of explosions and crash of falling stone and brick. Others danced and skipped among the corpses in the streets, and one was even heard, as he ran to the Coso, to shriek that he was the river Ebro and would extinguish the fires by drowning the whole city! The scene was pure Goya.

During the same day, the Spanish cannon replied from the Carmen and Santa Engracia gates, while the French made several feint attacks. Other French guns battered the Aljaferia castle, causing considerable damage and knocking down a large section of its weak walls and part of the main building facing west. As the bombardment reached a climax and the French infantry added to it with their fire from the trenches, the castle's commander, Mariano Cerezo, shut the main gates and calmly told his men: "*Caballeros*, here there is no other remedy than to die or vanquish." From his new headquarters in the Archbishop's Palace, overlooking the Ebro, near the Seo cathedral, Palafox appointed Mariano Renovales commander of the sector of the walls between the Sol gate and the Huerta de Campo Real and sent him a brief message: "The captain-general advises Don Mariano Renovales that this night the French will make an assault with ladders. Watch the whole line from the ditch of San Miguel to the vegetable garden of Campo Real. Such an assault is to be repelled with muskets, pistols, pikes and stones . . ."

The bombardment continued until shortly before dawn, then slackened for long enough to allow civilian volunteers, including one of the leading noblewomen in the city, the beautiful Countess Bureta, to help to evacuate the hospital patients and madmen to the buildings of the Lonja and Audiencia in the city centre; and the gunners to stand by their pieces in the much-damaged batteries.

As the first light of dawn broke on August 4, sixty French guns began to fire in unison as the infantry in the cover of the trenches formed up for the attack. Verdier had prepared three strong assault columns. On his right, the Polish soldiers of the first regiment of the Vistula, with French grenadiers and light infantry, all led by General Habert, were to storm the Santa Engracia monastery, capture the first few houses adjacent to the building on its left and make their way into the street called Calle de Santa Engracia which ran directly into the Coso. The centre column, commanded by General Bazancourt who had arrived on August 1, was made up of men from his brigade and was to advance over a wooden ramp thrown athwart the Huerva river and, if possible, across the bridge itself; then over the open space or promenade leading to the Santa Engracia gate. After capturing the gate it was to move to the left towards the little square called Plazuela del Carmen, occupying all the intervening houses.

The left column also contained many Polish troops, being composed of the 2nd regiment of the Vistula as well as French infantry of the line. Commanded by General Grandjean, its orders were to advance to the left of the Huerva river against a breach to be made in the section of wall between the Torre del Pino and the Carmen gate. After storming the breach, the column was to divide into two; half the men were to advance to the right to capture the Torre del Pino, move along the inside of the wall and fall upon the defenders at the Engracia gate from the rear; the other half were to move to the left to capture both the Carmen convent and gate.

After driving this initial wedge into the city, the French forces would fan out towards the market place to the west and the Plaza de la Magdalena to the east, while the centre attack was to be pushed home across the Coso and through the heart of the city to the river. Each assaulting column would be strongly supported by infantry in the trenches and by artillery. Once the columns had gained entrance into the city, they were to be followed by light artillery, who would be placed in the captured squares to sweep the streets ahead of them while

by a furious monk, Don Pedro Breton, wearing a sergeant's insignia over his tucked-up robes, and his eight companions who all fought to the death with pistols and cutlasses in the smoke-filled semi-darkness. While the few remaining Spaniards abandoned the monastery gardens and took refuge in the enclosure of Santa Catalina, the French made their way through heavy fire into the small square of Santa Engracia. As soon as they emerged into the city, they came under fire at point-blank range from a battery placed in the opening of the narrow Calle de Santa Engracia, and from defenders in the nearby houses who hurled grenades and stones down into the little square, causing great loss among the attackers.

Despite their casualties which increased at every step, Habert's men advanced over the corpses of their comrades and reached the wall of a corner house adjacent to the battery. In the confusion, the Spaniards had omitted to shut and barricade a door in the house which led to another side door and then into the street. The French rushed the door, swept aside the few defenders who were trying desperately to barricade it, bayoneted them and poured out into the street behind the battery, killing the colonel in command and putting the surviving gunners to flight. Lazan and Francisco Palafox, who had been present during the engagement, fell back with their men to the end of the street. There a second battery, protected by sand bags and huge bales of wool, had been set up outside the hospital a few yards from the Coso and now swept the length of the street with fire, keeping the French temporarily at bay.

While Habert's column was storming Santa Engracia, the centre column led by Bazancourt also crossed the Huerva by the bridge and rushed over the open ground of the *paseo* to the Santa Engracia gate. Although the defenders had abandoned the position, the great doors were shut and barred and the French were unable to make any progress. Instead they were forced to endure heavy fire from the nearby Torre del Pino and from guns along the walls to their left, and to wait at the foot of these walls while the battle raged inside the monastery.

On the left, Grandjean's Polish and French infantry stormed the breach between the Torre del Pino and the Carmen gates and divided into two forces as planned. On their left, they soon came to grips with the defenders of the battery in the gate; while, on their right, they stormed the Torre del Pino, capturing it and putting its defenders to flight. Now that they were masters of the tower, the French were able

to pour plunging fire into the Carmen battery where 150 valiant defenders had been grappling at bayonet's length with their attackers. The
Spanish position was hopeless but, before the French completely
mastered the sector, the defenders managed, by a heroic effort, to
remove to the rear their light field guns from the gate and the tower.
One gun was quickly pulled through the streets to the convent of
Santa Fé on the long Calle Azoque which ran straight to the western
extremity of the Coso. The other was placed in the Convalescents'
Hospital which, with the adjoining, heavily-manned convent of the
Incarnation, formed a strong redoubt which effectively barred any
French advance to the left, towards the Misericordia and Portillo
districts.

After fighting their way through a maze of narrow, barricaded streets
where, according to Verdier in his own report of the action, "each
house was a citadel from whence there came such a hail of bullets as
I have never seen before", Grandjean's men burst into the Carmen
convent and through it into the Plaza del Carmen, facing the opening
of the Calle Azoque. Meanwhile, Bazancourt's column, which had
been huddled outside the Santa Engracia gate under a murderous
fusillade for an hour, was at last saved from its predicament when
Habert's troops let them through.

The fierce resistance from every house and from behind every street
barricade slowed the rate of the French advance. Casualties were
heavy. The Spanish guns behind the barricades thrown across the Calle
de Santa Engracia were mowing down the attackers in large numbers
and, an hour after the French had burst so successfully through the
breaches, they were still unable to advance along the streets facing them.
Verdier was hit by a musket bullet in the thigh; Lefebvre, to whom he
handed over command, was severely bruised. But the French line was
extending to the right as men made their way through the market
gardens and grounds of the neighbouring convent of Santa Catalina,
the Botanic Garden and the cemetery of San Miguel towards the Coso.
The three columns were now masters of a line extending from the
Carmen gate to Santa Catalina and could be brought together for an
attack on the Coso; in addition, reinforcements were pouring into the
city from Monte Torrero and the trenches.

The defenders' position looked desperate. The French were bringing
their guns through the breaches and gates and, according to the usually
accepted rules of war, the commander of any garrison would have been

vinced him that the city's capture was imminent. He had already had ample opportunity to observe their fighting qualities during the siege and to see how difficult it was for the French to make quick progress through a city in which every building became a fortress and every citizen a warrior.

Leaving aside his pessimism, Palafox was presented with another reason for leaving the city when he learned that some of the expected reinforcements were on their way. 2,000 to 3,000 regular soldiers from Catalonia and Valencia were nearing the village of Villamayor, a mere seven miles from the left bank of the Ebro, and were only waiting for the right moment to break through the weak French blockade on that side. Palafox decided to make contact with them in person. In view of his great popularity and his influence among the Saragossans, it seems astonishing that he should not have sent a subordinate—perhaps one of his brothers—to accelerate the relief force. As he had already shown such considerable qualities of diplomacy and psychology in dealing with the different sections of the population and the various authorities in the city, it is even more surprising that Palafox should not have realised that news of his departure could have a disastrous effect on the defenders' morale—particularly as it was still far too early to tell whether the day's battle was lost or won.

Palafox admitted later that he had given up the city for lost, but he may have had at the time another—unconscious—motive for leaving it to fend for itself. He had only recently played the part of a saviour when he allowed himself to be brought back from Alfranca to be offered the supreme command of the defence forces. To leave Saragossa briefly and then return at the head of an army of succour—however small—would be to play the saviour's part again and raise morale even higher. We know from his behaviour on May 25, and from his resounding proclamations, that Palafox loved a stirring gesture, whether it was physical or verbal. This time, however, his gesture seems only open to one interpretation if we—rightly—except that of pusillanimity. In mitigation of his fit of despair, it must be allowed that the sudden tide of panic in the city may well have appeared to him as irreversible. Moreover, if Saragossa fell, he was still far more use to Spain outside it than as a prisoner or a casualty.

After learning of their brother's departure, Lazan and Francisco Palafox also left the city to join the force at Villamayor. When it was clear that nothing could prevent the French from breaking through the

Santa Engracia sector to the Coso, Lazan gave up hope for the city and managed to struggle through the throng of fugitives over the bridge, reaching his brother late that same evening. His own despairing view of the situation was made very clear in the short memoir he wrote later that year: "I was at the time on the Coso and placing all my hopes in the defence being put up by our battery at the Hospital, when I learned that it had been abandoned and was in the enemy's hands. Our defeated troops were flying in disorder towards the Angel gate to reach the stone bridge over the Ebro—the only retreat left to us. I was forced to follow the torrent and promptly made my way to the suburb, convinced that the enemy, who was already master of one third of the city, would not take more than one half hour to seize the rest. The confusion of the troops and people who were fleeing the city to cross the Ebro was such that all hope of driving out the enemy was lost. There was no longer any obstacle to oppose him and it was vital to leave the city at once if one did not want to be taken prisoner."

Just as Palafox was leaving Saragossa to its fate, the French columns, which had re-formed in the Calle de Santa Engracia, emerged in good order into the Coso. No shots were fired at them as they marched out with bayonets fixed, muskets at the ready, preceded by their officers and drummers. The whole length of the street was deserted and it seemed obvious that the rest of the city was for the taking. Although the noise of the continuing French bombardment could be heard in the distance, a deathly hush had settled on the centre of the city, broken only by the mournful, insistent tolling of the Torre Nueva bell, the beat of French drums, the tramp of French soldiers, and the crackling of burning timber in the shelled houses. After the last troops had left the Calle de Santa Engracia, three separate companies were formed. One moved along the left of the Coso in the direction of the market place, with orders to link up with the column fighting its way to the top of the Calle Azoque and then to march on towards the San Ildefonso gate; the second was to advance up the Calle San Gil to the bridge; the third was to move several hundred yards to the right along the Coso, to occupy the Sol gate and to let in the French cavalry. The city would then be divided into three sectors and the Spaniards would be cut off from their path of retreat over the bridge.

After stopping to dismantle a barricade, the right-hand column made its way towards the Plaza de la Magdalena, still without en-countering any opposition although the rattle of musketry fire was proof

that fighting continued around Santa Catalina. As the French reached
the square in front of the Magdalena church, with the vast ruins of the
seminary, devastated by the June 27 explosion, on their right, eight
men dashed out of a side street and came running towards them. They
were led by a man in monk's habit and they all carried muskets. Before
the French could recover from their surprise, the little group had discharged their muskets at point-blank range, hitting the leading officer
and the drummer. A moment later, they were swallowed up in the
French ranks; each man fought desperately until repeated bayonet
thrusts left them dying on the ground. A few moments later, heavy
firing broke out from nearby side streets and buildings. A new battle
had begun, as armed civilians, monks, women, even children came
running towards the French from three directions.

The flight over the bridge had been checked. When the exodus
started, several courageous officers and civilian volunteers made
strenuous efforts to reassure the people and regroup their scattered
companies, but all in vain: the crowd swept them aside and began to
pour across. Then, on the Arrabal side of the Ebro, a young cavalry
lieutenant, Luciano Tornos, added his name to the city's roll of honour
by defying the fleeing mob single-handed, sabre in hand, while on his
orders a cannon was dragged from the San Lazaro monastery and
trained on the bridge. The fugitives halted when they saw Tornos
brandishing the burning linstock. Then a monk ran past him holding a
crucifix aloft, urging his flock to return to their posts and duties. A few
minutes later, the tide of panic had subsided.

Meanwhile, the sound of fresh firing from the direction of Santa
Magdalena and reports that the French were being held back at the
Portillo and other gates sent armed men, led by Antonio Torres and
Colonel Obispo, running towards the Coso. Recently abandoned
houses were again occupied by the defenders who proceeded to fire at
the French column from the windows and cellar openings; a cannon
opened up from the shelter of an ancient medieval arch which stood at
the mouth of a street by Santa Magdalena; and new barricades began
to take shape in the side streets. The French position was soon critical.
The Spanish were bringing up their light cannon to sweep the Coso;
it was impossible to advance down any of the side streets because of the
hastily improvised barricades of mattresses, sacks, beds, tables and
cupboards; and another cannon had begun to fire volleys of grapeshot
from a small, easily defended street on their right, the Calle Parra.

The French tried to take cover from the barrage of musketry by crouching behind the remains of the makeshift barricades and sandbagged breastworks littering the Coso, but they were unable to escape the plunging fire from the many snipers ensconced high in the houses on either side. The number of defenders in the area rapidly increased until, a few minutes later, a crowd of Spanish regulars and civilians armed with knives, sabres and hatchets rushed at the French and drove them back in confusion.

Unable to hold the Coso, the French ran under heavy fire to the ruins of the seminary, where they were shot down among the rubble of the ruined corridors and halls; some of the pursuing Spaniards even stood on their comrades' shoulders to fire down at the French as they knelt behind the charred fragments of walls in the vast building.

During the battle for the ruins of the seminary, the centre column also encountered trouble. In the general chaos, it advanced down a dark, narrow street called the Calle del Arco de la Cineja, mistaking this for its real objective the Calle San Gil, which traversed the heart of the city. Soon the French became lost in a maze of dark openings and twisting alleys, and they were driven back into the Coso as shots rang out from the windows and roofs above and a storm of bricks, vases and even kitchen furniture rained down on their heads.

On the left, the French in the Calle Azoque were still held in check by the defenders of Santa Fé, and the column moving eastwards along the Coso was halted by a cannon and a large body of armed civilians from the Portillo sector. In a short time all the French in the Coso were forced back towards the opening of the Calle de Santa Engracia where they were able to hold only the first few houses by the hospital and San Francisco; here they were joined by the troops retreating from the seminary. The Spaniards completely dominated the Coso once more.

The attack by then had lost its initial impetus. The defenders stood firm at the castle, the Portillo, the Sol and Quemada gates; the retreat over the bridge had been stopped; and, even behind the French lines in the Santa Engracia and Carmen sectors, small groups of Spaniards had reoccupied several houses and were now sniping at the French rear. In the Calle Parra, a furious battle raged as the French troops advancing from the gardens of Santa Catalina charged the Spanish cannon, killed the gunners and attempted to drag away the gun until the Spanish counter-attacked and regained it. A detachment of thirty

Spaniards briefly managed to occupy the Torre del Pino again until their numbers were reduced to six; and another Spanish cannon was brought to bear on the Plaza de Santa Engracia. Whenever the French attempted to charge up a street, they would be blocked by barricades and sniped at from top storeys and roofs. Some of the most murderous fighting took place in a block of houses facing the Santa Fé monastery where Obispo and Sas launched a series of counter-attacks throughout the afternoon and into the early evening. Each time the French tried to storm the buildings, the defenders' deadly fire would send them running for cover. Then small bands of Spaniards, running the gauntlet of the French fire, would make sudden sallies, pursuing the French into the houses where they had taken refuge, smashing down walls and partitions with axes and musket butts and leaping through the windows as, sword in hand, they hurled themselves upon the enemy.

In the Coso, the French had brought up a field piece but, under heavy fire, were forced to drag it into the shelter of a nearby mansion's patio so that they could reload it undisturbed before pushing it through the main doorway again and firing it across the street. While the gunners were ramming the powder charge down the muzzle, an overseer of the Imperial Canal Company named Manuel Fandos, together with several companions, braved the French bullets by making a dash across the Coso to the doorway. The gunners were killed and the Spaniards, with the help of a mule found in the patio, hauled the gun out. The animal was shot as soon as it reached the street but Fandos and his men successfully dragged the gun fifty yards away to the shelter of another doorway. It was only one of the day's many heroic individual actions.

The fighting now spread from the streets and alleyways into the houses on the Calle de Santa Engracia. The French occupied the hospital, which they transformed into a temporary headquarters under the command of Lefebvre-Denouettes, and proceeded to fight their way into the palatial mansions of Saragossa's leading noblemen. They broke into Count Sastago's palace and then ran through its gardens to the grounds of the San Francisco monastery whose towers and upper floors were still held by the Spaniards. In the palace of the Count of Fuentes, the French were swept by a volley from the great staircase but they then stormed it; while fierce fighting continued in the gardens and cloisters of nearby Santa Catalina. Shortly afterwards, the Spaniards poured back into the Fuentes palace from its gardens and also succeeded in firing part of Sastago's mansion. Often, the French only occupied a

house to be driven out of it a few minutes later. In the rear, guards had
to be posted to fight off the Spaniards who kept returning over roof tops
and along side streets. With the exception of San Francisco, the
hospital and Santa Engracia, the French had no foothold they could
call permanent. The whole of Saragossa had become their enemy and
the horrors of street-fighting made a deep impression on the attackers,
vividly evoked by Belmas:

"The city was like a volcano as explosion ceaselessly followed
explosion. Here one could hear the cries of the victors and vanquished;
here there was victory, there disorder and flight; friend and foe all
fought pell-mell and without order. Each man defended himself where
he was attacked and attacked where he encountered the enemy;
hazard alone presided over this chaos. The streets were strewn with
corpses; the cries one could hear among the flames and the smoke
added still further to the horror of this scene of desolation, and the
tocsin, which rang on all sides, seemed to announce the death throes of
Saragossa."

Unable to establish any clearly defined front within the city, the
French army began to make the most of its temporary occupation of
houses and monastic buildings by pillaging them. Many of the inhabitants had been so confident that the French would never enter the city
that they had failed to remove their goods from some of the shops
nearest the gates. The French guardsman François Billon, whose
souvenirs were published in 1905, described how he saw some of the
first infantrymen to enter the city filling their shakos with watches,
rings, gold chains and earrings which they jokingly offered to their
friends and even to some of their officers. Wine cellars were invaded
and, whenever they could enjoy a brief respite from the fighting, men
began to get drunk on the thick, powerful Aragonese red wine. Verdier
himself, in his report on the operations of August 4, admitted that the
need to consolidate their position in the houses nearest the walls
"halted the first movement of our troops and gave them the facility to
gorge themselves with wine and pillage".

At nightfall, there came a lull in the fighting. The French had pushed
and managed to maintain a wedge into the city, holding the line of walls
from Santa Engracia to the Carmen gate at its base, their most advanced
point being the hospital and San Francisco monastery. Although they
occupied the monastery of San Diego behind San Francisco and the
Santa Rosa convent in the much-disputed Calle Azoque, they had been

unable to capture Santa Fé. Further to their left, several hundred defenders still kept them at bay from the great buildings of the Convalescents' Hospital and San Ildefonso monastery; and Renovales and his men prevented any eastward advance past the church of San Miguel.

From the Spanish point of view, the situation was still desperate but not hopeless. The French were contained in a relatively small area and the Saragossans had gained time in which to fortify every house and side street off the Coso. After the first panic, the inhabitants fought side by side with the city's few regular soldiers with astounding heroism and tenacity. But the temporary commander-in-chief, Antonio Torres, remained almost as pessimistic as the Palafox brothers. At ten o'clock that same night, he wrote a letter to Palafox and sent it by special messenger in the direction of Villamayor. A sense of anguish and reproach is evident in the latter part of his letter for, after informing Palafox that the French had been held back behind the Coso, he went on: "The French have committed a multitude of atrocities, which I have not time to relate here. Your Excellency does not ignore the fact that I lack the most necessary resources for defence . . . A part of the city is in the enemy's power. He is tranquil at present but only until tomorrow morning, and my position—the most critical in which a soldier has ever found himself—makes me hope that Your Excellency will not forget me. I am therefore led to believe that, tomorrow morning, Your Excellency or one of your honourable brothers will bring me the succour and supplies without which neither I nor anyone else will be able to save the city from the danger to which Your Excellency has exposed it by abandoning it to the mercy of its cruel enemies."

While the French entrenched themselves in the hospital and in San Francisco, leaving strong guard detachments at their rear to maintain communications with the breaching batteries and the camp, their artillery continued to fire shells and mortar bombs into the heart of the city. But all hope of a speedy end to the struggle had vanished. Between one o'clock in the afternoon and eight o'clock in the evening, the officially admitted French losses were 462 killed and 1,505 wounded: an enormously high proportion for a besieging army of only 15,000, of whom more than half were needed to guard the trenches, batteries and supply lines and to ensure the blockade of the city along its two-mile-long perimeter on the right of the Ebro and on the left bank.

Despite their battle-weariness and the continuing bombardment, the Spaniards worked frantically to strengthen their defences and were encouraged by the final result of the day's fighting. As Belmas wrote, and many French officers realised, the Spaniards "had seen that it was possible for them to resist full-scale attacks and they no longer feared them. The prestige attached to the conservation of the *enceinte* and which had led them to believe that all would be lost as soon as it was breached—this prejudice, so favourable to the besiegers, was completely destroyed". The piles of French bodies lying in the streets and heaped up on the Coso and in front of the Santa Fé monastery spoke eloquently of the further losses the French would have to suffer if the rest of the city continued to defend itself with equal determination. No less than twenty-four French corpses were counted on one of the several bonfires made by the Spaniards at Santa Fé. As the embattled French and Poles in the front sector kept watch on the Coso, they saw their comrades' dead bodies being carelessly flung into heaps or attached to ropes and dragged by children and youths in the direction of the river.

When dawn broke on August 5, the French could see that every side street across the Coso was barricaded. The muzzles of Spanish cannon pointed at them from between sandbags, through embrasures newly pierced in walls, from windows, doorways and gardens. A great pall of dark smoke hung over the city and several houses were still burning. On the steps of the Coso entrance to San Francisco lay the corpses of nine monks—victims, like those in other parts of the city, of French fury during the assaults on monastic buildings.

From his camp-bed where he lay recovering from his wound, Verdier sent the city another summons to surrender, threatening to reduce it to a heap of ashes. Torres took the message to the members of the *Junta* and to the *ayuntamiento* which continued to sit in its consistorial chamber. Shortly afterwards, the French could see a red flag and another with a white cross hanging from the top of the Torre Nueva. Torres had ordered them to be prominently displayed to show Spanish troops outside the city that Saragossa had not surrendered.

The French were still unable to complete the blockade of the city. Later in the day, to the tumultuous cheers of the populace and the sound of music, the Marquis of Lazan returned to the city with two wagons laden with gunpowder, three field guns and a fresh detachment of volunteers. He had managed to avoid the French cavalry patrols and had forded the Gallego river where it was left unguarded. He also brought Palafox's answer to Torres's anguished letter. Palafox wrote that he had assembled considerable forces, which were now near the city on the heights above Villamayor, and that his first aim was to restore communications with Saragossa. He had appointed Lazan to the command of a force of élite troops composed of Spanish and Walloon guards; he explained that, if he had not left the city on August 4, the battalion of volunteers he had gathered would not have arrived; and he announced that he was sending some supplies ahead of his main force. After an odd request that Torres should be ready to send him 400 field tents at short notice, he ended his letter by declaring reassuringly: "Hold fast, the salvation of the city is my sole care. All hope had already been lost for me but now I admire the prodigies you have achieved. May the Lord be blessed, soon perhaps we shall be free." The *Junta* and *ayuntamiento* were indeed reassured, Jorge Ibort and some more volunteers paraded in the Plaza del Seo, the powder was distributed, and soon fighting was raging again with undiminished intensity.

During the night, the Spaniards had reinforced the Portillo position in case the French should launch an attack in that sector; several cannon at the Sancho gate were placed where they could direct enfilading fire on the nearby streets; a twenty-four pounder was brought up in front of San Ildefonso to cover the approach to the market square; the barricade in the Calle San Gil was strengthened and several more were built behind it; and a large parapet was thrown up in the street in front of the Santa Fé convent.

As the French probed beyond their flanks and found that every house and monastic building held by the Spanish had become a well-armed fortress, Verdier realised that a new phase in the fighting had begun. After conferring in his tent with Lefebvre and Colonel Lacoste of the engineers, he ordered that the troops should advance only by sapping and piercing communications between each new house they captured and the next, since "it is the only kind of warfare suitable for waging against these madmen. The operation will be a lengthy one, but it appears the most sure".

The French were not allowed much time for sapping operations as the Spanish soon launched a series of furious counter-attacks. They continued to harass the French rear, and a Spanish charge across the Coso ended with the recapture of part of the Treasury building and the surrender of several French soldiers. While the French advanced towards San Ildefonso in a desperate attempt to break through to the market square, a murderous fire greeted them from towers, windows, balconies and roof tops.

The garrison in the Convalescents' Hospital still resisted fiercely. Although the French guns had opened fire on the building and were sending tons of masonry crashing down on the heads of its defenders, a group of about eighty men continued to hurl grenades at the French every time they approached the battered walls. French and Spanish guns exchanged fire across the Coso and one of the city's landmarks, a pillared shrine with a cross commemorating the Roman martyrs, was reduced to rubble. The Spaniards made strong attacks on the houses adjoining the hospital and the gardens of the nearby convent of the Daughters of Jerusalem; and, in spite of the French bombardment, the Santa Catalina convent remained in Spanish hands, as did the nearby Botanic Garden.

The entire population seemed to be taking a hand in the fighting, and the list of heroic civilians whose names were to be recorded in the city's annals lengthened. A seventy-six-year-old carpenter called José de la Hera, armed only with a knife, burst into a house being pillaged by a couple of French soldiers, killing one, snatching the other's musket and taking him prisoner. The beautiful Countess Bureta, who had already shown great courage in organising the evacuation of hospital patients during the terrible night of August 3, had set up barricades outside her house, in the street leading to the market square, and with a small garrison prepared to defend it to the death. She and many other women, besides tending the wounded, worked ceaselessly to bring ammunition and food and drink to the defenders in the front line.

The famous Agustina now reappeared on the scene. François Billon, who had been among the first to storm the breach at Santa Engracia under the eyes of General Lefebvre, was one of many French soldiers to be fascinated by her story. In his memoirs, he claimed that he had seen, met and spoken with Agustina during the fighting. As was confirmed by other eye-witnesses, she had been promoted, given a gunner's pay, and wore a shield of honour embroidered on her sleeve. After seeing her first from a distance during some street battle, Billon succumbed to her charms. No words could describe her, he wrote, for "in creating this marvel, heaven had exhausted in her all its resources of beauty, delicacy and vigour". Billon's account of his encounter with her is striking and picturesque. Part of it must certainly be romantic exaggeration but, even if it is entirely a product of a French soldier's overheated imagination, it does show that heroines like Agustina made a deep impression among the French. To find themselves fighting against women was a new experience for Napoleon's troops.

Billon recalled that he had entered a house on the Coso which was the scene of a struggle between some Spaniards, including Agustina, and fifteen French grenadiers in search of plunder. Agustina was in the act of ordering the outnumbered French to lay down their weapons or be killed when Billon and a detachment of light infantry stormed the house and saved their comrades. A sergeant held the girl by the throat after the rest of the Spaniards had been killed or driven off and, when at last he released her from his grip, she appealed to Billon:

"Pale with anger and surprise, motionless but always proud, Agustina summoned me in a lofty tone which, however, was tinged with a certain sweetness: 'Do with me what you will,' she said, 'but—*por Dios!*—if you have any heart, do not deliver up the heroine of the Portillo, who is under the protection of our Lady of the Pillar, to the brutality of your soldiers. I know that I am beautiful and your eyes tell me the same quite plainly. My honour and my life are both in peril: let it only be my life. But,' she added as she glanced rapidly around, '*Veremos!*' ['We shall see!']—I did my best to reassure her in this critical situation and then, very deeply moved and almost sincere, I added: 'Will you be my wife? It is the only way to avoid what you fear.'—'Then,' she cried loudly, 'I shall no longer be under the protection of Our Lady of the Pillar! . . . If only peace were made . . . But enough! You do not believe a word you say. I owe you a great deal—my life certainly, my honour maybe. Although French, you are far from displeasing me—I tell you so frankly—but your cunning speech makes me madly desirous to flee from you, with or without your permission and without waiting for the night.' She stood very close to me. Her serene and smiling face suddenly lit up and you could have said she was praying. 'O Virgin of the Pillar!' she cried as she flung her arms around my neck and kissed me, 'Adieu! . . .' All of a sudden, she jumped nimbly through a window and disappeared into the dusk.

"Out of respect for my rank, the grenadiers and *voltigeurs* had stood aside during this brief colloquy. I rushed out with them in pursuit of the fugitive but it was impossible for us to find any trace of her."

A day or two later, Billon met Agustina again as she was helping one of the city's heroic priests to give Extreme Unction to a dying Spaniard:

"Our sudden appearance scarcely moved the priest. He snatched up the wounded man's weapon and made a sign to those who surrounded him to aim their shots at me. Four of my brave *voltigeurs* fell and, if I escaped this volley, I considered that it was in no way the fault of my young heroine for she seemed to be aiming at me with great precision and coolness." Nevertheless, concluded the gallant Billon, he later learned that Agustina spoke of him to her fellow Spaniards with expressions of praise and gratitude!

Few of Billon's fellow-soldiers either lived or dreamed such a romantic interlude as the street fighting moved into its third and then its fourth and fifth day. The French were unable to advance, the Spaniards never lost control of the Coso, and the civilian defenders who had no muskets still had an inexhaustible supply of stones and bricks, from the rubble of their buildings, to hurl down at the French whenever they left the shelter of the captured houses. In the August heat, the corpses in the streets began to rot and sickened the French with their smell. Even worse—in building their barricades, the Spanish sometimes used dead bodies as well as horses and, during their assaults, the French would find themselves wading and slipping among masses of putrefying flesh. The threat of plague increased and Palafox ordered his French prisoners to venture out into the Coso and other disputed streets and drag the dead bodies away.

Belmas described the dispirited state of the French now that they found themselves hemmed in on the flanks and the front: "For nearly three days, almost all our troops were occupying the part of the city which they had seized. This position was dangerous as the soldiers were exhausted. General Lefebvre left only strong outposts in the front line and brought the rest of the army back to the rear to positions in which they entrenched themselves. There, a soldier was able to rest after a combat which had lasted thrice twenty-four hours and to recover a little. Our progress under cover continued slowly with the protection of the crenellated walls which formed our line. Our sentinels placed on the roofs and in the bell towers fired ceaselessly and we lost men in the most desperate manner for there is nothing more frightful than this kind of fighting. The heat, which was unbearable, still further increased the soldiers' fatigue. The besieged defended themselves with unparalleled fury. We could only gain ground by setting fire everywhere, by burrowing from house to house, by piercing the walls between one house and the next to establish communications and form new lines of embrasures.

It often happened that, as we smashed down one partition, we found the enemy behind it, defending himself with the bayonet."

On August 6, when the house-to-house fighting had extended even down into the cellars, where the last remaining defenders would take refuge after the French had mastered the ground and upper floors, Verdier received a note from Belliard, telling him of the evacuation of Madrid and ordering him to be ready to raise the siege. But, on the following day, after the fighting had died down temporarily, a second letter arrived countermanding the previous order. As it prepared to move northwards, the General Staff had decided that the attack on Saragossa was to be continued. The plan was to capture the city as soon as possible, to make it a point of strength on the line of the Ebro, and to await reinforcements from France. The French batteries, which were on the point of being dismantled, resumed their fire. The street fighting was to last for another entire week.

In an attempt to encourage an atmosphere of fanatical patriotism, it was announced that Palafox was on his way back with reinforcements, and posters appeared in the streets announcing that anyone who even mentioned the possibility of capitulation would be hanged without delay, that the city must be defended to the end, and that even if the enemy were victorious—which would be in contradiction to all the assurances vouchsafed by the most holy Virgin of the Pillar—then the inhabitants must cross the river, destroy the bridge and fight to the death in the Arrabal suburb. All who died would instantaneously go to heaven and, as an added compensation, they would then have the opportunity of sitting in judgement on the Virgin of the Pillar for having lied to them by promising them victory!

On August 9, a more concrete encouragement was given to the city. Although Lefebvre had heard of Palafox's approach and sent two battalions and some Polish lancers across the Ebro to meet him, he was unable to stop his progress. After skirmishing with the French, Palafox succeeded in sending 200 cart-loads of arms and ammunition into Saragossa. Shortly afterwards, he entered the city himself at the head of some 4,000 regular troops and armed peasants, including several hundred Catalan volunteers who had already distinguished themselves in their own province. To add to the Saragossans' joy, details of the great victory at Baylen were published on the same day in a special issue of the city's gazette. As they sheltered behind their barricades and kept watch on the Coso, the French could distinctly hear the cries and songs of the rejoicing Spaniards. The Pilar church was crowded to capacity; Palafox again kissed the hand of the holy statuette; and, in the streets, Saragossans composed songs of resistance in the manner of the traditional Aragonese *jotas*:

Que no quiere ser fran . . . ce . . . sa . . . a . . . a
La vir . . . gen del pi . . . lar
Di . . . ce . . . e . . . e que no quiere ser fran . . . ce . . . sa . . . a . . . a:
Que quiere ser Ca . . . pi . . . ta . . . na . . . a . . . a
De la tro . . . pa ara . . . go . . ne . . . sa . . . a . . . a!

Soon after their arrival, the Catalans attacked the French who were sheltering among the olive trees in the garden of Santa Catalina and in the Botanical Garden, chasing them from their positions with the deadly, long knives they particularly favoured for such action. Another Spanish assault on the Carmen gate disposed of many of the French occupying the battery there. The French continued to make fruitless forays against the Convalescents' Hospital and also launched an assault on the Vitoria convent a hundred yards to the north. On August 10, the French artillery opened up a furious barrage against the Misericordia but the infantry still failed to make progress. While Renovales and his men stormed the church and cloisters of Santa Catalina, hurling grenades as they ran through the building, another force attacked the main hospital and captured an adjacent house after extinguishing a fire begun by the French. Now that they had been driven back into an increasingly threatened position at the top of the Calle de Santa Engracia, the French were unable to keep possession of the first few buildings along the Coso.

According to the Spanish artillery colonel Manuel Cavallero, who also wrote a history of the siege, in the nine days between August 4 and August 13 the French only succeeded in capturing four houses on the San Francisco side of the Coso. One house, facing the Treasury, was only taken after six days and nights. Santiago Sas and his men held the palace and gardens belonging to the Count of Fuentes and the houses behind them as far back as Santa Fé for six and a half days despite repeated onslaughts. Most of the Spanish counter-attacks were in fact made at night. Both sides would make sudden dashes at each other's batteries, attempting to knife and bayonet the gunners, and would temporarily occupy the adjoining houses until they were driven out again. In some streets, the batteries were so close to one another that, on one occasion, a Spaniard managed to crawl along the ground through the scattered corpses and tie a rope around the muzzle of a French cannon in an eventually unsuccessful attempt to drag it away with the assistance of his companions who had run out from cover to help him.

On August 11, more carts with ammunition and food reached the city and Palafox made a tour of inspection along the Spanish line on the Coso. The French batteries outside the city continued to fire bombs and grenades deep into the city, badly damaging the houses next to the Seo cathedral and even hitting the church itself. According to the diarist Casamayor, so many cannon balls and bombs fell in the Ebro that shoals of dead fishes were to be seen floating on the water. But not even the constant shelling could deter many Saragossan housewives from continuing to wash clothes and linen along the river banks.

On August 12, a town crier informed the people that the Catalans had succeeded in dislodging the French from Santa Catalina and that those who lived in that district could now safely return to salvage any remaining possessions they might still find there. Fires were lit by the Spaniards in the hospital, where only a few French still remained, and twice they extinguished fires started by French artillery and grenades in the Sastago palace. On the same day, the former Captain-General Guillelmi's cook was hanged for treason, after being accused of firing rockets to show the French gunners where to direct their fire.

It now became clear to the besieged that the French were about to give up their attempt to take the city. While the Spaniards maintained pressure around Santa Catalina, the hospital and San Francisco, the French moved back all their men except for a few snipers. During the night of August 12, more than 300 Spanish prisoners, many of them nuns, straggled into the city from Monte Torrero where the French had released them. On the following day, while they continued to bombard the town, the French completely abandoned the hospital and San Francisco, setting fire to many houses on their retreat; the Spaniards promptly reoccupied the ravaged, plundered houses near Santa Catalina and in the Calle Azoque. Hostilities were mainly confined to shelling but this was maintained with such intensity that, in the words of Casamayor, "by nightfall, such were the fires all along the Coso that it appeared to be a single bonfire". The bombardment continued until midnight. A few hours later, before the first light of dawn, a tremendous explosion shook the city as the French set off a huge mine under the Santa Engracia monastery. It was their parting gesture.

In the morning, the city was completely free of French troops. They had left so suddenly that, as the advancing Spaniards picked their way through the ruins, the piles of corpses, dead horses and shattered gun-carriages, they found cases of ammunition left intact, heaps of unused shot, muskets, haversacks, and even supplies of dough for making bread. Lefebvre had received a formal order from King Joseph to raise the siege at once, to march to Tudela and then cross the Ebro to cover the left flank of the French main army as it withdrew from central Spain. The besieging army began to march at midnight, disguising its departure with a final bombardment of the town. After setting fire to their stores on Monte Torrero, the French were forced to abandon most of the light artillery they had brought into the city, to spike the heaviest siege guns and throw them into the canal, and to set the ammunition on fire as they were expected to move with speed and a heavy artillery train would have slowed their progress. The French losses were officially given as 3,500 but this may well have been a very conservative estimate. A week later, writing from his new headquarters at Milagro, Lefebvre stated that nearly all his high-ranking officers were wounded, killed or sick, and that "I have regiments commanded by captains". Spanish losses were probably at least as high.

Saragossa had been saved by the determination of its defenders and the results of Dupont's capitulation. Already, on August 13, Palafox was sure of victory when he addressed another resonant proclamation to the city, congratulating it on its heroism and especially singling out for praise the "sublime women of Saragossa" who "by their courage have surpassed anything that history has ever recorded". On the next day, the *ayuntamiento* ordered a fiesta to be held immediately in honour of the Pilar Virgin. August 15 was the festival of the Assumption. After four French soldiers captured on the bridge at La Muela had been hanged in the market square by the revenge-seeking populace—unable to prevent such reprisals, Palafox had urged in vain that the unfortunate men should simply be shot—and the head of a French cavalry officer stuck on a pike, together with the man's horse and weapons, had been brought to Palafox, the bells of the Pilar church summoned the citizens of Sara-gossa to a great *Te Deum* of thanksgiving. Palafox led a huge proces-sion from his palace to the basilica through streets lined with a guard of honour. Long afterwards the inhabitants continued to sing:

Que no quiere ser francesa
*La Virgen del Pilar.**

*   *   *

The news that the French had failed to take Saragossa inspired Spain, heartened France's other enemies, and added to Napoleon's already considerable fury. The whole summer became one of disaster and reverses so far as his plans for the Peninsula were concerned. Baylen and Saragossa were followed by setbacks and defeats in Catalonia and Portugal. On August 17, the French gave up their attempt to take the town of Gerona, and, later that month, Junot's men were decisively beaten at Vimiero in Portugal after a British army, led by the future Duke of Wellington, had landed.

While Napoleon raged against Dupont and Vedel, and Joseph's army retreated northwards, leaving sacked towns and villages in its wake, the whole of free Spain gave itself up to rejoicing. Castaños and Palafox were the great heroes of the day. It was a time of national euphoria. Although the English had driven the French from Portugal, it was pointed out that Spain alone had defeated the French, and it was widely believed that Napoleon would admit defeat and withdraw his remaining troops from the country.

Despite his success at Baylen, which he owed mostly to Reding, Castaños was slow to follow up his advantage by marching on Madrid. As the days passed the Madrilenes were still without news of the great army of liberation which should have been advancing to enter the capital and then pursue Joseph's retreating forces. On August 12, the Council of Castile met and declared that the forced abdications of Charles IV and Ferdinand were null and void; so too were all decrees issued by them while they were in France as well as those of Joseph and Napoleon.

The following day, 8,000 Valencian and Murcian troops entered Madrid in triumph but it was not until another ten days had passed that Castaños and his army of Andalusia marched into the capital. The Madrilenes at once enthusiastically resumed celebrations on an even greater scale with bull-fights (now again permitted), processions, firework displays, dancing and music On August 24, Ferdinand was officially proclaimed King of Spain with great pomp and ceremony and,

* "The Virgin of the Pillar
  who does not want to be French."

after further public rejoicing, Spain's statesmen and the leaders of the provincial *Juntas* began to discuss what form of government they should give their country during the rightful King's enforced absence.

Spain needed two things quickly: an efficient central government, and an army strong enough to expel the French who were showing no inclination to move any further back than their line along the river Ebro. A council of war was held in Madrid and decreed a mass levy of all men between the ages of seventeen and forty. French property was confiscated and a public appeal was made for funds, war materials, horses and weapons.

Opinions varied over the type of régime that most suited the country, but Spain's politicians, churchmen, civil servants and generals eventually agreed that each provincial *Junta* should send two deputies to form a supreme *Junta* with overall responsibility for the civil and military affairs of the nation.

The new, central Supreme *Junta*, popularly known as the *Suprema*, decided to meet in the royal residence at Aranjuez, where Godoy had so ignominiously fallen from power and Charles IV had abdicated in favour of Ferdinand. It was composed of twenty-four members, the number later being raised to thirty-five, and deputies included Francisco Palafox, Calvo de Rozas, and the great intellectual and reforming statesman Jovellanos; its president was the eighty-year-old Floridablanca. The task of composing proclamations and manifestoes was given to the celebrated poet Manuel José Quintana.

From the beginning, the *Suprema* wasted time in procedural, constitutional and legal debates. The members represented every tendency in current Spanish political thinking and they engaged in endless arguments about the respective merits of constitutional or absolute monarchy, plans for reform and the position of the Church. Despite a huge public response to the appeal for donations, little progress was made in the formation of a national army to liberate the rest of the country. Instead, while Quintana wrote one stirring appeal after another, and the deputies made endless speeches on irrelevant issues, the local *Juntas* began to quarrel with one another and look with increasing suspicion on the *Suprema*. The generals were unable to agree on any coordinated plan of action, and argued in their turn with the *Suprema*. The hoped-for new army of half a million with 50,000 cavalry failed to materialise, and no single commander-in-chief for all Spain's armed forces was appointed. To make matters worse, the French along the Ebro began to increase their strength and Napoleon announced his personal intention of leading an army to recapture Madrid and crown Joseph King.

Joseph's retreat from Madrid had dismayed and infuriated his brother, who had hoped to regroup the French forces in the centre around Madrid and beat off the threatened attack by Castaños. Napoleon had then wanted the armies to hold a line along the river Duero, which ran from Portugal through Leon and Castile, but events moved too fast for him. He had also been angered by Verdier's failure to remain at Tudela, so as to contain Palafox's forces and protect the French flank; by the end of August, the entire French army—except for the troops in Catalonia—was behind the Ebro with its headquarters at Miranda de Ebro. On August 9, Joseph had reached Burgos, where he was joined by Bessières with his army which he had withdrawn from Leon. From Burgos, Joseph wrote to inform his brother that he only wished to retain command of the French armies in Spain long enough to be able to defeat the rebels and recapture Madrid. But, he added, once he had re-entered the capital, he would give up the crown, since the entire population rejected him, and he preferred to return to Naples. A few days later, he was thoroughly dejected by the news that Napoleon had made Murat the new King of Naples. Joseph tried in vain to convince his brother of the impossibility of keeping an unwanted foreign ruler on the Spanish throne: 100,000 gallows as well as hundreds of thousands of troops would be needed to keep him in power, the entire population would oppose him, every house would be a fortress . . .

Napoleon ignored Joseph's prophetic objections. In spite of Saragossa's gallant defence and Dupont's defeat at Baylen, his low opinion of the Spanish army and their generals was unchanged. He had hoped that the forces he had sent to Spain would be sufficient to dominate the whole country, while he turned his attention to Austria which seemed likely to declare war on him once again. Now that he was forced to take personal control of the Spanish situation, he was determined that there should be no more half measures. He would bring to Spain several corps of his Grand Army, stationed in Germany, annihilate the scattered Spanish armies, overrun the whole Peninsula, drive the English out of Portugal and lead his men on to Madrid.

Huge French reinforcements soon began to enter Spain. Before the end of August, Napoleon had ordered two corps of his Grand Army and two divisions of heavy cavalry to be ready to leave for the Peninsula. They were followed by division after division of Napoleon's most ex-

perienced, war-hardened fighting men as well as by artillery, ammunition and supplies in huge quantities. On September 7, an Imperial decree
ordered the formation of a new Army of Spain consisting of seven corps.
Among its commanders were the great Ney—bravest and most iron-
willed of Napoleon's generals—and other such prestige-laden leaders
as Jourdan, Soult, Suchet, Lannes and Victor.

While the Supreme *Junta* argued throughout the month of October
over the niceties of constitutional as opposed to autocratic government,
and the Saragossans wisely began to build new, stronger fortifications,
Napoleon met the Russian Tsar Alexander I at Erfurt in Germany. He
convinced Alexander of the need to recognise Joseph as King of Spain
and dissuade Austria from declaring war on France. He also made
peace proposals to England but these came to nothing as the British
Cabinet insisted that the *Junta* was Spain's lawful government. On
November 3, Napoleon was back in Bayonne. On the following day,
he entered Spain for the first and only time in his life.

By the end of October, several Spanish armies had begun to move
against the French but, instead of 500,000 men, Spain could only put
130,000 into the field. The British Government's observers at Aranjuez
became increasingly dismayed as they saw the way in which the *Junta*
was losing the opportunity to mount a full-scale, coordinated attack on
the French lines and failing to provide a single, overall command for
its scattered forces. Instead, while millions of patriotic Spaniards were
making generous donations to the war effort and English guns and
money were reaching the country, the Supreme *Junta* was devoting its
time to such measures as the restoration of an Inquisitor-General and
restrictions upon printing!

Napoleon began his offensive less than a week after arriving at
Vitoria, where Joseph had established his court. The unhappy King was
pushed aside and told to let his brother win back his throne for him,
while Napoleon's generals began to cut the Spanish armies to pieces.
On November 10 and 11, Marshal Victor cleared the French right flank
by routing General Blake's Galician and Asturian forces near the town
of Espinosa, compelling the Spaniards to retreat over the Cantabrian
mountains into Leon. Again on November 10, at the small village of
Gamonal a few miles from Burgos, another small Spanish army under
an inexperienced young nobleman, the Duke of Belvedere, was swept
away by Soult. Napoleon drove on to Burgos and sacked it horribly.

The horrors of the summer were soon repeated on an even greater scale. The French soldiers were given licence to plunder and rape in revenge for previous defeats and, as the veterans of the Grand Army began to find their fellow-soldiers nailed to barn doors or lying mutilated and charred on bonfires, they needed little encouragement to behave with equal savagery. Napoleon's surgeon-in-chief to the Grand Army, Percy, was another of those sensitive French officers who never forgot the horrors of the war in Spain as Napoleon began to avenge Baylen. After a brief stay at Burgos, he wrote: "Expressions are lacking to depict the horrors and the abominable excesses with which the soldiery soiled itself at Burgos on the first and second day of its entry into this justly famous town which would have provided us with everything we needed in abundance without this brigandage. The monks and the inhabitants fled in terror; foaming with rage and no longer hearing the voices of their leaders, the soldiers flung themselves like a devouring volcanic lava into churches, houses and convents, and spared nothing. Tabernacles, sacristies, furniture, floors, tombs—everything was smashed, torn away, ripped up and thrown aside in the search for gold and jewels." In Miranda de Ebro, already occupied since the end of August, Percy saw the newly arrived soldiers setting fire to houses and breaking open tombs. South of Burgos, as it advanced towards Madrid, the entire army seemed to have become sodden with drink: "The Imperial Guard, especially the infantry, has become drunk. They have found wine everywhere and abused it. The roads are strewn with dead-drunk grenadiers of the guard, some having lost their caps, others their muskets, and at each halt they are still drinking." Like Tascher before him and others to follow, Percy was unable to refrain from crying: "We do everything possible to be abhorred and yet, the people are good, gentle, hospitable and even timid."

While the French officers did their best to restore some sobriety among their men, operations began again on the frontiers of Aragon. After immersing himself in the administration of his shattered city and the building of new defence works, Palafox was called upon to play a vital part in an ambitious scheme to drive the French back to the Pyrenees. Although his battle experience in the field was limited to the disastrous skirmishes at Alagon and Epila, Palafox was given a position of great importance in the Spanish plan of campaign and made responsible for the raising of a new army of Aragon, stiffened by men from Valencia and Murcia. As Castaños had decided that his army of 30,000 men was too weak to launch a frontal attack on Moncey's men behind

the Ebro, he went to Saragossa to ask Palafox for reinforcements. The
two leaders agreed to launch a combined attack upon Moncey's left
flank but soon began to argue over tactics. Castaños fell ill for a time;
Palafox showed his complete lack of experience as a strategist by
making impossible proposals for an advance to Pamplona to surround
and cut the French off from the Pyrenees; and Francisco Palafox made
the confusion worse by arriving on the scene to issue a stream of contradictory orders. When the news came that the French, who had re-
taken Logroño, were again on the way to Aragon, while Ney marched
south to threaten Spanish communications with Madrid, Castaños's and
Palafox's forces, numbering 45,000, fell back to defend a line between
Tudela and the small town of Tarazona at the foot of the mountains
south of the Ebro.

Battle was joined on November 23, a few hours after Palafox had
returned to Saragossa to organise a reserve force for his front line. There
was little coordination between the various regiments, and a three-
mile gap was left in the line. Lannes joined Moncey for the attack;
Lefebvre-Desnouettes was given command of the strong French
cavalry force and avenged himself for his repulses at Saragossa by routing the Spaniards before him, in a huge charge of over 3,000 horsemen.
One of the Spanish generals on the left of the line did nothing to help his
comrades who were cut to pieces, Castaños retreated towards Madrid
with the remnants of his forces, and the Army of Aragon under Palafox's
generals fled back in disorder to Saragossa.

History was repeating itself: it was the rout of Tudela, Mallen and
Alagon repeated on a far greater scale. A few days later, Moncey and
Ney appeared with their men before the walls of Saragossa. This time
the inhabitants were under no illusions: a second and even more murderous siege was imminent. Almost simultaneously, Madrid capitulated to
Napoleon and the Supreme *Junta* fled southwards. All the Spanish
armies had been defeated and Saragossa was now the only important
city between the Pyrenees and Madrid left to defy Napoleon's triumph-
ant forces. Once again, Spain and Europe looked to the city as the last
great symbol of the country's will to resist.

PART FOUR

THE SECOND SIEGE

IV

AFTER THE raising of the siege by Verdier, the news of Baylen, and of Joseph's retreat from Madrid, Saragossa fully shared the general euphoria which swept Spain. The French had suffered such severe reverses, the Saragossans had fought so bravely and stubbornly, and the whole population had endured so much that it seemed inconceivable at first that the French should ever return to repeat their fruitless attempt to break the heroic city's resistance.

When the dead had been buried and while the last French guns were fished out of the canal and organised attempts made to bring day-to-day life back to normal, the Saragossans were gratified to learn that their city and their leader had become famous all over Spain and Europe. The normally exaggerated local pride of the Aragonese was still further inflated by the chorus of praise and deluge of compliments which descended upon them from every corner of the country. A Madrid theatre, the Coliseo del Principe, staged a highly successful play called *Los Patriotas de Aragon*; poets and versifiers in every town wrote odes extolling the heroism of the Saragossans; Agustina was famous and honoured; and the *ayuntamiento* of Madrid sent a rapturous message saying that the city's efforts had been "without parallel in history". The defenders were told that they, together with the heroes of Baylen, had the distinction of having overcome "the victors of Marengo, Austerlitz, and Ulm". The citizens of Madrid sent voluntary donations of money and clothing, and a stream of carts and wagons brought food into Saragossa from the surrounding regions. Francisco Palafox and Calvo de Rozas were received with honour and public acclaim when they arrived in Madrid, and then in Aranjuez as the Supreme *Junta* began its deliberations Palafox—his former mistakes and his temporary abandonment of the city on August 4 now forgotten—was raised to the status of a great general in both public and official opinion.

In Saragossa itself, Palafox issued a decree in the name of Ferdinand VII stating that henceforth, because of their valour, no citizens of Saragossa could be sentenced to the death penalty, except for treason, no matter how grave their offence. In return, it was publicly proposed to raise a statue to Palafox until the *ayuntamiento* sensibly replied that, although it wished it could gratify this demand, the fact remained that more pressing tasks had to be faced by all true patriots. Instead of putting up statues, Palafox and the authorities told the population to put up new fortifications.

With the French standing fast in their northern-central sector of the Peninsula and Napoleon sending his soldiers of the Grand Army over the Pyrenees, Palafox and his senior officers realised that it was only a matter of time before the enemy returned to the offensive. New decrees were issued: a temporary tribunal of public safety was set up to uncover and judge cases of treason, collaboration with the French and sedition against the city's authorities; and another body headed by Palafox was formed to deal with questions of public health. A number of prominent citizens, officers, pharmacists and doctors were empowered to take all necessary measures relating to public cleanliness, sewage disposal and the burial of corpses, and to prevent citizens from using the now polluted waters of the canal. The engineer San Genis was called on to plan a new system of fortifications and he enlisted several young students of mathematics and engineering to assist him. The preliminary work began early in September. This time, Saragossa was to be treated as though it were a military fortress of the first order. No pains or expense would be spared to make it the most strongly armed, strongly garrisoned and best supplied citadel in Spain.

As work began, a number of distinguished visitors came to Saragossa. Francisco Goya, who had been born at the village of Fuendetodos only thirty-five miles away, journeyed from Madrid to inspect the ruins and hear first-hand stories of the siege. Agustina's feat inspired one etching in his *Disasters of War* series and another plate recorded the incident of the French corpses being dragged off the streets at the end of ropes. Two other artists, later appointed court painters to Ferdinand VII, also arrived. They were Juan Galvez and Ferdinand Brambila and, after much sketching and a careful study of the ruined buildings, they prepared a number of etchings entitled *Las Ruinas de Zaragoza*. The series, which was eventually published in Cadiz in 1814 and which had great success, depicted some of the most famous incidents and personalities of the siege. The seventy-six-year-old carpenter who had killed one French soldier and captured another, the battle of June 15, Agustina and the cannon, all these were drawn, as well as portraits of Santiago

Sas, Jorge Ibort and the Countess Bureta. By far the most interesting and impressive of the prints which were eventually made from their sketches were those of the great ruined buildings of Saragossa. In their detail, their architectural accuracy and perspective, they were master-pieces of precision and prove that, even in the early 19th century, cannon and mortars could rival the bombs and heavy guns of a later age in their devastating effect. In a number of extremely dramatic com-positions, Brambila and Galvez showed the terrible results of the French bombardment on the beautiful edifice of Santa Engracia, the rubble-heaped Coso, the ruins of the great seminary, the shattered cloister of Santa Catalina and the pathetic relics of other historic buildings such as the church of the hospital in which only a few arches and fragments of wall were left standing after the August 3 holocaust.

The story of the siege reached England and aroused great public admiration. In October, some distinguished representatives of the British Government reached Saragossa. One was General Charles William Doyle, bringing with him a young lieutenant, William Caven-dish, and the other was a diplomat, Sir Charles Vaughan, who had landed at La Coruña with another official British emissary in September. Their mission was to consult with the Supreme *Junta* and coordinate the British and Spanish war efforts. The three men went to Aragon after meeting the *Junta* and a number of generals including Castaños, and stayed some ten days in Saragossa as Palafox's personal guests. After his return to England, Vaughan published the first account of the siege in English, in a thirty-two-page booklet which was reprinted, circulated abroad and did much to impress the English with the stubbornness of Spanish resistance.

Part of Vaughan's diary at the time is devoted to his stay in Saragossa and it is well worth quoting at some length since it is the only contempor-ary English first-hand account of the city and of how Palafox appeared both to his own people and to an intelligent and perceptive English diplomat, accustomed to judge men and situations.

From the beginning, Palafox made a highly favourable impression upon his three English guests. Vaughan wrote that he was "much struck with his person, his address and his very lively intelligent countenance. His uniform was a plain blue coat embroidered with silver, he had a handsome sword-belt, and wore in his hat a cockade which was partly English, as it had upon it the names both of King George and King Ferdinand".

As Vaughan rode by Palafox's side through the city, he was deeply impressed by the signs of the recent fighting: "When I arrived at Saragossa about two months had elapsed since its termination. Marks of destruction everywhere met the eye. In some parts whole streets had been levelled with the ground, and still lay in one indiscriminate heap of ruins. It was difficult indeed to find anywhere a house that had not been struck by a cannon-shot. But in the principal street, the Coso, those houses which had escaped entire destruction were completely covered with shot-marks, both of musketry and cannon. Of the Franciscan convent, an immense pile of buildings of stone, nothing remained but the outer walls. The roof of the cloisters and part of that of the Church, which they supported, had fallen in. The miserable mud-walls of the city had entirely vanished, and nothing remained of them save the gates, which had been constructed of more solid material. The last remaining tower of the magnificent Church and Convent of Sta. Engracia fell while I was at Saragossa, and standing not far from the spot . . . The beautiful plain of the Ebro, in which Saragossa stands, was disfigured by the loss of its valuable groves of olives, and by the appearance of large mounds of rubbish, which marked the former sites of convents or country houses."

The inhabitants of the war-ravaged city were, however, in good spirits: "In the midst of these scenes of devastation it was most gratifying to observe the unbroken spirit of the sufferers, who (regardless of their own individual losses) seemed only to think of the honour of their country, and the means by which it might best be preserved. So far were they from showing despondency at the heavy calamities which had already befallen them that I found them in the middle of October preparing with the utmost zeal and alacrity for another siege."

Vaughan had many occasions to study the population as he was taken by Palafox to watch them drilling with their volunteer battalions: "The Aragonese seemed to me, of all others that I saw in Spain, the best formed for soldiers. They generally exceeded the middling stature— their persons are robust but sinewy and bespeak great activity. Their features are regular and large, their complexions dark but clear, their countenances sombre and impassive, their deportment grave and manly. They have the reputation of being extremely religious and very temperate. They have a high sense of honour, but at the same time are obstinate and revengeful. Their dress is a jacket and breeches of a dark colour, generally, a black waistcoat, and a scarlet sash around the waist. They wear stockings that cover only the calf of the leg, a hat with a very broad brim, and a light sandal upon the foot, fastened around the ankle with black laces."

Naturally, Vaughan heard accounts from his hosts of the feats performed by the female defenders: "Nothing could be more interesting than the conduct of the women, at one time acting as heroines, and then, when the season of peril was past, again appearing in their natural characters. Many females who, with a bayonet lashed upon a pole, had charged into the place of greatest danger during the siege, had so completely resumed their natural manners that, but for the shield of honour embroidered upon their gowns, or some scar that disfigured their persons, no one could have dreamed that they had taken part in such dreadful scenes."

Another aspect of the Spanish revolt was noticed by Vaughan: the kind of innate democracy and mutual respect between various social classes which had already struck Fischer, Laborde and other travellers before the war started. When he joined Palafox's table for dinner, Vaughan met priests, working people, artisans and farmers who had all played their part in the siege, and he noticed that "it was no uncommon thing during dinner for the chair of the Captain-General to be surrounded with people of humble condition . . . the inhabitants of Saragossa used to remark to me that their city was but a gloomy place before the siege, but that one common danger had now united all ranks of people. Superior courage and more than ordinary devotion to the cause of their country had now, it seems, raised some of the most indigent and humble of the inhabitants to places of trust, and opened to them the doors of the best families of the city. It was no uncommon thing during dinner for the chair of the Captain-General to be surrounded with people of humble condition".

There was no doubt about Palafox's enormous popularity among his people and Vaughan stressed the free and easy relationship which existed between him and the crowds as he rode ceaselessly around the city encouraging the workers as they strengthened the walls and built new fortifications. He also noted the great energy and endurance displayed by Palafox as he dealt with all the details of administration. As Vaughan watched him at work, he summed him up in his capacity as leader of soldiers and civilians who had reached his high position through circumstances rather than any previous professional skill and experience. His own assessment of Palafox's character and abilities is the longest

and most important we have from a contemporary. Vaughan was perfectly aware that Palafox's conduct of the siege and, in particular, his
two periods of absence from the city, had aroused criticism in several
quarters and that the French had tended to see him as a man completely
under the sway of fanatical monks and priests. But he could find little
but praise for him. In his description, he makes it clear that, in comparison
with many other military leaders, Palafox was one of the most attractive he had met in Spain:

"General Palafox is almost the only prominent character that
Spain has produced under the singular change that has taken place in
her government. The perilous circumstances of the times operated on
him as an imperative summons to withdraw himself, in the prime of life,
from scenes of gaiety and dissipation, to direct the exalted patriotism
and determined courage of the people of his native province . . .
Whatever may be the estimate made of his military talents by those
who are best able to appreciate them, his defence of Saragossa (despite
the ungenerous language of his enemies) made his *public* character the
admiration of the world . . . In his exertions as an officer he was most
active and indefatigable, and in his conversation there was a spright-
liness and vivacity that we rarely met with among Spaniards. But this
vivacity never betrayed him for a moment into a forgetfulness of the
duties of his station, or of the important trust confided to him . . . It
was a cheering and most interesting scene to ride with him through the
streets of Saragossa. The joy and exultation of the people, as he passed,
evidently sprang from the heart. The approbation indeed which they
lavished upon their General was reflected back again upon themselves,
for he had only the task of directing their exalted courage and patriotism. To have acquitted himself to their satisfaction was no mean reward,
and is a sufficient answer to the unworthy attempts to depreciate his
character that appear in the French *Bulletins* . . . I make no apology
for having dwelt thus long in attempting to give some outline of a
character so distinguished as that of General Palafox—a man whose
name will ever be dear to the country to whose service he gave up his
life. He may be held up as a pattern for imitation to any people who
may be at any time engaged in a struggle for their independence."

From Vaughan's remarks and other accounts of Palafox's hold over
his fellow citizens, it is clear that Saragossa's leader had what no other
Spanish general at the time possessed—a charismatic personality. At a
time when most Spanish generals and political leaders were either in-

competent or simply unfortunate, it was Spain's good fortune to have a man as attractive as Palafox to represent the defiant Spanish people in the eyes of their allies.

*   *   *

When the French and Spanish armies began to come to grips at the beginning of November, Saragossa's new defensive works were far from complete. In their mood of exultation during the first few weeks following the raising of the siege, the Saragossans were reluctant to face the possibility of another French attack. Palafox's engineers and officers found difficulty in recruiting personnel for the monotonous tasks of digging new earthworks, raising new walls and building new strong-points along the city's perimeter. At first, only men above the age of thirty-five were allowed to be employed for the work, and even then, their numbers were diminished in September and October by the need to gather in the various harvests. In addition, the labourers had to be paid and the treasury was low in funds. At the time of Vaughan's visit in late October, the prospect of an imminent resumption of hostilities had convinced many civilian volunteers to join in the work, but it was not until news of the defeat at Tudela that the population as a whole helped to complete the fortifications.

As the defeated troops of the various Aragonese, Valencian, Murcian, and Andalusian regiments streamed back into Saragossa, bringing alarming reports of a rapid French advance on the city, dismay and confusion spread rapidly. The battle had been mismanaged from the beginning and the fact that the Andalusian forces to the left of the line had taken practically no part in the fighting encouraged rumours that Palafox's men had been betrayed. Angry groups of soldiers and civilians gathered in the streets and squares to indulge in mutual recrimination. The Aragonese soldiers angrily accused their allies of jealousy and of having preferred their own provincial interests to the national cause. Passions were running high and the previously excellent morale of the city would undoubtedly have fallen very low if Palafox had not again shown his gifts for leadership and conciliation by convincing the entire population to make a last supreme effort to finish the fortifications before the French arrived.

Men, women and children worked day and night. Although much of the surrounding countryside had been laid waste during the first siege, a great number of trees and several small country houses still stood in the plain on both sides of the river. Large companies of workers hurriedly began to complete the task of cutting and razing them to the ground, using the timber for barricades and shelters in the city. Palafox issued stirring proclamations, urging the people to remain calm and confident and telling them, on November 24, that "new days of glory are being prepared". On November 27, he addressed a proclamation to his "army of reserve", forbidding all talk of defeat and threatening to punish all cases of cowardice with the greatest rigour. On the 29th, another decree ordered the entire population to take part in the city's defence; enlisted volunteers were recalled to their barracks; the mayors of the city's various wards were commanded to take charge of stocks of food and ammunition; dire penalties would be imposed on anyone causing alarm and despondency; for the next three days, women and men over sixty from outside Saragossa and children under fourteen were to be allowed to leave the city; civilians were to prepare matting, panniers and palisades for barricades and battery defences; and the women of Saragossa were ordered to sew shirts and sandbags and make wadding for the cannons. In addition to the evacuation of women and children, Palafox ordered Antonio Torres and Mariano Cerezo to take the remaining French detainees to the small castle town of Alcañiz, fifty miles distant. In order to forestall any angry objections from the people, Palafox told them that, although they knew well enough how to kill French soldiers on the battlefield, it was not in the Saragossans' nature to "tarnish their glory" by killing unarmed French civilians.

On the afternoon of November 30, the French again came in sight of the city. After the battle of Tudela, Marshal Lannes had left the army to return to France, as he was still suffering from the serious effects of a fall from his horse some time previously and as he believed that he had completed his mission. He handed back command of the victorious 3rd Corps of the Army of Spain to Moncey, who advanced as far as Alagon where he halted to wait for further supplies. Ney had been chasing Castaños's fugitive army in the mountains but, once he lost track of it, he marched into the Ebro valley and joined Moncey in his advance on Saragossa. As soon as the two marshals reached the city, Ney received a despatch from Napoleon ordering him to return to Castile in order to resume his search for Castaños, and to leave the conduct of the siege to Moncey. In the meantime, over 20,000 men of the 5th Corps under Marshal Mortier were to be sent to reinforce Moncey in his attack on Saragossa. With only 15,000 men left to him,

Moncey realised he was far too weak to begin a siege and prudently decided to fall back on Alagon, build up the supplies which were due to reach him from Pamplona, and to wait for Mortier's corps.

There was little fighting during the French army's short halt outside the city. A few cannon were fired from Monte Torrero, there were a number of insignificant skirmishes, and Lefebvre-Desnouettes lost four cavalrymen in an unsuccessful attempt to stop a large party of Spaniards from burning down a convent building on the heights west of the city. On December 2, the anniversary of Napoleon's coronation, instead of making their expected attack the French marched back to Alagon, to the great surprise of the inhabitants. Palafox realised that Saragossa had been granted a welcome reprieve and ordered the people to make even greater efforts to transform the city into one vast citadel.

The French did not return until December 20. During the three weeks' breathing space, the new defensive works were almost completed. A plan had originally been drawn up for an entirely new line of fortifications to be built along the line of the Huerva and the Imperial Canal, and then to the Ebro, but Palafox had neither the means nor the time for such a vast undertaking. Instead, he and his engineers decided to transform the line of the city's walls and turn the battle-scarred monasteries outside the walls into strong bastions. The Aljaferia castle was repaired, and a deep ditch was built around it, supplied with provisions and ammunition for 1,500 men, and connected to the walls of the city by a covered way and by a trench. The Sancho and Portillo gates were protected by ditches, earthworks and new battery emplacements. In front of the original, weak walls which ran all along Saragossa's western perimeter from the Portillo gate to the point where the Huerva river dipped away from the city, a completely new line of walls over a thousand yards long was built. It was a far more formidable rampart: not only were the outlying monastery buildings of the Barefoot Augustines and Trinitarians incorporated into the new wall as projecting bastions from which the defenders could pour their fire into the flanks of an attacking force, but a third semi-circular bastion with a battery was built half-way between the two monasteries. The wall itself was preceded by a steep ditch fifteen feet deep and twenty-one wide, and was built of beaten earth strengthened on the surface with a covering of broken stones and bricks. In addition to its parapets, it was provided with a terrace wide enough for guns to be handled along its top.

During the first siege, the main target for French attacks had been the gate and monastery of Santa Engracia. Although shelling and the explosion of the French mine had reduced at least half the building to ruins, the rubble was now used to build a new line of defence along the Huerva river; this was intended to protect the *paseo* which led to the gate, while the monastery itself was converted into a strongpoint to be defended by several hundred men and a number of cannon. Across the Huerva, in front of the gates and at the southern end of the bridge, a redoubt was built with a high parapet, a ditch, and a battery of eight cannon. This extremely important strongpoint was called the "Pilar redoubt" and an inscription was placed above its entrance, reading: "Redoubt of the Virgin of the Pillar, unconquerable because of such a sacred name. Saragossans: vanquish or die for the Virgin of the Pillar."

The monastery of San José was also repaired and transformed into a strong fortress to guard the second bridge across the Huerva. The vast building, much of which still stood despite damage from shelling and fire, was 120 yards long and eighty yards wide. It was surrounded by a steep ditch, new walls were built to a height of ten feet, embrasures were pierced in the walls and main edifice, and it was linked to the city by a palisaded, covered way. It was given twelve heavy cannon and a garrison of 3,000 men under the command of the heroic Colonel Mariano Renovales.

The remaining walls as far as the Ebro and the district known as the Tanneries (*Tenerías*) were strengthened and defended by several batteries, one by the Quemada gate being named after Palafox. The small Goiechoea oil press outside the walls was linked to the city, and other batteries were placed in the main oil press within the walls and in the Botanic Garden to cover the bridge of San José.

On the left bank of the Ebro, measures were taken to turn the whole Arrabal suburb into a miniature citadel. Heavy batteries were brought across the bridge; the two great convent buildings, the Jesus and San Lazaro, were provided with loopholes for gunners and protected by ditches and palisades; a line of earthworks and barricades was built around the suburb, and a garrison of 3,000 men was stationed within. On the river itself, a few large launches, mounted with light cannon, were manned by sailors from Cartagena.

The only remaining point of strategic importance outside the city was the hill of Monte Torrero which the French had captured so easily in June. Here, work had lagged behind although a large redoubt with guns was built on its summit. One of the nearby bridges over the canal was destroyed and another defended by a battery, and the whole position was defended by a garrison of 6,000 men commanded by General Saint-March with his division of Valencian troops.

As the month of December progressed, large numbers of Spanish regular troops continued to arrive in the city. Many Valencian and Murcian soldiers joined the garrison after the battle of Tudela, as well as the survivors from Palafox's Army of Aragon and Castaños's Andalusian army, and other bands of volunteers appeared almost daily from all parts of Spain. By the time the French were ready to return, Saragossa contained over 32,000 regular troops divided into four main divisions, one of which was commanded by Palafox's old friend and fellow officer Butron. The artillery corps had 1,500 men, there were 2,000 cavalry, and a corps of engineers with eighty sappers and a number of architects and workmen who had been employed by the Canal Company was formed under San Genis. In addition to the regulars, Saragossa would also be defended by many thousands of irregular volunteers, armed peasants and citizen recruits.

Military administration was under the control of a newly appointed intendant, who now had considerable sums of money at his disposal and an impressive supply of food and ammunition. Artillery was plentiful: in addition to the guns used in the first siege and other field pieces which had been brought into the city, the Saragossans had recovered all the French heavy siege guns from the canal and now had a total of over 160 guns of various calibres, including mortars and howitzers. On November 25, a large convoy of gunpowder and muskets reached Saragossa. General Doyle, who had visited the city with Vaughan, sent 8,000 British muskets, and more arrived soon afterwards. To avoid the risk of another explosion like the one which had devastated the seminary on June 27, various gunpowder magazines were established in the larger buildings and it was decided that powder would be manufactured on a daily basis according to need. Monks, priests and women were detailed to make cartridges and look after the sick and wounded. Large stocks of sandbags were piled up and the wicker baskets used for the grape harvest were collected for transformation into gabions for the batteries. As the city contained an enormous supply of wool (one of Saragossa's main industries) and linen, many huge woolsacks were made for protection against cannon balls.

The city also possessed plentiful timber, metal and, of course, an inexhaustible supply of stones and bricks which could be used as

missiles for the mortars, street fighting and repairing breaches. Food
was stockpiled and every inhabitant was advised to see that his cellar
contained as many non-perishable foodstuffs as possible. Even the
horses of the cavalry were well provided with forage.

The main shortage was accommodation for the huge number of
soldiers and civilian volunteers who effectively doubled the city's population. Although many of the troops were given permanent quarters in
various official and ecclesiastical buildings, some soldiers were eventually forced to sleep in the streets and under the portals and arches of the
market place when there was no longer room for them in private houses.
Not surprisingly, as winter began, infections began to spread, adding
to the overcrowding in those of the city's hospitals which had escaped
destruction.

By the third week in December, Palafox commanded an enormous
and well-armed garrison, backed by many thousands of enthusiastic
volunteers, and immeasurably greater stores of ammunition than anything he had had during the first siege. Because of this furious last-
minute effort, Saragossa had been given a completely new strong line
of fortifications, and the people had recovered from their fright over the
defeat at Tudela. Even so, morale in the city was not always quite so
high as it had been during the glorious days of June, July and August,
and the problems of maintaining discipline among such a large and
mixed garrison and population were considerable.

The successes they had won during the first siege and the feats of
such local heroes as Agustina, Santiago Sas, Jorge Ibort, and Mariano
Cerezo, had gone to the heads of many Saragossans. Their chauvinistic
pride in being Aragonese and the legendary obstinacy of their race, not
to mention the fanatical worship of the Pilar Virgin, made the Saragossans jealous of the many thousands of allied troops and peasant
auxiliaries who crowded into the city, for they were afraid that the
"foreign" troops would rob them of further opportunities to cover
themselves with glory. Furthermore, the fact that it was the Saragossans
who had done most of the work on the fortifications, while the Valencian, Murcian and Andalusian troops paraded before their officers or
rested in their barracks, caused considerable public resentment.

To flatter Aragonese pride, Palafox decreed that a special élite corps
of the most prominent noble citizens should be formed under the old
Moorish-Spanish name of *Almogavaros*. He also issued an order that a
priest and a monk should be on permanent duty in the gateways and

batteries to inspire the defenders and, as Ibieca explained, "because their influence was necessary to prevent disorders". Gallows were set up in public places to warn prospective evil-doers, traitors and rumour-mongers, and a special force of "public security" was formed, its members distinguishing themselves by wearing white sashes over one shoulder and across the body.

As tension grew while the city waited for the French to return and contradictory reports concerning their movements and intentions increased, there were outbreaks of spy-mania. Palafox found himself urged by some of his most fiery advisers and civilian leaders, including various prominent monks and priests like his old tutor, Father Basilio, to hunt for traitors. When it became known that the French at Alagon were daily receiving huge stores of siege implements, artillery and ammunition, public pressure increased on Palafox to order a sortie against Moncey's base. Since Saragossa contained some 45,000 armed men, it was pointed out that it was perfectly feasible and quite safe to detach several thousand to harass the French base and supply lines. On December 11, after a false alarm of a French approach, Palafox did indeed instruct two of his generals, Saint-March and O'Neill, to assemble their men, together with a waggon train of provisions, during the night and be ready to leave the city. The troops duly gathered in the Campo del Sepulcro and stood to arms the whole night but the order to march was never given. The exercise was repeated on the next two nights but still the men remained inactive.

According to Ibieca, "Palafox was fluctuating and inactive". The truth, in all probability, was that he could not bring himself to risk more troops—even a strong force of regulars—in another conflict with the French on open ground. Each time he had fought them outside the city, there had been a humiliating defeat followed by a general flight. 45,000 men had been assembled for the battle of Tudela and had been unable to withstand the French. Instead, it must have seemed preferable to Palafox to trust in the strong new defences and allow the French army to reduce itself to exhaustion by another fruitless siege. As the Aragonese winters are among the harshest in Spain and notorious for torrential downpours in the Ebro valley, Palafox must also have been relying on the climate for support and anticipating epidemics to ravage the French camp. But it was still hard to convince the fiery Aragonese of the inadvisability of hurling themselves upon a strongly entrenched French base.

A proclamation issued on December 13 confirmed that there was much talk of spies and traitors and also considerable unrest in the city, and that Palafox had decided against a sortie. It began, ominously, with the words "Saragossa, although you are the happier the more enemies you face, you must not give shelter in your bosom to all the hidden traitors who try to dishearten you". After assuring the population that the city's soldiers, fortifications, and cannon would repel the enemy with ignominy, he urged them not to be led astray and take useless risks: "Saragossans, your general speaks to you: vile intriguers are trying to mislead you and, without knowing it, you shelter in your homes the iniquitous agents of that same Emperor who robbed us of our beloved monarch. It is necessary that I watch over you. Yes, it is necessary that I preserve you from the perils into which they try to draw us. No son of this worthy city can harbour any evil thought, either against the king or the fatherland; but concealed in disguises and false cloaks of loyalty, and even wearing the same clothes as yourselves, the men who wish to disturb our peace and our unalterable harmony have escaped my vigilance and introduced themselves into the city, for they are those whom Napoleon calls his *means of victory*." The proclamation ended with a decree ordering "foreigners" to leave the city within twenty-four hours if they had no residence permits, and stating that any found still in hiding should be treated as suspects and "enemies of the public safety".

The result of such a proclamation was an even more intense spy-mania. But it also encouraged more civilians to help in the completion of fortifications, in the cutting down of trees, and the demolition of houses and walls in the surrounding countryside. Every day's respite was valuable for when the French army came into sight again on December 20, it brought one of the most formidable trains of artillery and siege equipment ever assembled for an attack on a fortified position since the beginning of the Napoleonic Wars.

*   *   *

By the time he was joined by Mortier and the 5th Corps on December 15, Moncey had received most of his guns, transport mules and ammunition. They should have been transported by canal from Tudela but, as the Spanish had destroyed or taken away all the boats and barges, the heavy cannon had to be brought by land all the way from Pamplona. Alagon was soon transformed into an important, well-organised base camp with hospitals and workshops. Under the direction of General Lacoste, 100,000 sandbags were manufactured, as well as the thousands of gabions and fascines so necessary for the protection of batteries and for assaults across the enemy's moats and ditches.

Mortier's arrival with two divisions, commanded respectively by Generals Suchet and Gazan, a cavalry brigade, seven companies of artillery, a company of sappers and another of engineers for building pontoon bridges over the Ebro, brought the total besieging force to nearly 50,000. Most of the soldiers in Mortier's corps were veterans from Germany who were fighting in Spain for the first time, while most of Moncey's had been in the original expeditionary forces sent before May 1808. Several of Moncey's regiments had already fought in the first siege, including the Polish soldiers of the 1st, 2nd, and 3rd regiments of the Vistula. After detaching several battalions to guard the depots and hospitals at Alagon, and others to protect communications with Tudela, the two marshals ordered their corps to march on Saragossa. They brought with them nearly 40,000 infantry, 3,500 cavalry, 48 heavy guns, eighty-four field guns, and 1,100 engineering officers, sappers and miners.

Moncey's Third Corps and Suchet's division from the Fifth Corps marched along the right bank of the Ebro, while Gazan's division took the left. Operations began as soon as the French reached their designated positions. Gazan was ordered to blockade the Arrabal suburb; Mortier and Suchet halted on the heights of San Lamberto facing the Portillo sector of Saragossa, while Moncey moved towards the Huerva and Monte Torrero. After a brief reconnaissance, the two marshals decided to launch simultaneous attacks the next day upon Monte Torrero and Arrabal. As they quickly began to place batteries to bombard Monte Torrero, Saragossa's drums and church bells sounded the alarm and the garrison stood to arms.

Although Monte Torrero was such an important point, dominating the city and offering excellent emplacements for siege batteries, its defence was no more successful than it had been on June 28. At eight o'clock in the morning, the French bombardment began and in a short time it had dismounted several of the Spanish guns in the redoubt and set fire to a store of gunpowder. Several infantry battalions supported by field guns then stormed the hill, the storehouses of the Canal Company and the bridgeheads at its base. Two of the French commanders, Habert and Grandjean, were veterans of the great assault on the city on August 4. By eleven o'clock, the Spaniards had abandoned the hill top after a short but sharp resistance by two regiments of Aragonese volunteers and despite Saint-March's desperate effort to keep his men at their posts. The attack was perfectly planned and executed, and one of the main reasons for the demoralisation of the several thousand defenders and for Saint-March's decision to pull back was a well-founded fear that the French would cut off their retreat and then surround them with their whole army before the city could come to their aid. Only the difficult nature of the terrain, which was partly flooded as a result of some of the canal dykes having been broken, prevented Suchet and his men from overwhelming the retreating Spaniards. Three hours after the attack had started, the French were in possession of the star-shaped redoubt on top of the hill as well as all the storehouses and bridgeheads on the canal. They captured several cannon and only lost some twenty killed and fifty wounded.

The attack against Arrabal should have taken place simultaneously. After capturing the hill, the French tried to distract the city's attention by despatching a column 800-strong towards the San José fortress, but Renovales and his men opened fire and sent them running back to safety. Meanwhile, Gazan held back his 8,000 men while he continued to reconnoitre the approaches to the suburb where several fields had been flooded by the rising waters of the Ebro. As he waited for the right moment to advance, a force of Spanish cavalry was drawn up in the Plaza del Seo and the Coso, ready to ride wherever the suburb might be threatened, and look-outs in the church towers followed the French movements.

Eventually, to the sound of church bells ringing a general alarm, the Spanish batteries opened fire, as the first of Gazan's columns moved forward at one o'clock in the afternoon. As they advanced, they extended their line towards the Gallego river on their left and attacked the isolated building known as the Archbishop's Tower, a few hundred yards from the suburb, killing and taking prisoner many of its defenders (these were Swiss mercenaries: there were several hundred Swiss soldiers under the Spanish flag in Saragossa when the siege began). Seeing the capture of the house, a Spanish force near the Gallego on the road to Barcelona withdrew to the suburb, pursued by the French. Although the Spanish batteries fired grapeshot at the attackers at close range, the French ranks charged with great determination but were cut down in swathes within a few feet of the sandbagged batteries. While

French corpses piled up, almost under the muzzles of the Spanish cannon, new columns came running through the trees and garden enclosures which had been left standing outside the suburb, only to be mowed down in their turn or bayoneted on the edges of the Spanish parapets.

Realising that it was suicidal to continue such an attack over open ground, almost entirely without cover, against such strongly defended batteries and entrenchments, the French columns swung away to the left and seized a house close to the large, well-garrisoned Jesus monastery a short distance from the suburb. The defenders of the Jesus were now in danger of being cut off by the French from all communication with the main line of defences. The capture of the house had a demoralising effect on some of the Spaniards who began to panic, convinced that the enemy were about to seize the whole left bank of the Ebro as far as the stone bridge. A detachment of cavalry communicated their panic to the infantry, who surged back towards the bridge, and began to stampede through a confused mass of soldiers and civilians.

The defenders' sudden failure of nerve in the Arrabal was a highly dangerous moment for the city but Palafox was quick to react. He had been watching the progress of the fight from one of the towers of the Archbishop's palace. As soon as he saw the defenders running through the streets of the suburb to the river, and fresh French columns moving up for a new attack, he dashed out of the palace into the Plaza del Seo, mounted a horse, gathered together several hundred infantry and cavalry, unsheathed his sabre and forced his way through the fugitives across the bridge and into the front line. A soldier who refused to obey his officer's order to stand fast against the retreating cavalry was at once arrested and later shot. Palafox urged his men forward, his officers shamed the defenders into returning to the fight, and a sortie was ordered to recapture the house seized by the French. The Spanish cavalry charged, the infantry marched forward with drums beating, the batteries fired new volleys into the French lines, and the day was saved. Although he could have launched his reserve troops in an attack on the vital Jesus monastery, Gazan ordered a general withdrawal at four o'clock in the afternoon as the winter night began to fall. He had lost 700 dead and wounded in the fruitless charge against the Spanish guns and fortifications and was reluctant to risk the remainder of his troops, and his only reserve force, in another all-out attack when it was obvious that the defenders had been reinforced and had regained their determination to fight to the death.

The news that the attack on the Arrabal had been beaten off was joyfully received by the anxious Saragossans; many of them had gathered in the Plaza del Seo while thousands of women had run to the Pilar basilica to pray for the city's salvation (by official order, only women were allowed in the church while the fighting was in progress). The far more serious matter of the loss of Monte Torrero was conveniently forgotten as the crowds packed the sacred chapel and mutually congratulated one another on yet another victory over "the victors of Marengo, Austerlitz and Iena". Only one thing marred the crowd's satisfaction: the knowledge that the Spanish cavalry had failed to pursue the French as they withdrew.

The following day was dark, cloudy and stormy. French corpses, many naked after being stripped by scavenging peasants and civilians, still littered the fields and meadows around the Arrabal; but on the right bank the people could see the French regiments strung out in a long thick line between the slopes of Casa Blanca and Monte Torrero. In the morning, while bands of civilians seized their last opportunities to cut down the trees which still remained near the city, Palafox made a tour of inspection of the gateways and batteries along the walls. At eleven o'clock, a French envoy under a flag of truce, accompanied by two trumpeters, was blindfolded and brought to Palafox in the Pilar redoubt; he carried a letter from Moncey who had set up his headquarters on Monte Torrero. In his message, Moncey very courteously told Palafox that the city was invested on all sides, that Madrid had capitulated and that Saragossa would be wise to do the same, in order to "stop the shedding of blood, preserve the beautiful city of Saragossa—so interesting on account of its population, wealth and commerce—from the misfortunes of a siege and the terrible events which might ensue from it, since this would undoubtedly assure you of the love and blessings of the people who are under your government".

Palafox, who had just completed another manifesto to the citizens and garrison congratulating them on the previous day's feats, indignantly rejected the summons to negotiate a capitulation, crying out: "Capitulate? I do not know how to capitulate! I do not know how to surrender! After I am dead, we will speak of it!" The men around him shouted "Vanquish or die!" and "Long live Fernando VII!", with the envoy still present, then Palafox withdrew to his quarters to write an equally courteous reply to Moncey. He declared that Moncey would "cover himself with glory if, while observing the noble laws of war, he were to manage to defeat me", referred to the French losses, suggested that the French should capitulate instead, and told Moncey that the "wisdom which is so much a part of his character and which has earned him the sobriquet of the Good, will not let him behold such disasters with indifference". As for Madrid, Palafox concluded, what was Madrid? It was "only a city like any other and that is no reason for Saragossa to surrender".

After receiving Palafox's defiant reply, Moncey at once instructed General Lacoste to plan the siege of the city; the rest of the month was devoted to digging a system of approach trenches. After careful reconnoitring of Saragossa's defences, Lacoste proposed that three different lines of trenches should be dug. One would be for an attack on the San José fortress which, being detached, was reputed to be the weakest point in the Spanish defence system. If the French could capture San José, it would be a relatively simple matter for them to outflank the Goiechoea oil press outside the walls and the Quemada gate. They could then advance past the fortress to the banks of the Ebro and so combine an attack on the eastern sector of the city with another on the suburb. The second line of approach trenches was to be dug against the Pilar redoubt, which, if it were taken, would give the French access to the Engracia gate and allow them to support the attack on their right. The third line of trenches would be for a feint attack on the castle to distract the attention of the defenders. On December 23, the first approach trenches, designed to lead to the projected parallels, were begun under the protection of a battery of howitzers on Monte Torrero. At the same time, on the left bank of the Ebro, Gazan was ordered to complete the blockade of the Arrabal and entrench himself across all three roads leading out of the suburb; and a pontoon bridge was built across the Ebro to the west of the city.

While the French started to dig, the Spanish look-outs kept a close watch on their work and also on Monte Torrero where further batteries were being placed. A few small sorties were made, mainly with the object of cutting down more trees, and a mortar battery in the Botanical Gardens began to bombard the French positions on Monte Torrero. The Spanish bombs caused considerable losses and, according to the historian Belmas, "in two days we lost nearly as many men on the Monte Torrero as the attack on this position had cost us". One shell, landed on the summit, killing a colonel and seven officers, forced Moncey to take cover in a nearby church and then move his headquarters back to the safety of a Charterhouse of the Conception, three miles south of the city. But, despite the Spanish mortars, the French worked hard to make the canal once more navigable by building new sluice-gates to replace those destroyed by the Saragossans, and also brought up barges which could sail on to Alagon to collect some of the supplies which continued to arrive. Other boats at Tudela had been laden with materials for the siege batteries but these and the heavy guns had still to be brought by road while the canal remained out of service.

Since there were so many regular troops in the city, Palafox could easily at this stage have spared several thousand for a resolute counter-attack on the enemy lines, while the French methodically continued their preparations for an assault. Instead, he contented himself with a few small sorties while the mass of the huge garrison remained passive and awaited events. Such inactivity has been severely criticised by French, Spanish and British historians. Unlike those of most other cities which have endured sieges, Saragossa's defenders were roughly equal in numbers to the besiegers. Once again, Palafox showed himself to be a poor strategist. A new *Junta* of commanders was formed and General O'Neill, Saint-March and the Baron de Versage, who had joined the garrison with his men, discussed whether a large force of infantry and cavalry should not be employed outside the city to harass the French lines and their communications with Alagon and Tudela. But their proposals came to nothing. As the Spanish military historian Arteche drily remarked in his account of the siege, for some of Palafox's officers "it appeared preferable to face death rather than responsibility". While the garrison decided to stay put and prepare for battle only behind the city walls, Francisco Palafox managed to leave the city by boat to seek further reinforcements.

The last ten days of December were bitterly cold. Many soldiers on both sides fell ill and their hardships increased from day to day. The Valencian and Murcian troops in particular suffered from cold and the lack of fresh meat and vegetables. According to the municipal tribunal's secretary, Casamayor, who kept a diary during both sieges, by December 29 more than 6,000 men lay sick in the hospital, not including the wounded who were taken to the San Ildefonso monastery.

Even the Polish soldiers complained of the cold, saying that it was worse than anything they had known in their native country. Colonel

Brandt, an officer in the regiment of the Vistula, described the harsh conditions endured by the besiegers. Except for the little town of Tudela, forty-five miles away, "the whole country was absolutely devastated. The inhabitants had taken to flight; the weather was frightful; icy hurricane blasts alternated with torrential downpours without any respite. We were lying on the bare earth since straw was a luxury unknown in this country. The soldiers cut down olive trees, tore out the doors and windows from deserted houses to feed the bivouac fires". When General Lejeune, then still a colonel, arrived before Saragossa late in December, he found that the soldiers were "making incredible efforts" to build themselves shelters with the reeds and canes which grew in abundance on the shores of the Ebro and were used by the Aragonese for their garden enclosures.

Food was a constant problem. The bread ration was often replaced by a handful of rice or beans. Mutton was occasionally brought into the camp; according to Brandt, however, only "one sheep was allocated to thirty men but the inner parts of the animal were always lacking and this meat would arrive in an unappetising state of mouldiness". At first, there was plenty of wine for the men but this too soon vanished. Apart from wine, the most lamented shortage was that of salt. Lejeune wrote that he had even seen soldiers using the saltpetre from their cartridges to make their soup edible, and a young lieutenant, Daudevard de Férussac, who also kept an account of the siege, was sent with a detachment to search for some old salt mines which had been discovered in Roman times. After a hazardous exploration in the nearby mountains, known to be swarming with savage guerrillas, Férussac discovered a two-thousand-year-old disused salt mine in a grotto. He was welcomed as a hero when he and his men returned, bringing a large supply of salt crystals.

Dysentery, fever and typhus soon spread through the ranks and the sick were taken to the overcrowded base hospital at Alagon. One of the patients was Colonel Brandt and he left a horrifying description of conditions there:

"The military hospital was more like an assassins' cave than a place where one had any hope of being cured. This hospital was installed in a filthy monastery whose monks had taken refuge in Saragossa where they were probably helping to cause the wounds from which we came to die in their building. Typhus reigned supreme since the whole country had been infected by the miasma of the corpses which had remained unburied for so long since the battle of Tudela . . . from my bed, I would follow the details of the burial of the many sick who succumbed. They would be thrown through the windows in a state of complete nudity and they fell, one upon the other, with a dull, muffled sound as though they were sacks of corn. They would then be loaded on to carts to be carried to huge ditches which were being dug incessantly some hundred paces away. The Spaniards who had been requisitioned for this task acquitted themselves of it with diabolical joy. With their fingers, they would show me the already very numerous heaps of earth where graves had been completed and covered over, making signs to me that there would be no lack of further work . . . the dull echo of corpses falling from the windows of the funereal hospital haunted my dreams for a long time . . ."

*   *   *

By the end of the month, the French engineers had begun the three first lines of trenches and Palafox decided to make a sortie on December 31. The Spaniards with their large garrison had a good opportunity to overwhelm the French but, to the latter's amazement, no more than 1,500 infantry and 300 horsemen were used for the attack. On the Spanish left, Renovales led a mere 300 men; another 300 men attacked the French parallel to their right; 300 made an attempt to distract the French by the bank of the Ebro and near San José; fifty men rushed forward in the centre, and the remaining attackers emerged from the city near the castle.

Although the Spaniards on the left advanced as far as the parallel, which then consisted merely of an uncovered trench and a parapet of earth, they were halted by strong French columns moving up for a counter-attack. The centre sortie, from the Pilar redoubt, did not even reach the trenches. The fiercest fighting was on the right, where Butron led his men with great dash towards the heights of Bernardona. His force had to withdraw when the French threatened to outflank it and cut off its retreat but, as a small consolation, the Spanish cavalry killed and wounded thirty men in a French advance post before they rode back into the city.

The only effect of the sortie was to raise the city's morale. It was a symbolic gesture more than anything else, but Palafox treated it as though it were a great victory in an even more high-flown manifesto than usual: "When the enemy fell in their masses upon you, you obeyed my orders and even surpassed yourselves. You hurled yourselves upon them and, seconded by your valiant cavalry, you cut to pieces these famous Northern warriors who awaited you, firm of foot. Their fire did not frighten you and even less their bayonets. Your swords gave them the reply and our invincible city has the pleasure of seeing itself surrounded by the countless corpses of the bandits who besiege it. The bugle rang out and at once the edge of your swords sent their proud heads rolling to the ground, vanquished by your valour and your patriotism, etc., etc., etc." As a reward for the day's feats, Palafox told his men that they could wear a red cockade on their chests.

On December 29, Junot, recently created Duc d'Abrantès, had arrived in the French camp and taken over direction of the 3rd Corps from Moncey who was recalled to Madrid. While the Spanish celebrated the sortie of December 31, Junot drew up for Napoleon a pessimistic report on the siege's progress. He had found the French army and, particularly, the 3rd Corps in a sorry condition and made no bones about it: "Its situation is deplorable; it has not even 12,000 infantrymen left . . . This corps is composed of young men all extremely exhausted by the last campaign. They are unclad, without greatcoats and without shoes. Thus, they enter in their hundreds into the hospital which, by its total destitution, the absence of personnel, bad administration and the penury of aid, becomes a tomb for all who find themselves in it."

Junot had an even greater complaint. He was of the opinion that at least 30,000 fit men were needed to blockade and attack the city successfully but no sooner had he arrived than he found his army weakened by nearly 10,000! Mortier had received a message from Madrid ordering him to leave Saragossa with one of his two divisions and to proceed to Calatayud in order to maintain direct communications with the capital. He marched at once with Suchet's division, leaving Junot with barely enough men to maintain the blockade on both sides of the Ebro.

At the risk of using insubordinate language to Napoleon, Junot bluntly emphasised the difficulties of his position and the importance of having the men and the material he asked for: "We need 30,000 men to take Saragossa and numerous artillery to smash this immense assembly of stones and bricks, and to crush a population greatly swelled by all the families of the surrounding region. We must kill many soldiers for there are many of them . . . Saragossa is more important to Spain than Cadiz and, no doubt, Madrid. If Saragossa surrenders, it will tranquillise the whole of Aragon, Catalonia and the two Castiles. As long as she exists, these provinces will not be subdued. We must strike hard and promptly but we need great means for this . . . Saragossa is vital to Your Majesty's interests."

Despite Junot's many difficulties, including the fact that the administration of his own 3rd Corps was "totally null", and his remaining forces had to be stretched out in a dangerously thin line to surround the city, the digging of approach trenches made good progress under Lacoste's excellent direction. The Spaniards maintained a steady fire from the walls and made a sortie on January 2 but, although they reached the second line of parallel trenches near San José, they were soon driven back. Thick fog masked the French sappers and front lines from the Spaniards for long periods on several successive days, but it is certain that if Palafox had launched a really large-scale attack he could have struck a disastrous blow at the French army, now diminished by 9,000 men.

January 2 was the anniversary of the Pilar Virgin's arrival in Saragossa and was celebrated accordingly. Otherwise there was little cause for joy in the city. Palafox made a brief speech to the Tribunal of the *Real Audiencia* but, according to Casamayor, only five members could attend as the others were all ill. Many Valencian and Murcian troops were dying from disease, whole families lay sick and in most households there was no longer any fresh food to be had.

Minor sorties continued to be launched, and there was fighting in thick mist on the left bank. In a report to Palafox, Renovales mentioned another heroine: a young girl called Manuela Sancho, who used to bring gunpowder charges, shot and stones for cannon and mortars at a particular battery, had apparently remained quite unmoved at the sight of the gunners falling dead around her, and had then fired several guns herself before picking up a musket and joining the sharpshooters in the front line of defence.

A war of propaganda now began. After the French had managed to get some papers into the city announcing that Madrid was under occupation and the French court installed there, Palafox addressed a proclamation to the inhabitants of Madrid: "My luck holds good always, amid the roar of cannon and the enemy's bayonets. These dogs scarcely give me time to wipe my sword clean for it is always stained with blood, but this city will be their tomb; these invincible walls will be the reef on which they shall be wrecked and where they will find proof of our love for our Ferdinand. Yes, valiant inhabitants of Madrid! Yes, heroes! Yes, my brothers! Here we shall not surrender. We cannot die, we cannot succumb under the weight of misery and the number of our enemies: we shall live for posterity and when heaven grants my desires by removing such an infamous enemy from our sight, I myself shall fly to your aid . . ."

On January 6, the rumour ran through Saragossa that an army of relief was on its way. Fireworks were set off, several battalions stood to arms near Santa Engracia and a proclamation was printed in six languages—Spanish, French, Italian, Latin, German and Polish—for the benefit of the besiegers, and thrown into the French forward posts; it urged the men of the various nationalities who formed the regiments to "abandon a war which shames you". According to Lejeune, the recipients of these tracts merely laughed at them. On the same day, the French sentinels were further entertained by the sight of a tall, elderly priest in white robes who emerged from the city, holding a crucifix, and made his way calmly to within fifty paces. Before they could recover from their astonishment, he had held up his crucifix and begun to harangue them, urging them to abandon their attack on a city which was under the divine protection of the most Holy Lady of the Pillar and to exchange the side of error and the path to hell for the road to virtue and paradise. Most of the soldiers were unable to understand his sonorous flow of Spanish, and after the sentries had shouted at him to go away, a few shots in the air finally convinced the priest of the failure of his mission and sent him back to the city as fast as his dignity would allow.

While the Spaniards confined their hostilities to sniping during the day —except at meal times—the French siege works steadily progressed. By January 6, a second parallel trench only eighty yards from San José was completed, and the besieged could not prevent the French from digging closer towards the Pilar redoubt. In the centre, the French established a small stronghold after they observed Spanish sappers emerging from the city and hurriedly digging their own line of trenches on the left bank of the Huerva in order to enfilade the French zig-zag trenches on the right bank. General Dedon, commanding the army's corps of artillery, received thirty siege guns with munitions and, by January 7, several batteries were ready built. By the 9th, a battery in the first parallel facing San José included four twenty-four-pounders, and a further four cannon of similar calibre were trained on the Pilar redoubt.

Heavy firing was kept up by both sides and the French losses in the trenches averaged thirty men a day.

By January 9, in fact, the French had eight batteries ready to open fire against the Pilar redoubt and San José. The work was accomplished by the highly skilled engineers and troops with picks and shovels despite a constant bombardment from the Spanish guns in the Goiechoea oil press, the Palafox battery by the Quemada gate, and the guns in the Botanic Garden and Santa Engracia. Palafox had decided to save his regular troops, who were fast being reduced in numbers by disease, and instead used peasants to harass the French lines with their musketry fire. As many of them were poachers and hunters they were excellent marksmen, and any French soldier in the trenches who forgot or disobeyed his officer's order always to keep his head lowered was likely to receive a fatal shot.

Within Saragossa, the situation was rapidly worsening. The dense concentration of troops and the swelling of the population by the inflow from the countryside began to prove fatal to the city's health. Infection spread so rapidly that many new hospitals had to be established. There were still plentiful supplies of grain and oil, but even dried and salt food had become scarce, and all the stocks of beans, chickpeas, rice and salt cod found in the shops were now stored in the Lonja building for the exclusive use of the regular troops. The cold weather and the unhygienic conditions continued to kill off the Valencian and Murcian troops in large numbers. In the figures quoted by the Spanish historian Arteche, only 20,000 men were under arms on January 1, out of total force of 32,000 regulars. Of the remaining 12,000, some 10,000 were sick or wounded and about 1,000 had already died in action. A week later, epidemics were wreaking such havoc that Casamayor saw men dropping dead in the streets, and the position in the hospitals had grown desperate. Nevertheless, public order was maintained, the tribunals still functioned, the Pilar chapel was constantly crowded with worshippers, and Palafox continued to give his full attention to every detail of the defence from his headquarters in the Archbishop's Palace.

It was clear that a French attack was imminent as troops could be seen massing on both sides of the Ebro. The weather had become milder and humid, causing the epidemics to spread even more rapidly, and continuing mists had made it difficult for the defenders to aim accurately at the French trenches where the sappers were completing the earthworks and gun emplacements. At six-thirty on the morning of January

10, eight siege batteries and the mortars on Monte Torrero began to thunder against Saragossa. The bombardment was maintained without interruption. While mortar bombs rained down inside the city, adding to the destruction caused during the first siege, the huge twenty-four-pounders sent their heavy shot crashing into the walls and parapets of San José and the Pilar redoubt. Four batteries shelled the east and west sides and the south-east corner of the monastery building and its outer walls, and four others concentrated from a greater distance upon the Pilar redoubt. The Spanish batteries replied and managed to put two of the twenty-four-pounders out of action but, as the bombardment continued throughout the morning, the French rate of fire began to outstrip that of the Spanish.

The defenders of San José showed heroic tenacity as they stood firm behind the weak walls of their building. Although the outer walls were soon reduced to rubble, the gunners continued to man their pieces even though a hail of falling brick and stonework was killing and wounding them a dozen at a shot. As the French bombardment increased in intensity, Renovales's men were forced to cover their heads with sacks of wool to protect them against falling débris which threatened to bury them and their cannon. But the infantry in the building, and in an advanced trench thirty yards in front of the monastery, steadfastly maintained their musket fire on the French trenches and batteries.

At half-past one in the afternoon, the French set up another battery which battered the west wall of San José until four o'clock, when large parts of the building were in ruins. Still the resistance continued. The guns which remained serviceable were by now almost without protection and their crews exposed to the full fury of the French bombardment and musketry fire, but they continued to keep the French troops pinned down in their trenches. At nightfall, it was plain that the French would have to postpone their attack until the next day. The survivors of the garrison were relieved by troops from the city, and Renovales gave orders for the breaches in the walls to be filled up and for the batteries to be remounted.

The bombardment of the Pilar redoubt had less effect as the French batteries were at a greater distance from this strongpoint. The Spaniards were at first convinced that the French would make an immediate attack on San José and a sortie was ordered against the right of the French line, so as to take the trenches from the rear. The counter-attack was supported on the Ebro by a launch with a crew of twenty men and three cannon which sailed towards the right bank and a small country villa occupied by the French and which the Spaniards had neglected to demolish. The gun boat did open fire on the house but was forced to put about when several of the crew were shot by the French outposts.

At seven o'clock, the French batteries ceased their fire against San José, and Renovales used the lull to repair the fortifications and parapets as much as possible and to clear the mountain of rubble which would have helped the French to clamber up to the breach in the outer walls. Then, at half-past eleven, a French patrol climbed out of the trenches and made its way through the darkness towards the ruined monastery, thinking that it had been evacuated during the evening. They had advanced to within twenty paces of the walls when two musket volleys from the defenders made them hastily retreat. Firing promptly broke out again on both sides and lasted until two o'clock in the morning. In another sortie, 200 men ran out of the monastery and dashed over the mere thirty yards of ground which separated the outer walls from the first French breaching battery; but a deadly discharge of grapeshot from two four-pounders, which the French had brought up to protect the battery's flanks, forced them to abandon the attempt to spike the heavy guns.

French mortar bombs continued to fall in the city throughout the night. There was a new exodus of civilians from the houses nearest the walls; the nuns of the Santa Monica convent abandoned their home and fled through the streets towards the Pilar which was already packed to capacity with terrified inhabitants; and the *ayuntamiento* ordered precautions to be taken against fires and did its utmost to reassure the people who remembered the horrors and miseries of the first siege's bombardments only too vividly.

In the morning of January 11, the French guns resumed their task of destroying what was left of San José. Renovales had withdrawn several guns during the night after realising the impossibility of repairing the battery emplacements, and the position was now defended by musketry, one howitzer, and two four-pounders. All the work of repair was soon shattered. The sandbags piled up in the breaches were ripped to pieces by bomb fragments and grenades, a section of the upper floors collapsed and, at two o'clock in the afternoon, the four batteries which had been bombarding the Pilar redoubt began to train their guns on the building. In such an inferno, it was amazing that resistance should have

continued at all, but it did so as the Spanish burrowed into the piles of
rubble and kept firing their muskets until they were literally buried alive
when not blown to pieces.

At four o'clock, the French launched their attack. Seeing that his
position was hopeless, Renovales ordered most of the garrison to withdraw, leaving only a few men to cover the retreat. The French infantry,
supported by two field guns, now charged forward. Two of the three
French assault companies, using scaling ladders, clambered down into
the steep-sided ditch around the building while the third made its way
to the back of the building where the captain in command found a small
bridge which the Spaniards had neglected to remove or destroy. As the
column dashed over the ditch into a small courtyard leading to the
church, which had escaped complete destruction, a fierce volley from
the defenders forced the French to fling themselves flat on the ground
after they had tried in vain to batter down the door with their axes.
Meanwhile, the men in the ditch began to pour through the breaches
into the building where fierce hand-to-hand fighting ensued, with the
Spaniards firing through cracks in the ruined walls and from casement
windows even though the walls and floors were giving way around
them and under their very feet.

Thirty Spaniards were killed and the remainder either fled across the
open ground to the city's walls or were taken prisoner. The scene inside
the shattered building was horrifying: as the French took possession
they had to pick their way through blood-stained beams and sandbags
hideously littered with arms, legs, heads and limbless trunks. Some of
the defenders had been buried alive or knocked unconscious by falling
débris and their bodies had then been torn to fragments as the French
guns continued to pound the heaps of rubble. In his memoirs, Lejeune
expressed the general feeling among the French when they surveyed
their conquest after the last Spaniard had been killed or captured: "So
stubborn were the attack and defence of this convent that from that
moment onwards we had a foreboding of the amount of work and perseverance that would be needed if we were to complete the conquest
of Saragossa."

The loss of San José was not the only serious blow to be suffered by
the city: the engineering officer San Genis, who had done so much to
give Saragossa new fortifications after the first siege, and who was
highly popular among the whole garrison, was shot dead in the Palafox
battery while he watched the French sappers digging a communication

trench between their second and third parallel. During the bombardment of San José and the city, the Saragossans were convinced that the French were about to launch a full-scale assault. To the crash of bombs and the whistling of cannon balls was added the sound of drums beating the alarm in the streets and the bell of the Torre Nueva tolling mournfully. A small pile of grenades and other ammunition blew up in the little square in front of the church of San Juan de los Panetes, which was used as a powder store, there were more rumours of treason, and the city's prison governor had six gallows with dangling nooses set up in the market square.

Palafox continued to do his best to keep morale high while his colleague Versage looked after the internal administration of the city, organising its police force and the establishment of new hospitals in private houses. In the belief that the French would soon attempt to break into the city, Palafox ordered the mayors of the various districts to gather squads of workers to dig ditches and set up barricades in the streets. Work was to continue night and day; each squad was to be relieved every four hours and shirkers could expect the harshest punishment. On January 14, Palafox issued a proclamation in which he reproached the civilians for still not showing enough enthusiasm for manual labour even at this late stage: "One thing only is lacking to make your heroism complete and that is to excercise it with method. You take pleasure in risking your lives in combat but refuse to devote yourselves to the work of fortifications, thinking no doubt that honour consists only in the handling of weapons. Saragossans, I must warn you that this is a very fatal error . . ." Palafox promised that he would reward those who took part in such work or looked after the wounded and sick just as much as those fighting in the front line. If only, he continued, the city had had more workers! The fort of San José might not have fallen and mines could have been laid to blow up the enemy as they advanced towards it. Not even all the olive trees near the city had been destroyed: "The olive groves to the front and left of the fort— what damage they did by not being cut!"

The bombardment continued day and night. There were no more prayers or masses in the churches except in the Pilar basilica which was crowded to the point of suffocation. The *Real Audiencia* and the *ayuntamiento* met no longer. On January 13, the bombardment was so heavy, that a large stock of gunpowder had to be removed at great risk from the monastery of San Agustín to the Seo cathedral. The French gunners altered their aim and shells now fell in the centre of the city, in the cathedral district and around the market place. The Saragossans huddled in insanitary basements and wine cellars where the foetid air, humidity and overcrowding did much to increase the spread of epidemics. Typhus began to break out and the number of soldiers seen dead in the streets increased daily.

The next French target was the four-sided Pilar redoubt with its ten-foot-deep ditch and battery, and 400-strong garrison. The batteries on the right engaged in a duel with the Spanish guns, which brought the hitherto intact cupola of the San José church crashing down on the heads of the French garrison trying to silence the guns of the Palafox battery which had been slowing down work on the third parallel along the Huerva embankment to the right of the monastery. A new battery of two twenty-four-pounders and two sixteen-pounders was set up to blow breaches in the walls, and other batteries joined in the bombardment of the Pilar redoubt.

The situation in the redoubt became desperate. Most of the gun carriages were knocked into splinters, the parapet was flattened and the ditch became filled with rubble. While the defenders replied mainly with musket fire, the women in the city frantically sewed new sandbags for the redoubt—even using Palafox's palace as a factory. In a single day, the defenders at the redoubt lost thirty dead and eighty wounded. A panic started but, as the defenders began to abandon their position, they were driven back by an officer sabre in hand. They lined the parapet once more but a French grenade landed among them killing eleven soldiers of an Aragonese battalion. A few French skirmishers moved forward and were repelled. The defenders made an ineffective sortie. The ground became heaped with corpses.

By eight o'clock in the evening of January 15, the last remaining portion of the redoubt's walls had been razed to the ground and the parapets had virtually disappeared. The defenders were now reduced to fifty men and, by the light of the gun flashes, the commander of the redoubt could see a detachment of French and Polish soldiers running towards him with scaling ladders and planks. A mine laid in front of the redoubt exploded without any effect; the attackers easily crossed the rubble-filled ditch, climbed over the flattened parapet, and drove out the Spanish at the points of their bayonets. The French, with losses of only one man killed and two wounded, were masters of the whole right bank of the Huerva. They could now continue the plan of attack which

Napoleon himself had devised and which, at this stage, involved a concentration of men and guns against the Santa Engracia sector and the
walls near the Quemada gate. More guns were brought up and began
to pound the Palafox battery, dismounting most of its cannon and
making large breaches which Spanish civilians hurriedly did their best
to fill with baskets, sandbags and bricks.

During the late afternoon of January 16, after another day of terrible
shelling, extraordinary rumours which had been current for some days
previously seemed now to be confirmed. Palafox had received a
smuggled message from his brother Lazan, writing from Catalonia and
promising to bring aid from Gerona and to attack the besiegers from the
rear, as well as several other reports all painting a rosy picture of the
general situation in Spain. A special issue of the city's gazette immediately published the good news and excited crowds braved the
bombardment by flocking to the royal printing house, near the Angel
bridge. According to the gazette, the French had been utterly routed in
Catalonia, General Reding was on his way with an army of 60,000 men,
Lazan had routed the French and invaded France, Generals Blake and
La Romana had beaten Napoleon, who himself was in danger of capture, and had killed 20,000 of his men, including Ney and Berthier, and
a huge sum of money for the Spanish army had arrived in Madrid!

As copies were passed from hand to hand, rejoicing broke out in the
city. To the astonishment of the French, all the church bells began to
ring joyful carillons, the batteries along the walls fired three successive
salvoes in unison, regimental bands played in full view of the French,
the defenders and crowds of civilians paraded the streets, fired their
muskets and blunderbusses in the air, cheered or shouted sarcasms at
the French from the walls, the streets were illuminated and lanterns
placed on the Torre Nueva. The French bombardment slackened for
a while and then resumed in all its fury at ten o'clock when the last
revellers had resumed their posts or taken shelter again. While Lejeune
and other French officers anxiously discussed the reason for this unexpected merry-making, "the silence and obscurity of the night were
once again interrupted only by the sound and flash of cannon". The
following day, according to Casamayor, saw the worst-ever bombardment. Since it had started on January 10, more than 6,000 bomb and
grenade explosions were counted in the city. The French compared the
trajectories of the bombs and shells with fireworks, and Daudevard de
Férussac, who was on the left bank of the Ebro, described how he and

his comrades would see as many as a dozen flaming projectiles from the French mortar batteries soaring through the air at the same time.

In spite of their successes, the sufferings of the French and Polish soldiers had increased and they now began to find themselves almost as short of fresh food as the Saragossans. Junot, known as a firebrand and said—with some reason—to be "a bit cracked" by his soldiers, grew increasingly impatient and spoke of making an immediate and final assault on the city. On January 16, while Saragossa celebrated the false reports of Spanish victories, he received news that Lannes had fully recovered from his injuries and would be returning to direct the siege. This threw him into an almost pathological state of fury and resentment which, according to Lejeune, represented the beginning of a mental illness that no one yet suspected but which was to become very obvious in his later career. Forgetting that he had told Napoleon that at least 30,000 men were needed for the siege, he announced a full-scale attack on the city for the next day. Thoroughly alarmed, his officers had great difficulty in dissuading him as he was determined to reap the glory of capturing Saragossa before Lannes's arrival.

A furious argument took place in Junot's headquarters. Lacoste remonstrated vigorously, urging Junot not to abandon the plan laid down by Napoleon and pointing out that the city probably contained a 100,000 souls of whom half would be armed (the French did not know the extent of the ravages caused by illness), whereas the French only had 20,000 men fit for action, since, leaving aside those who had left the siege for field operations, no less than 13,000 were lying sick in the hospitals. Junot flew into an even greater fury as Lacoste and the other commanders refused to withdraw their objections and insulted them by shouting: "You are my enemies and you betray the Duc d'Abrantès by reserving the honour of this conquest for *that marshal* [Lannes]." Finally, after a further argument, during the course of which Lacoste threatened to report him to the Emperor, Junot agreed to postpone the attack. But it was an ugly incident and did little to raise the spirits of the officers. To add to the general depression, foraging detachments kept returning exhausted and empty-handed, often having been attacked by peasants and guerrilla bands, and the bread ration was reduced by half.

The furious bombardment, however, continued, while the expected Spanish army of relief failed to appear. On the morning of January 17, a new French battery placed behind the ruins of San José opened fire on the Palafox battery which had been built on two levels beside the city's main oil press near the Quemada gate. Several Spanish guns were blasted off their carriages and had to be withdrawn until the damage was repaired by bands of civilians working throughout the night with only one four-pounder to protect them in case of a French attack. But a small boat did manage to escape, sailing down the Ebro under fire from French patrols on both banks—the French were still unable to seal the city off completely from contact with the outside world—and news still reached Palafox from time to time: in his memoirs Lejeune mentioned how a smuggler from a nearby village used his dog to carry messages back and forth until it was wounded by a French sentinel.

From January 18 to 21, the French sappers pushed forward, completing a third parallel trench and digging zig-zags down into the ravine of the Huerva and towards the Palafox battery and Santa Engracia—all this in spite of constant musketry fire which made the work extremely dangerous except in the early morning when a welcome mist afforded some protection. Additional batteries were built to shell the easternmost section of the city and to batter a breach in the walls of the monastery of San Agustín; others were constructed to the left of San José, to make further breaches and silence the Spanish mortars in the Botanic Garden which continued to damage the trenches.

The French losses from sickness were now almost equal to those suffered inside Saragossa. Junot had barely enough men to maintain the blockade and protect his engineers and sappers, but still Palafox failed to make a decisive move. Instead, he continued to make both the civilians and the garrison devote their time to building further defences and barricades within the city, in expectation of street fighting.

On the afternoon of January 21, those troops not manning the walls and batteries were drawn up on the Coso amid cheering crowds and it was generally expected that they would make a sortie at any moment. Peasants and citizens took their muskets and pikes and hurried to the suburb while the small cavalry force lined up along the river. Several hours passed, the crowds grew increasingly despondent, a few men went to the walls to snipe at the French lines, but still no order for a sortie was given. To soothe his disappointed people, Palafox issued another proclamation. It was simply one of his customary hymns of praise for the defenders: "Adventurous inhabitants of this city of God! For you is reserved the great satisfaction of being men of good will! Your wives and your children cover you with blessings and the whole peninsula and the remotest nations are anxious to appear by your side and imitate you. Spain is reborn in Saragossa and may this holy temple of the Pilar be the strongest bulwark and the admiration of the entire universe . . . It is enough to be born in Saragossa to be valiant; it is enough to fight in the shelter of its walls—which you will make perfect —to win the laurels of immortality . . ."

On January 22, to the great relief of the French army, Marshal Lannes reappeared and took over command from the irascible Junot who now led only the 3rd Corps. Lannes immediately inspected the vast system of trenches and batteries, and the whole line of batteries fired salvoes to celebrate both his arrival and the news he brought of another French victory over a Spanish army at Ucles, fifty miles south-east of Madrid.

The following day, after Palafox had inspected the defences and decided that the French lines had been considerably weakened by casualties and sickness the Spaniards made their boldest sortie since the siege began. The attack was made at four o'clock in the morning by three separate columns but—amazingly and inexplicably—no column contained more than 300 men. One force advanced towards the trenches in front of the castle but this was a feint attack, merely intended to distract the besiegers' attention. On the Spanish left, a second column dashed from the walls towards the bridge by San José and the French trenches of the third parallel. It succeeded in reaching a small house beyond the Huerva, capturing it and forcing its French occupants to escape through the windows until the Spaniards in turn were driven back to the city by a company of Polish soldiers.

The main attack was delivered in the centre from the Santa Engracia gate. Charging with great impetus and led by Captain Mariano Galindo of the Volunteers of Aragon who had commanded the Pilar redoubt until its capture, the men forded the Huerva on both sides of the destroyed bridge behind the Pilar redoubt, crossed the third parallel, and fell upon two batteries in the second. Although they were driven off from one battery, the Spaniards succeeded in cutting down the gunners in another and spiking two twelve-pounders. They advanced several hundred yards into the French lines but they were too few to make any further progress. The guards in the trenches quickly recovered from their surprise and cut off the Spanish retreat. Twelve Spaniards were killed and thirty, including Galindo, taken prisoner. The twelve-pounders were quickly unspiked and, with the other guns, resumed their fire on the city. Had Palafox only sent several thousand men, the French might have had to call off the whole siege. Why he did not do so is perhaps the greatest mystery of all. Certainly, there is no reason to suppose that he would not have found all the volunteers he wanted for such an attack.

The situation on the Spanish side continued to deteriorate whereas Lannes put new heart into his army. According to Casamayor, over a hundred people were dying daily from sickness, and to judge by the way in which the deaths accelerated in the following month, this may well have been an underestimate. Even though most of the population were sheltering from the bombardment—now almost in its third week—many must have been killed in the streets and on the walls by shells and musket fire. The number of corpses was so great that it was impossible to give them a prompt burial and, in order to avoid infection from the dead, the people were ordered to keep the bodies, sewn up in canvas sacks, in the doorways and porches of churches until they could be thrown into huge pits. Fortunately, the continuing cold weather prevented decomposition. The atmosphere in the cellars, where civilians cooked their meagre rations, ate, slept and whiled away the hours when the bombardment was at its most intense, became so foul and germ-ridden that many preferred to risk their lives in the open air.

The sufferings of the besieged might be increasing almost hour by hour but the situation among the besiegers was not very much better. The French colonel of engineers Rogniat, who took part in the siege and described it in a short book published in 1814, stated that, at the time of Lannes's arrival, the French were facing their most serious crisis since returning to the city:

"Our most terrible enemy was famine: several times, our soldiers were reduced to half rations of bread and they were without meat; no village would obey requisition orders and the feeble state in which we found ourselves around Saragossa since the departure of Suchet's division, a departure which had reduced us to 22,000 men who had to lay siege to 50,000, did not allow us to send out detachments strong enough to capture victuals. At no period did the numerous garrison we were besieging show greater confidence and energy. Their conviction that they would soon be delivered by the army of relief, whose bivouac fires they could see crowning all the surrounding heights, doubled their warlike ardour which had in no way been dampened by the loss of the city's outer works; for the Aragonese placed much less trust in their fortifications than in their houses in which they believed themselves to be invincible."

The army of relief was no myth even though it consisted mostly of peasant levies. Every night, the French could see rockets being sent up and bonfires being lit in the hills in answer to the signals being made from towers within the city. There was now a serious threat to the French lines of communication. The whole of Aragon was in revolt: Francisco Palafox had succeeded in gathering together several thousand volunteers near Alcañiz and had armed them with muskets which had arrived from Catalonia; Lazan was at Lerida with 4,000 men and, on the left bank of the Ebro, a regular army colonel Pereña was moving southwards from the province of Huesca with several thousand armed men as well as cavalry. Various other bands of insurgents were attacking French patrols and foraging expeditions. To deal with the rebels, General Wathier of the French cavalry rode with 700 horsemen towards Alcañiz; but, on January 20, a small French column was forced by the vanguard of Colonel Pereña's forces to retreat near the town of Perdiguera, twelve miles north of Saragossa.

Lannes at once decided to recall Mortier with the whole of Suchet's division, which was still guarding the lines to Madrid as Napoleon had ordered. Mortier quickly marched his 10,000 men back towards Saragossa, crossed the Ebro, and soundly defeated Pereña's forces; a few battalions were then sent out to disperse smaller Spanish gatherings. And, on January 26, Wathier's force routed several thousand of Francisco Palafox's men at Alcañiz, occupied the town and—even more important for the soldiers outside Saragossa—captured a huge food supply of nearly 20,000 sheep, 1,500 sacks of flour, large quantities of oil, fresh vegetables and other provisions. The immediate threat to the French was now removed and Lannes ordered Gazan to begin digging approach trenches for an attack on the Arrabal suburb.

Now that he had coordinated all military efforts around the city and in the province, Lannes decided to give Palafox another chance to capitulate with honour. He wrote him a letter informing him of the defeat of General Sir John Moore at La Coruña, of two other Spanish reverses in the field, and of the dispersal of the armed peasants in Aragon. The letter was entrusted to his aide-de-camp, a dashing young officer called Saint-Marc, who presented himself and a bugler outside the Santa Engracia gate. After a short wait, he was blindfolded and allowed into the city, and was then conducted by Palafox's cavalry through a large and hostile crowd. Amid shouts of "Hang him! and "Kill him!" and—according to Saint-Marc's own report—even occasional cries of "What a handsome lad!", he was taken to the palace of the Inquisition. It was an unnerving experience for the young man as he was led through the long corridors and endless chambers of the building until at last the blindfold was taken from his eyes and he found himself alone in a room entirely hung with black, with only a Velazquez painting of Christ on the Cross to distract him from his anxious meditations. Finally, Palafox made his appearance with members of the *Junta*. After handing over the message, Saint-Marc was left alone again without any explanation for several more hours until he was once more blindfolded and escorted beyond the walls. Although he did not know it at the time, the reason for his long wait in the Inquisition building was that Palafox did not trust the people if they saw a French officer in the city, and had preferred to wait until nightfall before sending him back. Saint-Marc's story confirmed reports in the French camp that Palafox always behaved chivalrously and with honour—all the more pity, it was said, that fanatical monks and priests were forcing him to continue a futile resistance which could only end with the destruction of the whole city.

As expected, Palafox rejected Lannes's summons to surrender but what really surprised the French was that his answer was accompanied by the city's gazette for January 16, with its glowing accounts of fictitious French defeats. If the Spaniards could believe this, they would believe anything! But several French officers pointed out that it was precisely because the Spaniards *would* believe anything that they could put up such a fanatical resistance. Belmas quoted the general French opinion: "During this war, the character of the Spaniards was such that the imagination of the leaders was always obliged to conceive absurdities equal to the people's credulity—from this came that boastfulness and confidence which increased as danger became all the more imminent."

The French were now preparing to cross the Huerva, whose steeply sloping banks were entirely devoid of cover on the French side and subjected to constant fire from the Spaniards. Despite the danger and the loss of several officers of the engineer corps, two trestle bridges protected by sandbags and panniers were laid across the river and still more trenches were dug. On the night of January 25, a third bridge was built across the Huerva and a hundred grenadiers and several sappers crossed over. They advanced as far as the walls of the Santa Engracia garden where they made embrasures and exchanged fire with the Spaniards for the rest of the night. The daring operation was a prelude to the main attack.

Inside the city, everyone was frantically building new lines of defence, piercing loop-holes for cannon and muskets in the houses, and setting up still more barricades in the narrow streets. The monks worked day and night to make cartridges, a huge repair shop for arms and a special furnace forged grape- and canister-shot for the cannon.

Meanwhile, the French made great efforts to facilitate their communications between the two sides of the Ebro. A bridge of boats above the city had been built back in December but had been destroyed by high waters. It was now rebuilt and was strong enough to allow even the heaviest-calibre guns to pass over it. In addition, a flying-bridge was built below the town, sufficiently sturdy to bear two twelve-pounders at a time. Artillery as well as large numbers of men could now be brought quickly and safely from one bank of the river to the other as needed, and further siege batteries were set up to blast breaches in the walls.

At dawn on January 26, thirteen French batteries with a total of fifty heavy guns, as well as the mortars which had been sending bombs into the city since January 10, opened fire simultaneously. To the people of Saragossa, each new French bombardment since the first siege began had seemed worse than the last. This one was no exception. Shells and cannon balls crashed into houses by the cathedral and into various churches. Several bombs exploded near the piles of corpses stacked up in church porches and soon fragments of half-decomposed bodies littered the streets. Considerable damage was done to the buildings near the University in the Plaza de la Magdalena, the working class district of the Tanneries was pounded mercilessly, shells fell in two chapels of the Seo cathedral, and the Pilar became packed to stifling point with sick, wounded or simply panic-stricken civilians and nuns. The battery in the Botanic Garden was soon pulverised, the gunners in the Palafox battery and in Santa Engracia were blown to pieces or buried under the collapsing walls, a French battery opened a breach next to the Palafox battery, a second was made in the garden wall of the Santa Monica convent and a third in the wall of a second garden belonging to the same convent which overlooked the first from a raised terrace. The French guns soon made gaping holes in the walls of Santa Engracia and its garden but, after a time, a thick mist prevented the French from sighting

their guns accurately. The Goiechoea oil press outside the city was set
on fire and its defenders retreated into the city along their covered communicating trench.

The bombardment continued all day, but Lannes decided to postpone the attack on the breaches until January 27. The French were
greatly impressed by the defenders' steadfastness under such heavy
fire. Most of their cannon were silenced and their batteries completely
destroyed but still the Spaniards continued to shoot back from their
ruins, as Lejeune described: "Such was the intrepidity of the Spaniards
that at the very moment when a cannon ball made its hole in the wall of
a house, those who were inside it at once used this hole as a loophole
through which to fire their muskets, even though it often happened
that a second cannon ball would send the wall crashing down on its
defenders. Everywhere, they could be seen building barricades in the
midst of the débris." After the French batteries had resumed firing at
dawn on January 27, three breaches appeared suitable for attack between
the Santa Monica convent on the French right, and Santa Engracia on
the left (here sappers had laid several mines underneath the monastery).
At eleven o'clock, three separate companies of assault troops were
ready in the trenches and in the Goiechoea oil press, which had been
occupied during the night. As usual in such attacks, only a few hundred
men were detailed to make the preliminary assault. Once they had
made their way through the walls and secured the breaches, they
would be followed by the regiments standing by in the trenches and,
eventually, easily-handled light field guns would be brought into the
city to support the infantry. By twelve o'clock, a morning mist that
concealed the city from the troops in the trenches had lifted. The mines
under Santa Engracia exploded, the assault columns charged forward,
the city's church bells rang the alarm and the defenders fired from the
walls and houses overlooking the French.

On the French right, the troops emerged from the Goiechoea press
and ran across the few yards of open ground separating them from the
convent. Two Spanish concealed mines exploded but caused no casualties. In a few seconds, the soldiers had clambered over the ruined heaps
of wall to the top but, as they reached it, they found that there was a ten-
foot drop on the other side into the lower of the convent's two gardens.
The garden was swept with cannon and musketry from the surrounding
terraces and a gun loaded with grapeshot fired at the French from a
mere twenty five yards' distance. It was a deadly, untenable position.

To the right of the French, two other Spanish cannon opened fire from the upper terrace of the convent and nearly 800 men were blazing away at them with muskets and blunderbusses from the windows and embrasures in the building. A small isolated house outside the walls of the Tanneries district by the Ebro was also firing into the flank of the attacking force. The French sent men to capture the house but, although they occupied it briefly, they were forced to evacuate it because of heavy fire from a battery in the Tanneries. The French commander in the breach was wounded and the whole column withdrew to safety, leaving a handful of men to entrench themselves in the ruins below the wall.

The centre attack was launched against the breach in the buildings forming part of the walls facing San José, a few yards to the left of the remains of the Palafox battery. The French *voltigeurs* rushed through the breach to find themselves in the premises of the city's main oil press, then emerged into the Calle Pabostre which ran on the left to the Quemada gate. The French advanced to the left and right under heavy fire, seized a few houses and smashed their way into a triangular block of small houses facing them. There they came to a halt.

The attack on Santa Engracia was a complete success. The mines had brought down half the outer walls of the monastery, and a detachment of Polish infantry of the 2nd regiment of the Vistula under the command of Chlopiski (one of the best Polish officers in the whole French army: he had beaten Palafox at Epila in June and later became a general in the Polish army), preceded by sappers and followed by the whole regiment, ran across 200 yards of open ground. When they reached the demolished walls, they found to their surprise that they were faced by a second wall with a breach only large enough to allow the passage of a few men at a time. Despite terrible enemy fire, the Poles entered the main building and, after a fearful massacre, rushed into the little square, the Plaza de Santa Engracia, on their left. They captured the houses and the little Capuchin convent in the square and attacked the whole line of walls between Santa Engracia and the Pino tower from the rear. In a short time, the French reached the Carmen gate and burst into the Trinitarian monastery, massacring its gunners and driving out its garrison.

Although the attack on Santa Monica had failed, the French had quickly driven two large wedges into the city. But the real struggle had only begun. As the Spaniards prepared to counter-attack, Lannes's men were discovering that every house, church and monastic building had become a fortress and that, as Belmas wrote, "the thickness of Saragossa's ramparts was to be measured by the entire space covered by the whole city".

*   *   *

In 1801, a Spanish military manual of instructions and regulations for the Royal Corps of Engineers stated, with regard to sieges of fortified cities: "When the enemy shall be definitively established in the breach, should the governor believe that he may exceed the limits of an honourable resistance through raising it to the level of the heroic by defending the streets and houses, he will then have claims on Our Royal Gratitude." From the moment the French entered Saragossa for the second time, any hopes they might have entertained that Palafox would ask for a capitulation with the honours of war was soon dispelled. In any other part of Europe, the commander of a garrison would be satisfied that he had done all that was in his power to defend his city and he would surrender in order to save the lives and possessions of the population. Such relatively humane rules of warfare, which had become generally accepted in 18th-century Europe, were not for the Saragossans. For them, resistance had to attain "the level of the heroic".

Saragossa was already prepared for a fight to the death. There was little comparison between the way in which the interior of the city was now fortified and its state in the previous August. A vast amount of work had been accomplished. Every church and monastic building was a fortress, every block of houses a citadel, every house a small fort and every room a redoubt. Entire districts between the walls and the Coso were labyrinths of tunnels from house to house, trenches, ditches and barricades. Every house had loopholes for muskets; every man, woman and child capable of offering resistance had some weapon or other, even if it was only a knife, an iron bar, a cudgel or a pile of stones.

The reproaches contained in some of Palafox's manifestoes indicated that, unlike the first siege, many civilians were inclined to let the huge number of regular soldiers do all the hard work of preparing the city for defence. It was believed by the French that most of the civilians would also leave the fighting to the soldiers. But once again, now that their own homes, possessions, churches and shrines were directly menaced, the ordinary citizens came to fight alongside the soldiers in the front line.

In the city's centre, while the bell of the Torre Nueva summoned men and women from their houses despite the continuing bombardment, Palafox quickly organised mixed companies of soldiers, civilians and priests, while women hurried to the walls with bundles of muskets and cartridge belts. As the French and Polish soldiers poured into Santa Engracia, they soon found themselves faced by monks, peasants, citizens, and even women, just as they had been on August 4, 1808. Once again, soldiers and civilians battled from room to room, through the ruined cloisters, along the corridors and even up the staircases in the least damaged parts of the building. The defenders fought behind temporary barricades of wool sacks, and even behind piles of books snatched from the shelves of the monastic library. A Polish soldier was battered unconscious on a staircase by a monk wielding a heavy crucifix; the priest Santiago Sas was seen in the midst of the fighting, arms bare, covered with blood, and sabre in hand, shouting that he had already killed seventeen Frenchmen; Augustina was again reported to be in the thick of the *mêlée*, and a French captain was shot at point-blank range by a priest hidden behind a pile of rubble.

The fighting was equally fierce in the Trinitarian monastery. No quarter was given on either side as the French forced their way over the ditch and through the embrasures and windows into the building. No church was sacred, no chapel or altar or great crucifix was left undamaged by bullets and bayonet thrusts as the Spaniards fell back, foot by foot. Lejeune was one of several officers to be struck by the nature of this war in which men, women and even children fought to the death in chapels and holy shrines and at the feet of statues of the Saviour and saints. He had been badly bruised by a ricocheting cannon ball and, as he staggered back through the ruined church of Santa Engracia where bodies lay shot and bayoneted on the steps of the altar, he caught a haunting glimpse of a life-size marble statue of the dead Christ and the praying Virgin: "A halo had been formed by the thick cloud of dust and smoke which the wind made swirl around the statue which seemed to have become alive. The dust partly concealed from me the dead and dying men whose blood came streaming down the steps of the pedestal, and the sad realities of this tableau appeared to me only as a sublime vision whose unexpected apparition struck me with admiration." Later, that same day, the French discovered the body of a young monk who had been shot dead among a pile of dying men as he attempted to give them the last rites, still holding the ciborium and consecrated Hosts in his outstretched hand. It was only one of many

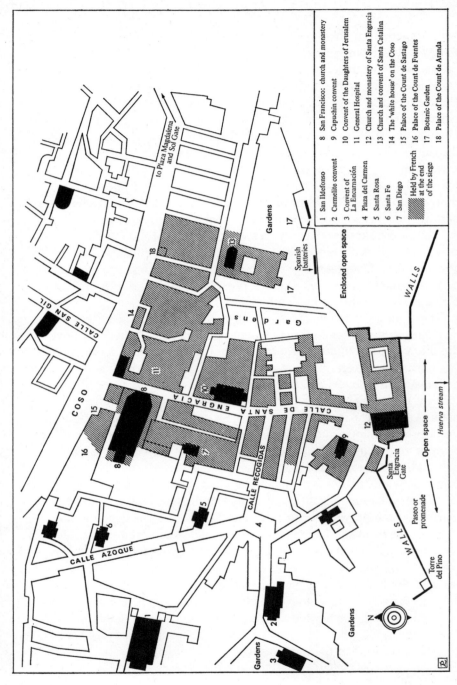

Saragossa during the second siege: the Santa Engracia sector

1 San Ildefonso
2 Carmelite convent
3 Convent of La Encarnación
4 Plaza del Carmen
5 Santa Rosa
6 Santa Fe
7 San Diego
8 San Francisco: church and monastery
9 Capuchin convent
10 Convent of the Daughters of Jerusalem
11 General Hospital
12 Church and monastery of Santa Engracia
13 Church and convent of Santa Catalina
14 The 'white house' on the Coso
15 Palace of the Count de Sastago
16 Palace of the Count de Fuentes
17 Botanic Garden
18 Palace of the Count de Aranda

Held by French at the end of the siege

Enclosed open space

Open space

Huerva stream

Paseo or promenade

WALLS

Spanish batteries

Gardens

COSO

CALLE SAN GIL

CALLE DE SANTA ENGRACIA

CALLE RECOGIDAS

CALLE AZOQUE

Santa Engracia Gate

Torre del Pino

to Plaza Magdalena and Sol Gate

N

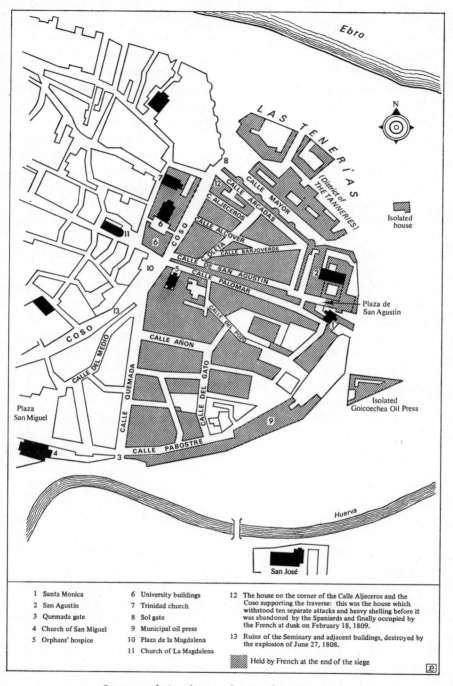

Ebro

LAS TENERÍAS

(District of THE TANNERIES)

N

Isolated house

CALLE MAYOR
CALLE ARCADAS
CALLE ALCOVER
C. ALJECEROS
COSO
CALLE COLETA
CALLE BARJOVERDE
CALLE DE SAN AGUSTIN
CALLE PALOMAR

8
7
12
6
11
10
6
5
2

Plaza de San Agustin

CALLE DEL POZO
CALLE AÑON
CALLE QUEMADA
CALLE DEL GATO
CALLE DEL MEDIO
COSO

13

9

Isolated Goicoechea Oil Press

Plaza San Miguel

CALLE PABOSTRE

4
3

Huerva

San José

1	Santa Monica	6	University buildings
2	San Agustin	7	Trinidad church
3	Quemada gate	8	Sol gate
4	Church of San Miguel	9	Municipal oil press
5	Orphans' hospice	10	Plaza de la Magdalena
		11	Church of La Magdalena

12 The house on the corner of the Calle Aljeceros and the Coso supporting the traverse: this was the house which withstood ten separate attacks and heavy shelling before it was abandoned by the Spaniards and finally occupied by the French at dusk on February 18, 1809.

13 Ruins of the Seminary and adjacent buildings, destroyed by the explosion of June 27, 1808.

Held by French at the end of the siege

Saragossa during the second siege: the eastern sector

similar incidents which were to be repeated over more than three weeks.

By the end of the day, the French had lost more than 600 men. After their initial gains in the fierce fighting which immediately followed the storming of the breaches, they had made scarcely any progress. The houses in the streets running off the Plaza de Santa Engracia were still full of armed Spaniards, the French had only captured a few of the houses in the Calle Pabostre, all the approaches to the Coso were blocked and, on the French right, the Santa Monica convent remained strongly garrisoned and its breach unassailable. A huge cloud of smoke hung low over the city; the palace of the *Real Audiencia* with its precious historical archives of the Kingdom of Aragon had been set on fire by French shells and was blazing fiercely; civilian stretcher-bearers carried the wounded through the shattered streets towards the cathedral area; a town crier made his rounds declaring that the French had lost 6,000 killed, and the people's morale remained high in spite of all the horrors of the continuing bombardment and the epidemic.

The French plan of attack inside the city was simple and straightforward but the first day's fighting in the streets was enough to convince Lannes that it would be a slow and desperate undertaking and that great care would have to be exercised if the French were not to suffer unendurable losses. The first main objective was the Coso but, to reach the boulevard, several large and strongly defended buildings would first have to be taken to provide the attackers with bases for further operations. On the French left, it was essential to push forward to the end of the Calle de Santa Engracia and capture the hospital and the San Francisco monastery, thus gaining domination of the central strip of the Coso.

In the centre, the whole of the Calle Pabostre must be taken so that the French could advance up the Calle Quemada to the Coso. On the right, the Santa Monica convent and the adjoining San Agustín monastery with their hundreds of defenders and their cannon constituted formidable obstacles which would have to be overcome before the French could advance along two straight streets—the Calle Palomar and Calle de San Agustín—towards the end of the Coso and the Sol gate. It was hoped that operations in the area of the Sol gate and the Tanneries district could be combined with an attack on the Arrabal. If the suburb were captured, then French guns could bombard the city's centre around the Pilar and Seo churches at devastatingly close range and support an attack on the easternmost end of the city which could be launched by sending troops across the bridge. Work had already begun on siege works on the left bank of the Ebro, now that Gazan's division no longer need fear an attack by Pereña's men from the north.

Few gains were made by the French on January 28. Their batteries continued to bombard the city, the *Real Audiencia* was still burning, huge explosions were heard all over the city, more Spaniards died of sickness, and the interior of the Pilar basilica became unrecognisable because of the numbers of refugees, sick and wounded who were camping in it and trying to get as near to the sacred shrine as possible.

While the breaching batteries went on pounding Santa Monica and San Agustín, the French troops remained confined in the Plaza de Santa Engracia, unable to advance into the nearby streets; but a few more houses were captured in the Calle Pabostre. At first, the French contented themselves with occupying only the ground and first floors but, after the Spaniards counter-attacked, coming over the roofs into the attics and then making surprise attacks down the stairs, they were forced to cover every floor and post men in the attics, from where they exchanged fire with Spanish snipers all day long. At two o'clock in the afternoon, a fierce Spanish attack on the Trinitarian monastery caused a slight panic among the French and their commanding officer was wounded, but a colonel restored order and the building was held. Under Lacoste's directions, embrasures were pierced in its walls and the doors and windows facing the city were blocked and sandbagged.

In other parts of Saragossa near the walls, the French found it impossible to cross even the narrowest streets, so fierce was the fire from the houses and roof-tops. French soldiers on the ground floors would find themselves exchanging fire with the Spaniards a few yards across the street, while the Spaniards in the upper floors made holes in the ceilings and dropped grenades on their heads. Still the French were unable to advance towards the Coso.

Later on the same day, Palafox issued another proclamation. Again, there was a note of reproach in his message after he had declared that the whole of Spain and all Europe were applauding the city's efforts: "With much bitterness of heart I must warn you that you were in danger of having the palms of so many famous victories snatched from your hands. Yes, Saragossans, you are in peril because of your lack of subordination and constancy. Scarcely did the enemy set foot in the city than you came running with your habitual valour to repel him but many of you did not obey your leaders' orders and others withdrew arbitrarily. It is true that your honour and courage brought you back promptly but what matter—had you exposed the city to capture in that time! . . . Yesterday, we would have dislodged the French from the city if you had obeyed your leaders . . . If, despite my just expectations, there be any inhabitant or dweller in this city who will not repair promptly to the points of battle or who will abandon them, then from this very instant I declare him a traitor and as such he will at once suffer the pain of the gallows and the confiscation of his goods". After these exhortations and threats, Palafox proceeded to bribe the more reluctant civilians by promising them officers' ranks according to the number of combatants they could each muster: a hundred men would earn a captaincy, thirty a lieutenancy and so on.

The French pressure against the Santa Monica convent increased and new mortars were brought up to bombard the building. During the night, French troops made a reconnaissance of the breaches but were forced to withdraw; and a new attack started against the first blocks of houses on each side of the Calle de Santa Engracia. On January 29, five more houses in the Calle Pabostre were taken without any resistance but Spanish snipers killed the occupying troops every time one of them showed himself at a door or window. A large breach had been made in the upper wall of Santa Monica, and a detachment of Polish infantry and sappers now charged it. During the night, the Spanish commander, Villacampa, had done his best to repair the breach but, as the intense bombardment had made this impossible, he had then built a second line of defences strengthened with wooden cases filled with earth, and had pierced embrasures in both cloisters of the convent. As the Poles came dashing forward to storm the wall, many were mowed down by musket fire and a hail of grenades and stones and the survivors had to retreat. After further determined efforts, a few houses were captured in the Calle de Santa Engracia, but as the French reached the end of the first block they found themselves unable to cross a narrow little street separating them from the next.

Meanwhile, Palafox formed a new corps of priests and civic leaders to encourage the defenders, and ordered the Dean of the Pilar basilica to have the church cleared of refugees: "I have learned with great emotion that the temple of Our Lady of the Pillar is suffering indecent profanation on account of the people who have taken refuge there:

chapels have been converted into latrines, the whole church is a dormitory, and the Holy Chapel seems to be a place for conversation rather than prayer. Even worse: yesterday they were frying sardines on the steps of the High Altar, in front of the Holy of Holies . . ."

During the night, the French made another attack, aiming to establish themselves in the breach made in the wall of the upper garden of Santa Monica, but were forced to give up the attempt because of the heavy musket and grapeshot fire maintained by the several hundred defenders; fighting also raged in the nearby streets as the French tried to attack the building from the rear. On the left of the Calle de Santa Engracia, the French at last managed to cross the little side street which had been holding them up. They charged into a house but were only able to occupy the cellar and ground floor as the Spaniards had destroyed the staircase and still held the upper floors. French sappers pierced loopholes in the walls so that they could fire into the rooms of adjoining houses but the Spaniards promptly filled them up again.

Lannes soon decided that the only practical way to make progress in the city was by using large quantities of gunpowder. After issuing orders expressly forbidding the French to attack in the open, he decided to tunnel and sap each block of houses in turn. His men should lay mines to destroy both the houses and their defenders, and then send forward small detachments to entrench themselves in the ruins; new mines would then be exploded under the next target until—if necessary —the entire city was reduced to rubble and the whole population buried under it. Command of the mining operations was entrusted to Lacoste. Each time a new house or block of houses was taken, the troops moving forward would be replaced in their rear by reserves to guard against Spanish counter-attacks. When two sides of a street were captured, communication between them was to be assured by a covered trench or double row of sandbagged parapets which would act as a protection against the Spaniards if they fired down the length of the street. When captured houses were not too severely damaged, they would be made intercommunicating by holes pierced in the dividing walls, and their doors and windows would be sandbagged.

On January 30, this new approach was put to the test. Six barrels of gunpowder were placed in the cellar of the house in the side street off the Calle Santa de Engracia where the French still held only the cellar and the ground floor. There was a huge explosion which brought down several adjoining houses as well, but as the French moved over the smoking heaps of rubble, they came under murderous fire from other houses nearby and were forced to retreat. More actual progress was made in the Calle Pabostre as the French slowly fought their way towards the opening of the Calle Quemada, but the last house on the corner still remained in Spanish hands, despite furious attacks and shelling. Then, on the evening of January 29, the French managed to break into its kitchen after exploding a small mine against the outer wall. As soon as they climbed through the breach, however, they found that the Spaniards had pierced embrasures for their muskets through the wall of the dining-room. While the defenders fired at point-blank range, those on the upper floors dropped grenades down the chimney to explode in the kitchen. The French then tried to run a mine underneath the building but the Spaniards countermined and forced them to abandon the attempt. On January 31, the house still held out although a French battery bombarded it throughout the day.

The two most important actions fought on January 30 were a successful French attack on Santa Monica and an unsuccessful Spanish counter-attack on the Trinitarian monastery. The bombardment of Santa Monica was so intense that, according to Ibieca, three whole storeys of the building collapsed at once, burying many of the defenders and raising such a thick dust that the survivors almost died of suffocation. New mines were exploded and, in the afternoon, after they had occupied the lower garden of the convent, the French stormed the breach in the upper wall and began to enter the building. The Spaniards retreated to the cloister, where they held out for two hours, firing back through the new embrasures they had made and throwing grenades. The commander of the garrison was wounded, the fighting extended to the church and finally, after firing a last volley, the Spaniards retreated once more, through a little door guarded by civilian volunteers. The French tried to pursue them outside but were greeted with such a barrage of musketry from adjoining houses and streets that they shut and barricaded the church door and prepared to spend the night in the ruined building.

In the afternoon, the Spaniards made a furious attack against the Trinitarian monastery, which was vital to them since it commanded the approaches to the Misericordia and the Portillo sector. The castle, a few hundred yards away to the west, had been left unassailed by the French and its guns were therefore able to bombard one side of the building. After a breach had been made in the wall, the Baron de Versage

with several officers and churchmen, including Santiago Sas, led a
motley force of soldiers, civilians, peasants, monks and women in to
the attack. At first, he had been reluctant to assault such a strongly
defended position, maintaining to Palafox that he had insufficient regular troops for the attempt, but he finally had to give way to the impatient
urgings of the crowd.

Versage's force, supported by musket fire from the roofs and windows
of the nearby houses, made a wild rush forward but could not penetrate
through the breach. They then attacked the main door of the church
which was under fire from a four-pounder. But, when they finally
battered it down with axes, it was only to find that the French had built
a heavily sandbagged barricade behind it and were waiting for them
with loaded muskets and fixed bayonets. As another crowd of Spaniards
dragged the four-pounder closer and a screaming horde of armed women
joined the men in a desperate rush at the barricade, the French moment-
arily wavered but a few moments later reinforcements arrived from the
rest of the building and their volleys drove the attackers away in confusion. Although some women still ran forward and monks and priests
waved crucifixes and urged the men to make another attempt, the
French proved too strong for the disorganised mob and Versage had to
call off the attack, leaving many dead and wounded in front of the
barricaded church door.

When he received details of the attack and the participation of so
many women, Palafox issued two more short proclamations. One was
specially addressed to the female warriors: "You also thirst for glory . . .
I could tell you that it is no new thing to find valour among persons of
your sex but there is even more energy to be found in you, women of
Saragossa, than among other women. Band together, worthy women,
and do not leave the laurels and palms of triumph to men alone. The
French soldiers will fear you and it will be shameful to them to be vanquished by you . . ." The proclamation ended on a somewhat surprising note: "I desire you to look upon me as your father: that alone
is lacking to make my happiness complete."

*   *   *

After Santa Monica, the next fiercely disputed strongpoint was the
monastery of San Agustín where the remnants of Villacampa's heroic
force had been relieved by some men of an Estremaduran regiment as
well as by armed civilians. On January 31, as the French entrenched

themselves in Santa Monica, some soldiers heard a knocking on the outside wall of a chapel near the main entrance. Believing that the Spaniards were about to lay a mine or pierce loopholes through which to fire into the church, a French officer gave orders for a hundred pounds of gunpowder to be placed against the threatened wall. The charge was exploded in the evening, making a huge hole in the wall and killing eight Spaniards who had been digging behind it.

The French immediately rushed through the breach into neighbouring houses and captured an entire block between the Calle Palomar and the church of San Agustín. They spent the rest of the night laying a 200-pound charge against the side wall of San Agustín. After the explosion at five o'clock in the morning, a detachment of grenadiers entered the breach, and were closely followed by the main attacking column.

The battle inside the church of San Agustín became one of the most famous incidents of the second siege. After slipping through the hole blown in the wall, the French soldiers found themselves in the sacristy and from there pursued the defenders into the church. They then rushed for cover behind the main altar as other Spaniards came running into the building. After a first exchange of fire, the French remained behind the altar while the Spaniards flung an improvised barricade of chairs and benches across the nave and took up positions in the side chapels, the choir, the organ loft and even the massive, sculptured wooden pulpit which was one of the most prized features of the church.

Grenades were thrown on both sides, and the building was soon filled with smoke from the explosions as bullets smashed into the organ pipes, shattered the stained-glass windows, thudded into stone statues of saints and splintered the elaborate wood carvings in altars and chapels. Then the French suddenly emerged from their cover, and charged down the aisle; a furious battle ensued at the foot of the pulpit which the Spaniards had occupied. The last defenders in the nave and side-chapels were shot, bayoneted or bludgeoned to death, but the survivors fought a desperate rearguard battle up the winding stairs leading to the bell tower. The main French column ran out of the church only to find that every corridor in the monastery was barred by barricades of wool sacks and timber, each of which had to be stormed in turn. And, while the Spaniards on the tower staircase prevented the French from climbing more than a few steps, other defenders came running towards the church from a nearby building. The French fought them off and invaded the rest of the monastery, but the men in the tower reached the top and proceeded to fire their muskets and hurl down grenades. According to Ibieca, they remained there for several days, as the tower held a supply of food and ammunition.

Now that they had captured the convent and monastery, the French were able to advance along two straight streets, the Calle de San Agustín and the Calle Palomar, which ran to the eastern extremity of the Coso.

After four days fighting, the French at last succeeded in smashing their way into the ruins of the house on the corner of the Calle Pabostre. They then began to move down the Calle Quemada towards the Coso. It was impossible to drive the Spaniards out of all the overhanging upper storeys, so the French made their way along the right hand side of the street by clambering through the holes which the Spaniards had pierced in the dividing walls on the ground floors. At the end of the Calle Quemada, the French had to brave the fire from a large orphan's hospice on the Coso and then began to run towards the Plaza de la Magdalena.

As soon as the French appeared on the Coso, nearby church-bells ran the alarm. To the sound of drums, several thousand civilians and soldiers, led by Palafox and including a large number of women, assembled by the ruins of the seminary and the Magdalena church and then fell upon the French. They fired cannon at the advancing column, civilians shot at them from the roofs and hurled pieces of timber and stones, hand-to-hand fighting developed, and the French were soon driven back. They had to abandon the entire Calle Quemada after such a fierce struggle that in one house alone, according to the diarist Casamayor, the bodies of nineteen Spaniards and sixty-one Frenchmen were later found. Several houses in the Calle Pabostre returned to Spanish hands and, further east in the city, the French were brought to a halt in the Calle Palomar and Calle de San Agustín after they had captured a few houses.

In the left sector, the process of mining continued. After five days of continuous fighting, the French had made scarcely any headway along the Calle de Santa Engracia where three great buildings with large, well-armed garrisons still blocked access to the Coso: the convent of the Daughters of Jerusalem, the hospital and the San Francisco monastery. In spite of all the heavy damage they had suffered in the first siege and the bombardment in the second, their battered, half-ruined structures still constituted formidable obstacles.

Lannes remained determined to spare his soldiers' lives as far as possible and to avoid costly confrontations in the streets. In a letter to Napoleon, he paid tribute to the tenacity and courage of the Spaniards: "Never before have I seen such furious ardour displayed by our enemies in the defence of this city. I have seen women who rushed to the breaches to get themselves killed . . . Your Majesty, this is a war which fills one with horror . . ."

While Lacoste directed the sappers, Lannes repeated his orders that the men were not to expose themselves in futile charges and pitched battles. Even heavier mines were used to bring building after building crashing down on the heads of the defenders; the French could then make a dash through the smoke, dust and confusion, and entrench themselves in whatever cover remained among the ruins. On January 31, another cluster of five houses which were being defended with great obstinacy was brought crashing to the ground after a 200-pound charge of gunpowder had been exploded. And, on the following day, two large mines were prepared by Lacoste's men to the left and right of the Calle de Santa Engracia. The mine on the left was placed at the end of a tunnel under the tiny Calle de las Recogidas which the French had been unable to cross for the three days since they had first reached it. Several houses were blown up, burying all their defenders, but a huge fire at once broke out preventing a French advance for several more days. On the right of the Calle de Santa Engracia, two houses facing the Jerusalem convent across a little street had been captured and 200 pounds of gunpowder were now placed inside to destroy the adjoining houses. There was another tremendous explosion and nearly a dozen buildings crumbled away into heaps of rubble. As Polish infantrymen charged forward to occupy the ruins, Spanish snipers simultaneously shot Lacoste and an officer standing beside him as they watched the progress of the attack from the window of a nearby house. The officer was killed outright, Lacoste died a few hours later. It was the second serious blow the French had suffered that day. Not only had their troops been swept back from the Coso but one of the army's most popular and talented officers, and a leading military engineer, had been lost to them.

Following the successful repulse of the French from the Coso, Palafox issued yet another proclamation. It was a strange composition. After urging the public to show gratitude towards God, the Pilar Virgin and the valiant civilians and soldiers who had saved the people from "the terrible day of horror and frightfulness that was being prepared for Saragossa", and painting a graphic picture of the inhabitants being led off as slaves, children being torn to pieces in the streets and virtuous women being raped, Palafox came to more mundane matters. Each "valiant defender of the fatherland" was to be rewarded with five *reales* a day and a ration of wine; a few rich citizens had contributed the money and Palafox himself had given "my watches, my silver ware and all I possess, keeping only my sword to avenge the insults heaped on us by this infamous and cowardly nation".

The whole population of Saragossa was again showing its heroic determination to fight to the last man but it certainly needed encouragement. The number of deaths from disease had reached several hundred a day, and the rate was increasing rapidly; often the corpses were not discovered until several days afterwards. The weather had become warmer, bringing a greater risk of infection, scurvy was rampant, men were dying by the score from gangrene because of the lack of medical supplies and attention, and all the time the French batteries continued to fire grenades, shells and cannon balls into every part of the city.

According to rumours in the French camp, Palafox could only make the people fight on by means of a reign of terror. His old tutor, the priest Basilio Boggiero, and the heroic and fanatic Santiago Sas were especially blamed for their influence over him. Hangings and secret executions were said to be frequent, the gallows in the market place always had fresh victims dangling from its six nooses and there was talk of another evil and ruthless churchman—the sinister Father Consolación—and of a former lemonade seller on the Coso known as Tio Marin who were compelling Palafox to rule by tyrannising the people. Palafox himself was said to be grief-stricken by the executions he was forced to sanction but the members of his *Junta* and his closest advisers were inflexible. Certainly on February 3, there was a particularly unpleasant example of the spy- and treason-mania which was kept at fever pitch in Saragossa.

A French bomb had fallen in a warehouse and set fire to it. As the citizens came running up to fight the conflagration, they discovered several beds of which there was a desperate shortage in the hospitals. Although he protested that he had received no official order to hand over the beds, the unfortunate warehouse superintendent was seized by the outraged mob, accused of treachery, taken to the city prison and garroted in his cell. The next day, his body was dangling from a gallows in the Coso, with a sign pinned to his chest: "Murderer of the human race for having hidden 20,000 beds."

During the night of February 1, Palafox made an attempt to send a message for help to the Duke of Infantado who was reported to be at the head of a large army at Cuenca in New Castile. Seven picked men left the city in a small rowing boat at three o'clock in the morning but they were soon sighted and fired upon by the French batteries on both sides of the Ebro. The boat was boarded, and three Spaniards were killed and three taken prisoner. But, although he was severely wounded on the head by blows from an oar, the seventh Spaniard managed to escape by swimming away; he reached a nearby village with his message, but died a few days later. On February 4, Palafox issued another manifesto. Without any preamble, he announced further rewards for those who particularly distinguished themselves in action. The army's commanders, officers and mayors of the city's wards were to send in daily reports of the most heroic deeds which had come to their knowledge. In the name of Ferdinand VII, Palafox would then personally invest the twelve bravest men as knights in the Pilar chapel, their titles being hereditary.

Lacoste was replaced as head of the engineering corps by his second-in-command, the cold, humourless but extremely capable Colonel Rogniat, and fighting continued with great ferocity. It was at its bitterest in the little streets adjoining Santa Monica, near the Puerta Quemada and around the Jerusalem convent. In the Calle Pabostre, Polish troops counter-attacked and managed to recapture the houses they had lost on February 1. According to the Spanish engineering officer Manuel Cavallero, who took part in the city's defence, two of the small two-storey houses in that street were only taken by the French after nine hours' continuous fighting. The French also returned to the Calle Quemada and occupied a few houses as they resumed their attempt to move forward to the Coso and the important stronghold of the orphans' hospice. They fought their way, house by house, through the maze of narrow, winding little streets between the Calle Quemada and the Calle Palomar, which was being swept by musket and cannon fire from a barricade near the Coso. As he watched the fighting, Rogniat was wounded but—he was luckier than Lacoste—only by a bullet in the hand.

Progress remained extremely slow. To speed it up, the French cleared a way through the rubble and over the ground outside the walls so that they could bring field guns into the city through the breaches.

As they waited for artillery support, the French and Polish soldiers became increasingly proficient in this new, deadly type of warfare in which soldiers became moles, burrowing into the ground while they made their way from one heap of ruins to the next. Each time they managed to move forward a few yards, they would build parapets with sandbags and whatever other material lay at hand and dig trenches to protect themselves against the unceasing Spanish musket fire. To fight near buildings was just as dangerous as to fight in them: any soldier who went too close to a house was likely to find himself pelted with stones and even grenades from the roof-tops unless the whole block had been occupied by the French. On the other hand, a soldier might have to wait until nightfall in his improvised shelter before making a dash across the devastated wasteland all around him.

When he took charge of mining and sapping operations after Lacoste's death, Rogniat realised that it was necessary to reduce the amount of explosive used in attacking enemy-held houses. The disadvantage of completely destroying several houses at once was that, although the defenders were killed, little cover was left for the French as they moved forward to occupy the ruins, and heavy casualties might be expected before they could build themselves a protective barrier. New orders were consequently issued: as soon as a house was captured and cleared from top to bottom, a man would be posted in the attic to watch the neighbouring rooftops while a sapper set a charge calculated to destroy only one side of the next house to be attacked, leaving the rest of the building standing. This, of course, meant that fighting from floor to floor and room to room—like that already experienced on January 28—could not be avoided.

The horrors of such fighting made a deep impression on the French and Polish infantry. For most soldiers, it was a strange, disconcerting, unprecedented type of warfare, quite unlike previous street fighting they had experienced or battles in the open countryside. No building could ever be regarded as safely occupied until all others in the block surrounding it had been cleared. The Spaniards were expert in making preparations to defend each house as it became threatened. Whenever the French assaulted the first of a block of houses, they could hear the Spaniards smashing the staircases, often replacing them with ladders which they would pull up after them once the enemy had broken into the ground floor or cellar. The defenders would pierce holes in walls and ceilings and have stocks of grenades and stones ready to hand on the top floors. They became extremely agile at running over the roofs and, at any moment, the French might find a shot fired or a grenade thrown at them from the top of a staircase, through a window or a hole pierced in the roof. In his memoirs, Brandt described this style of fighting: "When we broke into a house we had first to inspect it thoroughly from bottom to rooftop. We learned from experience that a sudden interrupted resistance could be a warlike ruse. Often, as we were installing ourselves on one floor, we would be shot at point-blank range from the next floor up through openings made beforehand in the ceiling. The nooks and hiding places which we frequently found in these old-fashioned buildings facilitated such murderous ambushes. Above all, we had to keep a watch on the rooftops. With their serge shoes, the Aragonese would circulate as easily and with as little noise as cats and were therefore able to return to make unexpected forays well behind the front line of operations. It was a veritable war of aerial fighters. We would be sitting tranquilly by a fireside, in a house which had been occupied for several days, when all of a sudden shots would come through some window or other as though they had come from the sky."

An excellent description of a typical room-to-room battle for possession of a house was given by Belmas in his detailed, day-by-day account of the siege: "If the enemy disputed the entry to a room, we would pierce loop-holes facing his own and there would be shooting from both sides. As the room separating the combatants quickly became filled with smoke, this allowed a sapper to crawl forward on his stomach and make his way under the enemy's musket barrels; the sapper would then stand up, beat with all his might on the musket barrels with an iron crowbar and force the Spaniards to pull their guns away. Our grenadiers would then move forward, throw grenades, fill in the loop-holes and force the enemy to seek refuge in another, more distant room where a new battle would begin. Whenever a thick wall stopped the dash of our soldiers, the sappers would reduce its thickness with pick-axes before making any opening and would then push the wall down, all at once, over the Spaniards. These different attacks had to be made simultaneously on each floor of a house so that we would not be exposed to the enemy's fusillades through the ceilings of the upper floors or to the grenades which he would drop down the chimneys. It was especially necessary to occupy the roof-tops in strength since the Spaniards would use them to make raids in our rear and cut our communications."

The Spaniards soon discovered another means of keeping the French at bay—fire. Most houses in Saragossa were built of brick and because they contained little wood except for their beams did not burn easily, but the Spaniards would compensate for this by covering the walls and floors with tar, resin and other inflammable substances and placing tar-soaked bundles of wood against the doors and windows. The houses would burn slowly, sometimes for several days, keeping the French back and giving the Spaniards more time to fortify the next block or line of houses behind the smouldering ruins. While the French were forced to wait for the fires to burn themselves out and for the ashes of the houses to cool, they had to endure ceaseless sniping through the flames and smoke. The Saragossans and Aragonese generally were excellent sharpshooters. Colonel Lejeune related how the Spaniards "seemed to look upon it as an amusement as they practised their skill in taking aim at us. They were such good marksmen and they fired so quickly that the shakos of our soldiers would be riddled with bullets as soon as they showed them above the parapets of their trenches . . . the patience of the Spaniards in this shooting practice was such that they even made breaches with musket shots in walls which they could not demolish by other means and which they supposed must serve us as shelter. So much lead was consumed in this manner that in some parts of our trenches it could be picked up by the shovel-load".

Since the French found it impossible, because of the barrier of fire the Spaniards had lit, to take most of the houses on the left of the Calle de Santa Engracia, they made determined efforts to capture the important Jerusalem convent by tunnelling under the narrow little street which separated them from the building. Two tunnels were dug under the convent and a third under a house to the right. The French sappers made rapid progress but, when they broke into a cellar, they heard the sound of Spanish sappers burrowing towards them. The French immediately placed a large charge of gunpowder in the cellar and abandoned it. The huge explosion destroyed several houses adjoining the convent, killing their defenders and burying the Spanish sappers alive, but it also wrecked the French tunnels and work had to begin all over again. And, as the new mining works were pushed forward, the Spanish commander in the Jerusalem convent set fire to what was left of the houses separating his position from the French and it was soon ringed with flames.

Believing that this new fire was a sign that the Spaniards had abandoned the building, a company of light infantry and sappers made an audacious charge through the flames and emerged in the grounds of the Jerusalem, from where the defenders fired at them behind a loop-holed wall. The convent was soon invaded, and fighting raged through its corridors, chapels and cells; as the fire spread to parts of the main edifice, both dead and wounded men were burned by the advancing flames. The commander of the garrison was killed, the surviving de-fenders retreated, and yet another fortress-convent was in French hands.

The capture of the Jerusalem convent made an indelible impression on Lejeune, whose memoirs give us such a vivid picture of what it meant for French soldiers, used to the open battlefield, to have to fight their way through a city which seemed to consist only of an endless series of churches, hospitals and convent buildings. Like some of his fellow-officers in Spain and, no doubt, like many ordinary French soldiers who neither wrote memoirs nor kept a diary, Lejeune was seized by anguish at the type of war he was forced to fight because of an entire people's resistance to Napoleon's armies:

"Never shall I forget the effect produced on me by the appearance of the interior of this convent as I beheld it through dense clouds of dust and smoke. The nuns' cells, once havens of peace and prayer, had now become the theatre of war. In this hour of desolation, the assailants were trampling over every symbol of piety, the holy water stoups, amulets, enormous rosaries and the rush mats which were the only couches and furnishings of these austere sisters. With every step I took on the pavements of their oratories, I trod on instruments of flagella-tion such as iron scourges with sharpened points which bore witness to their severe customs just as the needlework they had been engaged in to clothe the poor, and which now lay scattered on the ground, bore witness to their ardent compassion. A few, suddenly surprised in their flight or else kept back by the warlike women of the city, had remained with them among the defenders. As we approached, we saw the nuns snatch the objects of their worship and chaste love from the altars to save them from profanation. These saintly sisters who obeyed only the devoted instincts of their piety in this terrible moment would carry away only the crucifixes and images of the child Saviour. With heart-rending cries, they abandoned their abodes, left strewn with the many emblems of their pious sentiments and the goodness of their hearts. In all their little chapels, they had assembled pretty figures of coloured

wax, representing adorable little Infant Christs with snow-white
lambs, all adorned with ribbons and everything that their artless and
childlike imaginations could find most graceful. Over these cribs of
flowers, moss and greenery and over these cradles of the Saviour which
lay upturned in confusion, we now saw wounded soldiers falling and
the blood of dying men streaming amid bouquets of everlasting flowers,
wreaths of roses and blue ribbons."

As the French contemplated the pathetic remains of the captured
convent and made preparations for a new advance, their artillery continued to shell the city. Masses were still being held in the Pilar and Seo
churches where several cannon balls and even an occasional mortar
bomb had fallen, although without causing great damage. Many of the
Spanish regular troops had died of disease and more civilians were now
seen in the firing line. The monastery and convent buildings remaining
to the Spanish were inundated with sick and wounded but the survivors
stood firm. Even after days of the most desperate action, however, new
bodies still appeared on the gallows, as though the population needed
constant reminders that failure to fight meant treason.

After the capture of the Jerusalem convent, the French advanced
towards the Coso along the Calle Quemada, the Calle Palomar, and
Calle de San Agustín, and Rogniat's engineers prepared new tunnels to
attack the General Hospital. On the left of the Santa Engracia sector,
more houses were set on fire, and several were captured from the
Spanish, but no attempt was made to push on towards the Portillo, or to
occupy the large area of houses and gardens lying between the Calle
de Santa Engracia and the Calle Quemada.

French aggression remained confined to limited sectors of the city.
Even though losses were comparatively low, they were a constant
drain on the few regiments entrenched in the city, and no attacks in
new sectors could be launched for the very simple reason that Lannes
did not have enough men. He needed 5,000 to maintain the blockade
of the castle and hold the line between it and the Trinitarian monastery;
Gazan could not spare a single one of his 7,000 or 8,000 outside the
Arrabal, and Suchet's 10,000 were busy keeping watch on the countryside and dispersing the bands of armed peasants whenever they
threatened the besiegers. Lannes had only two divisions of the 3rd
Corps—9,000 men in all—to pursue the attacks, guard the captured areas
of the city, and make new trenches and tunnels. Of this total force, only
half were employed at a time, the others resting in camp or providing

sentinels. Thus, only 4,500 were in action or on duty within the city walls at any time.

On February 6, a large mine was laid under the General Hospital. Although it had been so badly shelled during the first siege, large parts of the vast building were still standing and, in the great wards and corridors, several hundred well-armed men continued to stop the French from reaching the Coso. In the afternoon, the mine exploded and 400 French infantry of the line charged the breach and forced the defenders to withdraw. The hospital had cavernous cellars and, after they were cleared and the last hand-to-hand fighting had ended, the French sappers occupied them and began a series of new tunnels which were to run under the Calle de Santa Engracia and the San Francisco monastery.

Tunnelling had now become the most important part of the besiegers' offensive operations. The Spanish, soon realising this new threat, lost no time in counter-mining, and a deadly subterranean war began in earnest, as sappers on both sides burrowed through the earth at the constant risk of suffocation, often without space to hold up a lantern. As the French sappers pushed forward, the Spaniards would sometimes lie in ambush in their own tunnels, waiting for the enemy to break through the last few feet of earth and gravel, when they would fling themselves upon him with knives, pickaxes and shovels. Often, Spaniards and French simultaneously broke into the many cellars which honeycombed the ground under the houses near the hospital, and fearful massacres would take place in the dim light and even in total darkness once lanterns were smashed or knocked to the ground. Some cellars contained huge earthenware containers and, if they were broken in the fighting by random blows from a pickaxe or a pistol shot, the liquid would rush out to flood the cellars and tunnels; as men fell, they would die choking and drowning as their own blood mingled with hundreds of gallons of oil and wine. At other times, each side would lay small mines to blow up the other's tunnels and the explosions would bury men alive. Often, a French sapper would only be a few feet away as he heard the last desperate struggles of the Spanish sappers dying of asphyxiation after a mine had brought the roof of their tunnel down upon them.

Horrors were not confined to the ground beneath the streets and houses of Saragossa. Once they had advanced to the top of the Calle Quemada, and reached the Coso through the ruins of the houses destroyed in the seminary explosion of June 27, the French and Polish infantry, after attacking several adjacent houses, made a succession of attempts to dislodge a strong Spanish force from the orphans' hospice. Fierce fighting broke out in the block to the right of the Calle Quemada and, in one house, most of the day was spent in a desperate struggle for the staircase. The Spaniards then set light to the houses and withdrew into the hospice. The French tried to put out the flames but had to give up the attempt under heavy fire. After the blaze had died down, the Poles made a new attack, were repulsed, attacked again, and were repulsed again. On February 7, sappers started to mine the hospice but the Spaniards suddenly abandoned it after setting fire to it. As the French and Poles made their way into the building, they found themselves in a huge charnel-house. It also very nearly became their death trap, as Brandt described:

"Something horrible happened this February 7. The Spaniards had at last evacuated this hospice after it had been mined on all sides. The assailants penetrated into it without meeting any resistance but the spectacle offered to their eyes made even the most intrepid of them fall back. The beds and the floors in the rooms were encumbered with dead and wounded that the Spaniards did not have time to evacuate. But they had time to prepare the fire and already the flames were running towards us, consuming *everything* in their path . . . I commanded a detachment of twenty men covering the left of the column as we made our way through the adjacent courtyards and the outbuildings of the main edifice. A sapper sergeant who was acting as our guide went in the wrong direction and led us straight towards the centre of the blaze. We suddenly found ourselves enveloped in a thick smoke which gave out the abominable odour of charred flesh. Happily, despite the darkness in this pestilential obscurity, my hand found a window which I smashed and which gave us back a little air and daylight . . . after many detours we emerged safe and sound from this place of abomination."

The French were forced to abandon the whole building and wait for the fire to die out. Even though they had now reached the Coso, they were unable to advance along it until nightfall as the Spaniards were firing at them with musket and cannon from the other side of the Coso and from behind a large sandbagged traverse which ran halfway across the boulevard. Finally, the French made a dash forward and managed to reach the ruined seminary. Other troops had advanced to the end of the Calle Palomar and occupied the last block of houses overlooking the Coso, but Spanish cannon fire forced them out again. After they had fallen back, another Spanish cannon was brought up to the mouth of the Calle Palomar to sweep its entire length. Almost no French progress was made in the sector for the next two days. The Coso was still a formidable rampart, barring the French from the inner heart of the city.

Since the end of January, Gazan's men had been digging trenches and placing batteries from which to attack the suburb. Their initial target was the isolated Jesus monastery, which the Spanish had not had time to demolish. In spite of its exposed position, the Spaniards decided to defend it with 200 men and two cannon. While the French dug their trenches towards the unfortified outer walls of the monastery, the monks watched their progress. As the besiegers drew nearer and started to build batteries, snipers on the roofs and terraces began to take their daily toll and it soon became so dangerous to dig any further that work was continued only at night. Although Gazan's men were envied by the troops in the city for being able to work and fight in the open air, their hardships increased. After the cold, they suffered from damp; at night, they would be silently led to the trenches and made to dig for several hours in total darkness, knowing that any sound—even a cough or a spit—might attract flaming projectiles and grenades followed by musket volleys. Some of the soldiers in the trenches were not relieved for seventy-two hours and, when dawn broke, the men who had been digging throughout the night would fall asleep behind piles of earth they had heaped up in front of the trench, too exhausted to return to the safety of the rear lines.

When the Jesus garrison saw scaling ladders, sandbags, fascines and panniers being brought to the front trenches, they hurriedly began to demolish the outer wall of the monastery and surrounded the building with a ditch. On the night of February 7, when preparations for attack were almost complete, an approach trench for a storming party was dug within sixty yards of the walls. Next morning at eight o'clock, twenty-two guns opened fire on the monastery and suburb. Two hours later, large breaches had been made by the twenty-four-pounders. Several of the French guns were then turned against the quayside of the Ebro and the stone bridge. The assault companies ran out of their trenches and penetrated the building without any difficulty while the monks and many of the garrison made a precipitate retreat into the suburb. As the troops charged they came under grapeshot fire from a heavily fortified

Spanish battery to their left, near the river. A French officer and several *voltigeurs* charged the redoubt but without support they were killed or captured. After the whole monastery had been cleared of defenders and thoroughly searched for snipers, its captors began to dig a communication trench to connect the building with the main trenches and a new parallel against the suburb.

Daudevard de Férussac was among the new occupants of the building. Like Lejeune, who came to inspect it after its capture, he was highly impressionable. Both men, like other soldiers during the siege, had previously been too busy fighting or supervising engineering works and tunnelling to pay much attention to the contents of the houses and monastic buildings that had been taken. Now that there was a lull and they began to contemplate the horror and desolation of the scene which surrounded them, they could not escape a growing awareness of the enormity of their situation. While most soldiers simply looked for food and wine and cheerfully plundered whatever they could find, several officers were seized by the gnawing, anxious feeling that they were unjustifiable intruders as they observed the pathetic remains of the libraries, art treasures, and signs of Spanish piety around them. It was a feeling that was to grow stronger as the siege progressed. After fighting against civilians, monks and women, they began to look more closely at the evidence of the civilisation their enemies were defending—this strange, superstition-ridden but exotic world of Spanish Catholicism symbolised to the French by the cellars of the Inquisition and the hooded penitent with his scourge, and the priest who was capable of holding a crucifix in one hand and a sabre in the other.

The monastery had been used as a hospital and the cells, cloisters and even the church were filled with dead and dying men and women. More than 200 bodies lay heaped in the middle of the main cloister ready to be burned. After the French had lit this human bonfire, the soldiers tried to avoid the smell of burning flesh by going into the innermost recesses and crypts of the building. Daudevard was filled by superstitious fears as he kept watch on sentry duty: "The obscurity, the enemy's vicinity, the pick-axe blows of the workers who seemed to be digging tombs, the corpses over which one tripped as one walked, the ground covered with men stretched out asleep but who all seemed dead—such was the impressive and lugubrious scene which faced those who kept vigil like myself. I entered the monastery but there were new scenes of horror; there were great corridors to traverse where one walked on tip-toe, there was a glacial silence, there were flames which rose from time to time, there were half-extinguished fires which had been lit in the courtyards. All this set your nerves on edge. Such a glow, before you plunged into obscurity, made you see giant pictures on the walls where sinister figures reminded you of the shadows in the Greek caverns of Tenare."

Both Daudevard and Lejeune found their way to the large library in the monastery. Soldiers snatched pages from missals and ancient manuscripts to light as torches. By their glow, a sapper found a crucifix of solid gold, weighing more than a pound; the more literate-minded officers and men explored the shelves and discovered fine editions of the Bible, a set of the French *Encyclopédie* (officially banned by the Inquisition), works of history and science and wonderfully rare and beautifully printed editions of Greek and Latin poetry and medieval illuminated manuscripts among a mass of mystic, sentimental and superstitious religious works and saints' lives. While some soldiers perused them, others swept them off the shelves and carried them off as fuel for the bivouac fires. No one, complained Daudevard, had thought of setting a guard over the precious collection! Leaving this scene of destruction, he and Lejeune explored the crypts. The monks who had died were laid in catacomb-like niches in the walls, wrapped in the robes of their order before being sealed up behind marble plaques on which their names were engraved. Lejeune's anguish increased as he contemplated the vast, vaulted mausoleum: "We looked meditatively at the monks who had died or been killed during the siege and whom lack of time had prevented from being walled up in their sepulchres, and we could not avoid the painful impression caused in us by this sad spectacle. We kept silent. Each of us seemed to be thinking: 'Why are we troubling the peace of this tomb? Tomorrow, perhaps, *we* shall be laid in it. Come, let us go elsewhere to explore the ruins . . .'"

During the first siege, the French troops had mainly looted jewellery, furnishings in private houses, and wine shops. Now, they helped themselves to the contents of the great churches and monasteries. Paintings were snatched off walls and used instead of firewood or even as shelters from the cold. Wooden sculptures and crucifixes were piled on bonfires or used together with church furniture and altar-pieces in the making of barricades or breastworks in the trenches. Lejeune was particularly distressed by the way the soldiers treated so many of the fine books found in the monasteries. It seemed that vandalism was the order of the day—especially where libraries were concerned. Religious books had new uses: "These enormous volumes describing the history of the martyrs in great length and these parchment folios which were so numerous in the monasteries were extremely useful to us. We would pile the books up as easily as bricks and whether they were stood on end or on their sides, they would protect us perfectly from bullets. Several of our men owed their lives to the history of such-or-such a saint whose piety they never dreamed of imitating. This way of destroying the libraries which contained so many precious books and manuscripts was not the most distressing disorder we witnessed in this respect. At night, our soldiers who were without wood would burn these books to warm themselves, or else they would tear out the pages to give themselves light among the labyrinths of wreckage in which it was so easy to hurt oneself. Our educated officers lamented this vandalism and tried to prevent it but as wood was very rare in the buildings of Saragossa, it was often difficult to put other less precious combustibles within reach of the soldiers . . . It was thus that we lost a very precious and very ancient collection of original manuscripts and diplomatic papers of which only a few scattered leaves were found." Other more profitable discoveries, both for the antiquarian-minded officers and the simple soldiers, were gold and silver coins, many dating from Roman times, which the sappers would find as they dug their tunnels, particularly near the Coso which probably marked the limits of the old Roman town. Sometimes, as Lejeune described, the men would come across virtual treasure troves underground: "In this memorable siege, I have seen men digging horizontally twenty feet under the earth when their pick-axes would break antique vases out of which there would flow gold, silver and bronze medals which the Carthaginians, the Romans or the Arabs had hidden in similar times of public calamity. As the metal glittered in the light of the miner's lamp, it might well have interrupted his work or excited his cupidity but instead he would push both the treasure and the loose earth to the miner behind him, saying simply: 'Here! pass the treasure to the captain—it'll amuse him.' Captain Véron-Reville was a numismatist. He thus received some very rare medallions of which several were discovered at the foot of an ancient Roman wall which had given great trouble to our miners on account of the hardness of its cement."

When they were not finding such treasures, the sappers were only too likely to find the enemy. After the French had begun their mining

galleries under the Calle de Santa Engracia towards the vast, bombarded shell of San Francisco, the Spaniards vigorously counter-mined.
Sometimes, they would make sorties and further deadly fights with
pick-axes, hatchets and shovels would occur in tunnels and cellars.
Grenades would be thrown, tunnel walls and roofs would collapse,
counter-mines would be laid and exploded and still more miners buried
alive. Sometimes, after destroying the Spanish works, the French would
at once make efforts to rescue the survivors. Such gallantry was rare
but there were a few other cases of much mutual respect between
enemies. The conscript Billon stated that in one house, jointly held by
Polish infantry and the Spaniards, a Spanish officer defending the first
floor conversed down the stairs with a Polish officer and offered him a
glass of wine to drink to the ending of the war. The Polish officer
readily agreed, promises were exchanged to respect each other's
liberty, the Spaniard came down with a bottle and glasses, then just as
the two men were about to drink the first toast, an officer on a tour of
inspection arrived and insisted on taking the Spaniard prisoner and
conducting him to Lannes. After hearing the story, the Marshal assured
the Spaniard that he was free and, after giving him dinner, sent him
back under escort to his first-floor post.

Above ground, the French continued to make every effort to reach
the Coso and push their attack on the right towards the Sol gate. More
houses were blown up or set on fire by the defenders and, every now
and then, one of particular strategic importance would be captured by
the French after a swift dash through the wreckage, only to be abandoned after the Spaniards had replied with heavy cannon fire and
grenades from the next block of houses. As a company of Polish soldiers
emerged into the Coso from the ruins near the seminary, they tried to
build a barricade, until a storm of musketry and grapeshot forced them
to run for shelter again. Heavy artillery was brought into the city by the
French, and a battery of two sixteen-pounders was placed in the Calle
Palomar and began to bombard the far side of the Coso.

Because of the constant Spanish shelling, the French were unable to
occupy the entire ruins of the hospital. They began to move to their
right in an effort to link up with the men in the ruined houses at the top
of the Calle Quemada but several hundred yards of buildings still
separated them. After a few more small houses had been taken, French
sappers dug tunnels to mine the large mansion known as the "white
house" which stood between them and the Coso; but, after a breach

was blown in its walls, the attack was repelled and several more houses to the right were set on fire by the Spanish.

Although the defenders were still holding firm and disputing every square yard of ground with the greatest tenacity, Palafox continued to issue exhortatory proclamations full of reproaches and alarming statements that there were traitors in the city. There was a touch of paranoia in the speeches—the soldiers and civilians who were still able to fight were making the most heroic efforts to contain the enemy and still their leader felt obliged to threaten the direst punishments, to rage against traitors and cowards, and to promise rewards to those who did their duty. On February 9, he began his proclamation with these words: "The indifference and abandon with which some citizens look upon the fate of their motherland is the reason why the enemy today shame us by occupying the part of the city which they still keep despite their weakness and cowardice. The honourable, the true patriots exhaust themselves in vain without being able to extirpate this evil which is unworthy of the Aragonese: many soldiers follow this example by leaving their companies and hiding themselves in the houses of cowards, joining with them to dissemble their cowardice . . ." Such men, continued Palafox, must immediately rejoin their companies or be punished by being made to run the gauntlet between 200 of their comrades and then being sentenced to forced labour for six years. Malingerers would be punished with six months' forced labour, worse offenders would be executed and the company leaders and ward mayors were ordered to show the greatest rigour and vigilance in keeping their men together. Even while copies of the manifesto were being circulated, civilians and soldiers were allowing themselves to be blown up and even burned alive rather than abandon the houses that the French were trying so desperately to capture. Some of the French officers and historians of the siege afterwards stated that Palafox's hand was being forced by his bloodthirsty and fanatical priest-advisers but there may well have been another explanation: Palafox was working night and day to organise the defence, he was physically and mentally at the end of his tether and had probably begun to suffer from fever as the contagion brought the death toll to four, five, six and even seven hundred a day.

The French dug three tunnels under the Calle de Santa Engracia towards the San Francisco monastery. Sometimes, they had to halt all work for a time as the sappers' shovels hit layers of stones and pebbles which might give the alarm to the nearby Spanish sappers as the noise could be heard quite clearly. Spanish counter-mining speeded up, there were more deadly clashes and ambushes in cellars, and sometimes grenades were hurled underground causing such dense smoke that digging had to be abandoned for several hours.

On February 10, another large mine was exploded under the "white house". Its ruins were stormed and occupied by a battalion of French infantry but, even as they retreated, the Spanish survivors hurled grenades at them, and a cannon firing from across the Coso made it impossible for the French to do anything but entrench themselves as deeply as possible in the ruins and wait for support. On the same day, a huge mine was prepared under the foundations of San Francisco.

The French engineers had intended to lay it under the main tower of the monastery church so that as this collapsed it would crush the church and the rest of the building; but as the tunnel neared completion, the French could hear Spanish sappers only a few feet away from them. After a quick check, it was found that the Spanish tunnel had already passed the French and was four yards in their rear. The order was immediately given for the head of the French tunnel to be filled with 3,000 pounds of gunpowder—the greatest amount yet used at any one time during the siege. As it was known that not only soldiers but a large number of civilians were occupying the monastery, where workshops and a powder factory had been installed, French troops advanced through the ruins of the hospital as though they were about to make an immediate attack; in this way they hoped to bring as many Spaniards as possible to the point where the mine was due to explode.

At three o'clock, the mine was set off and a vast explosion rocked the city for several hundred yards around. A large portion of the main cloister and the monks' quarters were completely wrecked but even before the last bricks and stones had fallen back to earth and the massive cloud of dust had begun to clear, the French could see that the tower was still standing. The troops ran forward and began to engage the Spaniards at bayonet point in the remaining corridors and rooms of the building, while Spanish cavalry, alerted by the explosion, gathered in the Coso and market square in anticipation of a French charge.

The French had hoped that the explosion would terrorise the defenders into surrender or retreat but no sooner had they forced their way into the building than yet another terrible, long-drawn-out, hand-to-hand battle commenced. As the French fought their way through the ruins and the rubble-strewn corridors, the Spaniards retreated to the church, and then to the roof-tops. The commander of the garrison, the Swiss–French émigré Colonel Fleury, led a band of Aragonese volunteers and civilians on to the roof of the church and the neighbouring walls. Some fired down at the French from the cornice of the great dome, others pierced holes in the vaulted roof of the church and pelted the French with stones and grenades. Fleury also held the tower and managed to harass the attackers to such an extent that, by the end of the day, the French still only controlled part of the building and were forced to entrench themselves in its ruins, piling up heaps of sandbags to block all the corridors leading to the church. On the following day, fighting was resumed among a hail of bullets and grenades from Fleury's men and a constant fall of broken masonry and tiles. Some of the French pursued the defenders across the roof-tops, often falling and slipping to their deaths. When several Spaniards were cornered, they were seen by the French to throw themselves down to the ground from a height of eighty feet rather than surrender.

Not until February 12 was the French occupation of San Francisco complete. Fleury and his men held out in the great tower, throwing down bricks and tiles when they ran out of grenades and bullets. Slowly, the French fought their way up the winding steps, stormed the top of the tower at bayonet point, and after a last struggle in the confined space hurled the bodies of Fleury and his gallant companions into the void. It was the most terrible battle that the French had yet fought for a building—even worse than the struggle for San Agustín. The horrors of this latest conquest eclipsed all those seen previously, as Lejeune described in a section of his memoirs which deserves to be quoted in its entirety. No other accounts of the siege, in which the authors mainly confined themselves to dry details of sapping operations and tactics, give such a graphic picture of the desolation and carnage experienced by both sides:

"Rarely has war ever presented a more frightful picture than that of the ruins of the San Francisco monastery during and after the assault. Not only did the violent explosion destroy half the building and the underground cellars, in which many families believed themselves to be in security against the bombardment, for it also brought death to more than 400 workers and defenders among whom perished an entire company of genadiers of the regiment of Valencia. The soil in the gardens of the Count of Fuentes (his palace was adjacent to the monastery), all the surrounding ground and roof-tops, were a horror to behold

because of the quantity of human remains with which they were strewn.
One could not take a step without treading on torn and palpitating
limbs: a great number of hands and fragments of arms separated from
their trunks showed us the whole enormity of the catastrophe.

"One of the grenadiers who had just been pursuing the Spaniards as
far as the roof of the church, where we searched the long eaves and
gutters to see whether there remained any enemies in hiding or
wounded men to succour, showed us two hideous objects from among
the débris which, at any other time, would have made us recoil with
horror. 'Look!' he cried fiercely, 'see the hands torn from the arms of
these madmen: they are quite black from the gunpowder they have
been using against us!' As he moved them with his foot to pass without
treading on them, he stretched out his hand to pick up and curiously
examine a fine head of hair which was remarkable on account of its
sheen and thickness. He thought he had picked up a woman's artificial
coiffure but promptly threw away his spoil after seeing that the beautiful ebony-coloured hair was still attached to the remains of the pale,
lacerated face of a young girl. He had seemed no less moved than we
were by this painful sight when he added furiously: 'See this stream of
blood! See the deplorable results of such obstinacy and fury!' And in
truth, the blood of several Aragonese was streaming under our feet and
along the Gothic rain-gutters which projected from the side of the
building in the forms of dragons, vultures and winged monsters. For
eight centuries, these gutters had poured down nothing but torrents of
rain. Today, in hideous contrast, they vomited floods of human blood
over the assailants."

Equally terrible scenes took place in the great church with its
beautiful stained-glass windows and high altar in brown marble with
ornate baroque baldaquin and eight Corinthian columns:

"The explosion had made a large opening in a side of the walls near
the main doorway and had wrecked the entire pavement of the nave
and cloister. In this upheaval, everything had changed place. The
cornices, the pulpit, the side altars had all fallen and were partly buried.
The tombs and the human remains confined in crypts for centuries past
had been torn away and thrown up to ground level from the depths of
the cellars. As we came through the breach, the Spaniards were already
withdrawing into the church through the sacristy. In the middle of the
wreckage, they barricaded themselves behind benches, chairs and over-
turned confessionals. Reliquaries and even fragments of the tombs

exhumed from their crypts—everything served them as a rampart behind which to hide and fire muskets. A rain of bullets came down on us from all sides. The most deadly were those from the upper organ-lofts and galleries and, especially, the small openings in one of the great pillars beside the choir which contained the staircase to the bell-tower. Happily, the breach through the main wall of the church was very wide. Our column penetrated through it with ease and the whole place was invaded. The defenders were pursued by our bayonets with great fury from their entrenchments and the side chapels on to the roofs. We climbed up behind them on the great, narrow, dangerous, spiral stair-case where they fell one by one under our blows."

Yet another Goya-esque horror confronted Lejeune when he re-turned to the church after the fighting: "From one of the shattered ancient coffins, we saw protruding the livid, fleshless face and half the body of a bishop who had been buried in his pontifical robes. His bony, dessicated arms which pointed towards us, the deep and sombre orbits of his eyes, his frightening mouth all made him appear to us as a phantom similar to the shade of Samuel as he cried out in the silence: 'Saul! Saul! wherefore do you come to trouble my tomb?' This up-heaval, this scene of carnage among the bones, and this mitred spectre which trembled as the floor shook under our footsteps was the most imposing and extraordinary aspect of this scene of desolation which met our astonished gaze."

Less impressionable than their officers, the soldiers stripped the exhumed prelates and monks of their rings and vestments. Some soldiers sat shivering in the church with dead monks' cloaks or a bishop's robes around their shoulders, others drank wine they had found in the cellars and several played handball with empty wine-sacks. The scene demanded a painter with Goya's talent for the macabre, for what could be more surreal than this deadly, claustrophobic warfare in which a nuns' oratory became a battlefield; in which monks and priests would leap to their deaths from roof-tops and walls after dashing out the brains of enemy soldiers with their crucifixes and chalices; in which a French soldier would admire a page torn from an illuminated manuscript or precious volume which formed part of his shelter, while Spanish bullets whistled over his head; in which frenzied women and sick men on stretchers prayed before the brilliantly lit Pilar chapel, while cannon balls crashed through the vaulted ceiling; and in which, as an eye-witness related, some French soldiers shuddered with superstitious horror after noticing that a marble slab used as a table for their meal was engraved with a funeral inscription? As the French continued their work of devastation, the whole city seemed to have become a living, hostile organism in which every heap of rubble could conceal a Spaniard with his knife or grenade and in which even the bodies of the dead left their graves to greet the invader with silent maledictions.

On Feburary 10, Palafox drew up a further proclamation. It was even longer than that of the previous day and contained the same underlying note of hysteria and the same suggestion that traitors were teeming in the midst of the surviving inhabitants. For the first time, Palafox mentioned the possibility that his people might abandon him, in which case "the world will blame you". Should any man give up the fight or leave his post, Palafox would no longer regard him as a son and the Pilar Virgin would withdraw her protection! Let the people stand firm, for the weak would bear "the mark of scorn on his forehead and become infamous in the eyes of God and Mankind"! Help was on the way but did the Saragossans even need it? Let them be valiant and "go up the towers, look down, count the numbers of enemies besieging us, and you will see that it is shameful to find ourselves oppressed by so few".

The French also counted their enemies. When the whole of San Francisco was cleared of Spaniards, Lejeune and other officers climbed to the top of the great bell tower and looked over the ruined city towards the cupolas and towers of the Pilar basilica. They could see gallows laden with their latest victims in the Coso, other gallows in the market square, barricades and earthworks in every street, a few carts being dragged in the direction of the river, and the inhabitants listlessly picking their way through scattered corpses, paying as little attention to them as though "they had been stones on the road". All the French observers agreed that the city now resembled nothing so much as one vast cemetery and that only the priests and women seemed to display any energy.

Appearances were deceptive. The defenders continued to show a grim determination as they beat back new French attacks. The French were unable to move through the streets and gardens between their two main sectors, long portions of the walls remained in Spanish hands, and after days of bitter fighting and heavy shelling, the French were still unable to capture the Sol gate and reduce the Tanneries district to submission. With every house they captured after days of mining, the more the resistance seemed to intensify. Another large edifice—the long, massive University building—now became a vital objective. If it were captured, then the French could not only advance to the Sol gate but past the Magdalena church towards the Archbishop's Palace and the river.

Any attack on the University would expose the French to cannon fire from a thickly sandbagged traverse which projected into the Coso from the end of a block of houses between the Calle Aljeceros and the Calle de las Arcadas. The corner house where the traverse began was therefore an essential objective for the French. The only way they could move against it was from the direction of the Calle de San Agustín, but first they had to capture the intervening blocks. On February 9, they occupied all the houses near the Coso between the Calle de San Agustín and Calle Alcover and sappers went down into the cellars to begin tunnelling towards the University building. Above them, the Spanish cannon pounded away, and on the following day there was a furious battle ending with the French still unable to pierce through the block between the Calle Alcover and the Calle Aljeceros, where the corner house was situated. The next day, the Spaniards abandoned the last few houses between the Calle Alcover and Calle Aljeceros but, when the French tried to cross the second street and attack the traverse from the rear, they could only occupy one house after a whole day of uninterrupted fighting and shelling. Finally, after a surprise night attack the French penetrated into the corner house after blowing down the door with a charge of gunpowder, but they were soon forced out again.

On February 12, the French returned to the attack, captured the house next to the vital corner house and exploded more gunpowder to open the partition wall. The result of the explosion was that their own house was ruined and the corner house now stood isolated: any attacking force would be totally without cover. Leaving the house for the time being, the French went ahead with their attack on the university. Two 500-pound mines were exploded but, as the tunnels had not been dug far enough across the Coso, they only caused slight damage to the walls. The Polish soldiers forming one of two columns brought up for the assault charged impetuously and blindly through the dust and smoke. But, when they reached the building, they could find no breach and came under such heavy grapeshot fire from the traverse that they were forced to run to their left, losing thirty-eight killed and wounded before they could take cover in the Calle de San Agustín. After this unsuccessful attempt, a twelve-pounder was dragged through the ruined streets to bombard the University.

In the left sector, the French began to break into the palaces along the Coso to the left of San Francisco but came under heavy fire from the Spanish guns. For the time being, it looked as if the French had been brought to an almost total standstill. To make matters worse for the exhausted troops, there were rumours that a large army of reinforcements had been gathered by Lazan and Francisco Palafox and was moving towards the city. Mortier's division sent word of the Spanish approach to Lannes who with a small force left Saragossa to meet them, thus still further depleting the French line of blockade and, no doubt, further infuriating Junot who was left in command.

On February 13, Palafox issued a very brief proclamation in which he mentioned the possibilities of help and of an imminent sortie. He began by congratulating the defenders of the Sol gate and University, promising them a shield of honour as well as the means to help their wives, children, and relatives, remarking that "this new proof that you are receiving the prize for your labours should serve to encourage your fellow citizens and to awaken those whom treason and perfidy have plunged into a profound slumber". As for the enemy: "No doubt, as he has learned that reinforcements are on their way to us, he runs with haste to meet them. We must help our brothers—and how easy for us this is as the enemy have left so few forces in his lines! We can seize his artillery, destroy his works and emerge from the state of apathy in which we find ourselves! We shall assemble together at the sound of the bell, and we shall take advantage of the most propitious moment of the day to execute our enterprise. Be certain that if you assemble in very great numbers, the Virgin of the Pillar, our patroness, will grant us every kind of felicity!"

The idea of a large-scale sorties was sensible, and the French army had indeed been weakened considerably. But it had always been a good idea and every historian of the siege was fully justified in expressing surprise that Palafox had never put it into practice before his city was turned into a vast graveyard; this time, not even a few hundred men were to attack the French trenches as they had in the past. It was rumoured that Palafox's two brothers had reached the town of Piña, only six hours' march away, but throughout the day of February 14, the

look-outs on the Torre Nueva continued to report that no army of
relief was in sight. Lannes's force and Mortier's division had made
Lazan's army withdraw and the besieged felt too weak to launch a
counter-attack outside the walls. Instead, while the French bombardment of all parts of the city thundered on as before and the mortality rate
soared daily, all the Spaniards could do was to fight with the fury of
despair as they swore to let themselves be buried in the ruins rather than
surrender.

The French soldiers in the city also became discouraged as the
struggle dragged on. Billon reported that the young conscripts had
become greatly adept in the art of house-fighting and made a game of
crawling across the ground to seize and bend the barrels of the Spanish
muskets as they poked out of loop-holes, but for most soldiers it seemed
that the battle would never end until they too had become buried in the
ruins together with the fanatical Spaniards. As the French slowly
edged forward into the labyrinth of alleys and side streets, these always
seemed to become narrower and the Spanish firing more deadly.
Lejeune described how "nearly every Spanish bullet was fired at almost
point-blank range. They riddled our barricades, the planks, doors,
beams and shutters behind which they thought we were sheltering. In
a few seconds, every piece of wood was pierced through and through
as though it were lace and woe betide anyone who happened to be
behind this cover . . . Often, we lacked room to place the cannons,
howitzers or little six-inch mortars in the narrow streets to which we
could only bring them after they had been dismounted. Our gunners
overcame these difficulties with incredible skill and swiftness but the
vibrations from each shot would bring windows, tiles, chimneys and
even walls crashing down on their heads . . . several batteries had to
be covered and protected with wooden planks before their safety
could be assured".

In his account of the siege, Rogniat recorded the complaints which
were circulating with increasing frequency among the battle-weary
troops. In the camp where the soldiers would recover for a few hours
after they had been relieved in the front line, they were saying: "Has
anyone ever heard of an army of 20,000 men besieging another of
50,000? We are barely masters of one quarter of this city and already
we are exhausted. We must wait for reinforcements, otherwise we shall
all perish and these cursed ruins will become our tombs before we have
forced the last of these fanatics out of their final stronghold."

Lannes, who had returned to camp, did his best to encourage his men and pointed out that the spread of sickness and the havoc caused by the bombardment could not fail to subdue the city soon, and that even if the Spaniards did manage to hold out for a few days longer, they were doomed to surrender or be buried under the ashes of Saragossa. Meanwhile, as Gazan's engineers were fast completing their approach trenches for a final assault on the suburb, spring came to the countryside. While the soldiers in the city gasped for breath among the smoke and dust of collapsing buildings or wormed their way along underground tunnels, those in the camp noticed that the weather had suddenly become much milder.

Within a few days, a premature spring descended on the Ebro valley and the soldiers outside the city were able to inhale the fragrance of wild lavender, rosemary and fruit blossoms instead of gunpowder and the stench of burning bodies. Many large oil paintings from the captured churches and monasteries had been used during the cold weather in the construction of shelters against the wind and rain. Now, they were put on display, reminding older officers of the open-air art exhibitions formerly held by young artists in the Place Dauphine in Paris. Crowds of curious soldiers inspected portraits of Christ and saints, scenes of martyrdom, baroque paradises, scenes of damnation and redemption, sugary Madonnas and Child in the style of Murillo, kneeling penitents and hermits in the style of Ribera, and huge portraits of impassive Aragonese grandees and their ladies. The Polish soldiers, being devout Catholics, were particularly impressed by the religious paintings.

No more proclamations came from Palafox's headquarters but still the incredible resistance continued. On the French left, the Spaniards set fire to a row of buildings on the Coso and shelled the French as they tried to gain the ruined, once palatial mansions of the Counts of Sastago and Fuentes. To the right of the Calle de Santa Engracia, the French made strong efforts to break into the vast palace of the Count of Aranda —a strongly garrisoned building with two corner turrets—and began to dig a mining tunnel under the narrow Calle de Santa Catalina separating them from it and which it was impossible to cross in the open. In the Coso, the French began to fire down the boulevard for several hundred yards on both sides with a gun they had brought up to San Francisco, and another battery began to pour shells down the long Calle San Gil.

The fiercest fighting was still near the Sol gate and University. A breach was blown in the wall of the University but was judged to be too low and dangerous for an assault as it opened into an amphitheatre where the Spaniards had built strong barricades, and the approach to it was always covered by the traverse on the right. It became more important than ever to take the corner house supporting the traverse but each successive attempt failed. On February 14, after a day of struggling for possession of the Calle de las Arcadas, the Spaniards counter-attacked. They climbed over the remains of the old Roman or Moorish wall with scaling ladders, and recaptured several houses which, being supported by the thick wall, were difficult to demolish by the usual means. On February 15, the French began mining towards the corner house, and several soldiers risked their lives by crawling along the shaky beams and remnants of floors in a ruined house near the old wall in an attempt to attack the traverse from the rear.

Two days after beginning their tunnel towards the corner house, the sappers had to abandon it because of sewage water which was filtering through the earth. On February 17, an eight-pound cannon was brought up after further fighting in the Calle Mayor, and placed in a courtyard where a wall concealed it from the corner house. An embrasure was pierced for the gun and, each time it was pulled back to be reloaded, the hole was plugged by sandbags to protect the gunners from the deadly aim of the Spaniards in the house. Shot after shot tore through the house but the defenders remained in occupation. Brandt was among the Polish soldiers who stood by for the attack and marvelled at the way in which the Spaniards simply moved to an upper floor as the building below them was riddled by round shot. They continued to fire their muskets and to hurl grenades at such a rate that it was impossible to advance over the open ground against them. A breach was made on the ground floor and eventually attacked by fifteen Poles after a swift dash across the street, but they were driven out of the main door by a hail of grenades, stones and bullets.

The bombardment of the house was resumed while the Poles and Spaniards continued to contest every inch of the Calle Mayor and Calle de las Arcadas. By February 18, the only progress made in the rest of the city was along one or two small streets near Santa Catalina. The French had managed to establish themselves in the palace of the Count of Sastago but ferocious cannon fire from across the Coso kept them pinned down and only able to use the house as an observation point.

On February 16, the French had also managed to pierce their way through the walls to the left of San Francisco into the Count of Fuentes's residence only to find that the house further on their left had been set on fire by the defenders. Three weeks after they had entered the city, the French were still unable to cross the Coso even though they were now continuously shelling the other side of the boulevard. Similarly, they had been unable to capture the walls and houses between the Quemada gate and the gardens of Santa Engracia or the Santa Catalina district.

As the days passed, the pattern of the fighting remained the same. Each morning, another attempt would be made to cross some side street, to attack or mine some house, and to shell the corner house and far side of the Coso into submission. The French official reports gave the same monotonous details: another barricade built, another house taken or lost, so many more pounds of gunpowder exploded, so many more killed and wounded, a few more yards of ground occupied in the maze of ruins where only the numbers and names written in charcoal on the ruined walls gave any indication of direction to the French. Of prisoners there was no mention. The Spaniards did not surrender.

How long could such a resistance continue? Another week? A month? And how long could the French keep up the attack? They only occupied one quarter of the city's area although they hammered the remains with mortars, howitzers and cannon by day and night. Even the Pilar basilica was hit. Some of the oval frescoes in the cupola were damaged, the roofs of some side chapels were pierced, rubble littered the floor of the nave and the Pilar shrine as the people prayed on; but not even this proof that their holiest of holy sanctuaries was not immune to French shells seemed to dismay the defenders.

It became obvious to the French that disease was killing off the population in huge numbers. Apart from the piles of unburied corpses which grew daily higher in front of the churches, many other victims of typhus or gangrene lay dead in the streets where they had fallen. Captured houses and their cellars were found to be filled with dead bodies. Fortunately for the living, the air was sharp and dry and sufficiently cool to prevent the corpses from decomposing and stinking. They were "light and resembled cardboard statues covered with dust", observed Lejeune. He was haunted for a long time by the sight of a room in a house which had lost its outer wall: "The explosion seemed to have come as a surprise to a father and his daughter taking their siesta after a meal, beside a little round table, still covered with several bowls. The old man, fairly well dressed and partly wrapped in his cape, was sitting in a large black wooden armchair while his fully clothed daughter was lying at his feet on a rush matting. Nothing in their features bore the imprint of suffering and for the first few days as I passed in front of this motionless scene, I could never decide whether the figures of these two dead people were real or made of wax."

A few days previously, a company of Swiss mercenaries had emerged from the Arrabal to go over to the French lines and a hundred peasants of all ages and both sexes had left Saragossa by the Portillo gate and implored the French to let them return to their villages. Lannes ordered them to be given bread and two francs each before sending them back to the city, so that they could tell the inhabitants that the French had food in abundance and were disposed to be generous—if only Saragossa would capitulate!

The French were still unable to take the Aranda palace or the corner house. Even long-captured streets remained dangerous because of Spanish snipers. When a soldier had to traverse the street, he either had to crouch behind a double row of sandbags across its width or make a sudden dash from a door or opening in the wall to one directly opposite him. Several officers who could not run fast enough were killed in this manner. Inside the Fuentes and Sastago palaces and the ruined "white house", life was no safer for, at any moment, a fanatical Spaniard was likely to run across the Coso and hurl a grenade before being shot down a few yards from his target. Sickness also spread among the French and it was impossible for them to extend their attack to the left of San Francisco or, indeed, attack any new part of the city, even if they had wanted to, since every man was needed where he was. The only point where a new attack seemed imminent was on the left bank of the Ebro.

Ever since the capture of the Jesus monastery, the French had been moving their trenches closer to the San Lazaro monastery and the small, modest houses which made up most of the suburb. Lannes crossed the river to inspect the siege works on February 17 and was nearly shot by a sniper hiding behind a pile of ruins near the Jesus. Furious at the incident, Lannes went up to the attic of the building, demanded a supply of loaded muskets, and began to shoot. A Spanish cannon-ball came through the window, hit an officer standing beside the Marshal, and cut his body in two. Lannes was widely criticised for risking his life in this foolhardy manner—"a schoolboy prank," said the soldiers in the trenches.

On the 18th, at eight o'clock in the morning, fifty-two French siege guns began to bombard the Arrabal's defences. Mortars also hurled shells across the river and several more projectiles pierced the roof of the Pilar basilica, adding to the scene of desolation inside it. The outer walls of the San Lazaro monastery, which commanded the approaches to the stone bridge, were riddled with shot, but the French noticed that each time another gaping hole was made, Spaniards would use it as a loophole for their muskets. By noon, four large breaches had been made in the flimsy walls and three assault columns were ready to leave the French trenches.

After a final salvo, the troops rushed forward by companies. On their left, after losing several men since the position was exposed to Spanish fire from the right bank, they burst into a small oil press. They massacred the defenders and then stormed a nearby house. Sitting calmly among his dead companions was a young Spanish soldier, eating peas from his pocket. After his astonished captors had surrounded him, he haughtily complained that if a French soldier who had stolen his greatcoat did not return it to him at once he would complain to the French general in command! After taking their difficult prisoner—still eating his peas—to the rear, the French advanced along the narrow streets. In one house, resistance was so fierce that they were brought to a halt for an hour until a captain and several men climbed on to the roof and broke in upon the Spaniards from the attic.

The Spanish batteries were soon outflanked and attacked from the rear, and an assault column entered the garden of San Lazaro where the Spaniards were shooting down on them from the roof of the church. Lejeune was with the attackers: "With the help of a petard we brought down the door of the church which the monks were defending to the death. Behind them, a mass of men, women and children who had not dared retreat over the bridge had taken refuge at the foot of the altar and were crying for mercy. But the smoke was too thick for us to distinguish the victims we would have wished to spare. We wreaked havoc everywhere and death alone stifled their cries and restored silence to the sanctuary. At the same time, the great staircase, the corridors and the cells of the monastery became the scene of a combat as bloody as it was stubborn. The whole monastery was taken and at that very instant we could see the monks and soldiers who had defended it leaping into the Ebro through every window." Other defenders were shot down or bayoneted as they ran towards the bridge. Daudevard de

Férussac, who was with the assault column, saw a woman with a child in her arms coming down the stairs of the monastery through thick smoke. At the bottom step, she and the child fell riddled by bullets from both sides as the fight raged around them.

The adjoining convent of Altabás was stormed by another column. Breaches had been made and the huge, wooden doors opening into the courtyard had been battered by roundshot. As they came off their hinges, a swarm of peasants rushed out of the building and held them by brute force. Another cannon ball hit the doors and sent them crashing on the defenders. More men lifted them up again, then yet another shot knocked them down. Finally, the French guns blasted away the pillars on each side and the infantry charged over the great doors and the heap of crushed corpses underneath.

The French then made their way to the head of the bridge, which was under heavy fire from their batteries, while the Spaniards began to fall back and disperse. Hundreds of civilians and armed men rushed out of the suburb along the roads which the French had blocked with patrols as well as with sandbags; others jumped in the river and began to swim across; some, braving the intense fire, piled into small boats, and many fugitives on the bridge were killed. The Baron de Versage was struck dead by a cannon ball as he ran across the bridge from the city. Others followed him in a last-minute attempt to save the suburb, as cannon shot blasted away chunks of the parapet. While the bombardment of the bridge was at its height, despite the mass of people trying to struggle across it to safety, and the French cavalry charging through the streets after the fleeing defenders, a white-haired old nun with a calm and dignified expression appeared through the smoke and dust and slowly began to walk towards the bridge, begging the French soldiers to let her rejoin her sisters and die with them. A young officer took her to Gazan who treated her with great respect. She was the sister of a famous French actor and had been a nun in Saragossa for fifty years.

The battle for the suburb soon ended. The French only used a few hundred troops for the assault, captured over 2,500 men and seventeen guns and killed several hundred Spaniards for the loss of about eighty of their own. They were now able to shell the whole of the city facing them from across the river, and to give artillery support to the soldiers attacking the Tanneries and the Sol gate.

In the afternoon, two 500-pound mines tore huge holes in the walls of the University and the building was stormed and occupied. Among its captors was the conscript Billon, nicknamed "the Rector" by his comrades after he visited the library and chose several finely-bound editions of 17th-century authors to give as presents to his superior officers. Later in the day, after at least ten attacks, the corner house by the traverse was finally captured and the traverse abandoned by the Spaniards. In the left sector, the Spaniards once again set fire to the houses to the left of San Francisco, and flames soon spread through the Fuentes and Sastago palaces.

Saragossa was now in its final agony. Palafox was seriously ill from a fever and had been evacuated to the safety of a small house in the Calle de los Predicadores near the Sancho gate. According to Casamayor, he was first taken into a chapel in the Pilar basilica so that the faithful could kiss his hand from behind an iron rail. Meanwhile, his men continued to fight to the death. In one house, where half the outer walls had been blasted away, a dozen Spaniards hurled bricks at the French until the floor under their feet collapsed. Others fell to their deaths as they made their way towards the French along the upper floors of the blazing palaces on the Coso.

Day merged into night almost unnoticed by the combatants as the flames spread and dense clouds of smoke blanketed the city. Lannes's men had already said that they seemed to be fighting for nothing more than a vast cemetery but now it seemed that the dead themselves had come to join the few remaining defenders. Often, the French soldiers would step over the body of a Spaniard who had dropped almost at their feet from a last convulsion of fever rather than a bullet or a bayonet thrust, and several Spanish sentinels, who had been sitting dejectedly at their posts, were seen to drop their muskets and slump to the ground.

The shortage of fighting men to contain the French—even in their limited sectors—had become so acute that officers raided the hospitals and dragged sick men from their beds to replace their losses. Pale and emaciated human wrecks, shivering with fever, were posted as guards for the Portillo and Sancho gates and the castle, and the men they relieved were rushed to the scene of the fighting. Later, even the sick and dying were sent into battle. Sometimes, they would lie gasping on the ground after firing a shot; sometimes, they would only have the strength to hold their muskets while lying down; sometimes they had to wait for a spasm of illness to pass before they could reload; and sometimes a poor wretch would make a suicidal dash towards a French-held house, to hurl a grenade with his last remaining strength before he collapsed. Not even the smoke, the flames and the stains of gunpowder could conceal the deadly pallor of many of the men who faced the French among the ruins and flaring embers. It was as if the whole city had died and its remains were now being defended by a legion of ghosts. Those who had escaped the sickness were wasted by hunger and thirst, and gasped for breath in the furnace-like air as they hurled themselves forward in yet another counter-attack or climbed on to the roofs and ruined walls to shoot their last bullets.

On February 19, the French managed to extinguish some fires along the Coso in spite of a strong wind, and exploded a 1,600-pound mine under the Aranda palace, subsequently occupying its ruins. After the storming of the University the previous day, they had been unable to capture the adjoining church and monastery of the Trinity which they mined during the night. In the morning, they attacked the breach and fought their way through the church, cloisters and monks' cells but were still unable to advance on the left past the Magdalena church since the Spaniards had set several houses on fire and were strongly entrenched. But the French finally occupied the Sol gate and, despite heavy firing, a Polish detachment moved forward into some houses on the Ebro quayside.

On the same day, Lannes received a letter from Palafox on his sick-bed. It was brought by an aide-de-camp to the French headquarters and constituted a reply to the Marshal's summons to surrender which he had sent on January 24. Palafox requested a three days' truce and permission to send several officers out of the city to see for themselves what the state of affairs was throughout Spain. If he then decided to capitulate, he would do so only on condition that the garrison be allowed to march out with the full honours of war and to join the nearest Spanish army, taking their baggage with them.

Lannes's reply was sharp and to the point: "General, I have just received your letter. Your propositions have irritated me in the extreme. When a man of honour like myself says a thing, one should consider his word as sacred . . . as for reinforcements, I repeat to you, on my word, that you have nothing to hope for . . ." He informed Palafox that all the Spanish armies had been defeated and then ended on a milder note: "The sentiments of the French nation are too well known by the whole world for there to be any doubt about its loyalty and generosity: I am ready to grant a general pardon to all the inhabitants of Saragossa and I offer to respect their lives and possessions."

Hostilities resumed at once in the city, but Palafox handed over all his powers to a *Junta* of thirty-three officers, churchmen and leading citizens including the heroic Mariano Cerezo and headed by the Regent of the *Real Audiencia* Don Pedro Maria Ric (he was also engaged to the Countess Bureta). There was an anguished debate throughout the night as various officers commanding the remnants of the regular infantry, cavalry, artillery, and engineers, were called upon to give their views.

The prospects for further resistance could not have been more discouraging: according to the latest count supplied by a brigadier, a mere 2,800 infantrymen were fit for duty; the cavalry only had 260 horses, and no more than 1,300 pounds of gunpowder were left. An engineering officer pointed out that the only fortifications which could still offer serious resistance were the castle, the Sancho and Portillo gates. Even then, there was a clash of opinions. Palafox had declared that the last drop of blood should be shed and the fight be continued "*hasta la ultima tapia*" (to the last wall of the last house). General Saint-March supported him, stating that unless the French launched an all-out attack on all fronts, the city could still hold out for another three or four days. Would reinforcements arrive in that time? The *Junta* decided that they would not.

Rumours spread through the city that surrender terms were being discussed. The next morning as they looked out over the city from their towers, the French could see crowds ignoring the bombardment and massing in the square by the Pilar church, and noticed that many of the men accompanied by monks, were dividing into small groups and seemed to be arguing furiously. Suddenly, the explosions of several large mines shook the city: under the Coso, sappers were completing six mining galleries to demolish all the houses on the far side.

The *Junta* continued their discussions all morning and into the afternoon. According to Manuel Cavallero, several armed civilians were guarding the few boats still moored by the quayside in order to prevent any officers or other leaders from escaping down river. At three o'clock, several Spaniards advanced towards the French with white handkerchiefs attached to their swords, and asked for Lannes to send them the same envoy who had come into the city a month previously. An hour later, the French gave orders for a cease-fire along the whole line, and the same young Saint-Marc who had spoken with Palafox in the Inquisition Palace arrived at the Carmen gate and was led blindfolded to the *Junta*. The few inhabitants in the streets still had enough strength to hurl insults after him.

Saint-Marc assured the *Junta* that Lannes would show generosity to the city if it capitulated, and its members again began quarrelling bitterly. Just as they were on the point of agreement, a huge mine was exploded in the Coso by some sappers who had failed to receive news of the cease-fire. There were cries of "treason!" and "betrayal!" and an angry crowd marched towards Palafox's house. Saint-Marc was in serious danger of being attacked and lynched until several Spanish officers bravely forced their way through the screaming mob to his side, and a messenger from Lannes hurriedly made his way to the city to express regrets for the explosion. The crowd was calmed and dispersed and the *Junta* agreed to confer with Lannes and draw up the terms of capitulation. There was nothing else that they could do: Lannes had threatened that if they did not agree to his summons within two hours, he would launch a full-scale attack at his discretion. All morning and until the cease-fire in the afternoon, the French guns had been pouring their shells into the city. According to Casamayor, it was the worst bombardment of the whole siege. But as small bands of fanatical armed men were still roaming the streets, the *Junta* decided to wait until nightfall before going to Lannes's headquarters by the Imperial Canal.

The final negotiations were soon concluded. The Spaniards insisted in vain that Ferdinand VII should be recognised and mentioned in the agreement, and that the clergy should retain all their possessions and privileges. Lannes replied by showing them maps of the city and pointing out where his sappers had laid huge mines, each of 3,000 pounds, under the Coso. He then began to dictate the terms of the surrender. The victors were generous on the whole. As the French maintained the fiction that Joseph Bonaparte was legitimate ruler of Spain, those opposing him were considered traitors instead of soldiers of a country at war, but even so Lannes granted a general pardon to the whole population. The garrison was to march out the next day with their arms and lay them down 200 paces from the Portillo gate; officers could keep their swords, the soldiers their baggage; those who swore an oath of fidelity to King Joseph would join his armies and those who refused would be taken to France as prisoners of war; all civilians were to hand over their arms; people from the countryside could freely return;

private property and religion would be respected; civil servants would take the oath to Joseph and the laws would be administered as before. The document was signed and the members of the *Junta* returned to the city. As several soldiers and civilians were still agitating for resistance to be continued, the negotiators spent the night in the castle where several prisoners, including the former Captain-General Guillelmi, were set free. At last, public excitement died down and the whole city numbly accepted the inevitable.

On February 21, at midday, the surviving defenders marched out of the Portillo gate. The French troops, wearing their best uniforms, had been drawn up in battle order, facing the river and with gunners standing beside their loaded pieces, holding lighted linstocks. Brandt and Lejeune were among those who described the appearance of the city's last, valiant defenders. Brandt was particularly surprised as the first survivors emerged from the gateway: "A certain number of young men aged between sixteen and eighteen, without uniforms, wearing grey cloaks and red cockades, and nonchalantly smoking their cigarettes lined up in front of us. Soon we saw the arrival of the rest of the army: a strangely assorted crowd composed of people of all ages, of all conditions, some in uniforms, most in peasants' clothing . . . The officers, mounted on mules or donkeys, could only be distinguished from the soldiers by their three-cornered hats and long capes. These people were all smoking and chatting and seemed highly indifferent to their imminent expatriation . . . most of them had such an unmilitary appearance that our men were saying quite loudly that we should never have had such trouble in overcoming such a rabble."

Lejeune was more compassionate as he watched the procession: "Never, perhaps, was our sight afflicted with a more sad and touching scene. 13,000 sick men bearing the germs of the contagious disease in their blood, all hideously thin, with long, black, neglected beards and with barely strength to hold their weapons, slowly dragged themselves along to the beat of the drum. Their clothes were filthy and disordered. Everything in them gave the impression of the most atrocious hardships. But a sentiment of indefinable pride still flashed across their livid countenances, blackened by gunpowder smoke and dark from anger and sadness. Brightly-coloured Spanish sashes around their waists, large, round hats crowned with a few plumes from black cockerels or vultures over their eyes, and brown mantles or mule rugs casually draped over the various costumes of the Aragonese, Catalans or Valencians, still gave a little grace and even elegance to the clothes so tattered in such a noble cause—to the discoloured rags which covered these living spectres. Their ranks were encumbered by weeping women and children who frequently turned towards the Madonna whom they still implored. At the moment when these brave men laid down their arms and handed over their flags, many of them gave vent to violent sentiments of despair. Their eyes flashed with anger and their ferocious looks seemed to be telling us that they were counting our ranks and strongly regretting that they had ever weakened before such a small number of enemies."

Although the French occupied all the gateways and placed patrols in the main thoroughfares and squares, the main body of the army was withdrawn from the city and encamped behind the trenches in order to avoid infection. The whole interior of the city, including all the areas unoccupied by the French during the fighting, was a vast open cemetery and a stinking plague pit. As the guns fell silent, dying men and women staggered out of ruined houses and cellars to die in the open, gasping in vain for fresh air in an atmosphere poisoned by smoke and the stench of decaying corpses. A few famished dogs roamed the streets and were seen to tear canvas sacks from the bodies of the plague victims and begin to devour them. 6,000 bodies were counted in the streets. There was little looting by the French or Polish soldiers: the interiors of the houses were too horrible, the survivors too pathetic. Even the normally unemotional Belmas who laboriously compiled his detailed history of the siege from official reports and first-hand eye-witness accounts felt obliged to describe the state of the city as it appeared to its conquerors:

"The city was a horror to behold. We breathed an infected air which suffocated us. The fire which was still consuming several buildings covered the sky with dense smoke. The districts in which the attacks had been pressed forward were nothing but heaps of ruins mingled with corpses and scattered human limbs. Even the houses which had been spared by explosions and fires were riddled with loop-holes or bullet holes if not damaged by bombs and shells . . . above the few walls which were still standing, portions of roofs and suspended beams and planks threatened to fall and crush anyone who went near them. All along the Coso which marked the limit of our conquest, the ground was torn up by mines and bombs; doors and windows were filled or covered with sandbags, mattresses or furniture; all the adjacent streets were obstructed with barricades and rubble . . . The hospitals had been abandoned and the patients, half naked, were wandering in the

streets. The new market place presented one of the most frightful sights:
a great number of families whose houses had been invaded or ruined,
had taken refuge under the arcades; there, old men, women and
children lay pell-mell on the pavements among the dead and the dying.
In this place of suffering we heard nothing but cries wrenched from the
living by hunger, suffering and despair."

Two days after the capitulation, Brandt was sent into the city to
collect the wine ration for his comrades and with a comrade made a
brief exploration of the city's centre. They went first to the Pilar by
way of the riverside to avoid the barricades and still-smoking piles of
ruins:

"The square before the church was one of those scenes you never
forget. It was encumbered by praying women and children, by coffins,
and by dead for whom coffins were lacking. In some places, there were
as many as twenty piled on top of each other . . . One of them was open
and contained an old man clothed in a sumptuous white uniform with
red facings. Near him, her hair in disarray, his wife or daughter—a young
woman of great beauty—was praying fervently . . . The priests could
not fulfil all their tasks although they were officiating in great numbers
and were at all the altars. The lugubrious congestion continued under
the portals, and in the aisles; the floor of the nave vanished under kneeling black figures whose sobs mingled with the psalms. Near the main
altar, I also glimpsed a few kneeling French soldiers. The smoke of
incense and from countless candles slowly rose up to the vaulted roof
riddled in many places by our projectiles.

"The Calle de Toledo was perhaps even more sinister. It had been
the principal refuge for the population of the quarters which had been
invaded and bombarded. Under its arches, there lay children, old people,
the dying, the dead, household furniture of every description, and starv-
ing domestic animals all in an indescribable confusion. In the middle of
the street there was a heap of corpses, many in a state of complete
nudity; here and there were brasiers where a few poor wretches were
cooking their food.

"The children, above all, thin and with eyes bright with fever, were
painful to see. Sombre figures, wrapped up in their great capes, were
conversing with animation but fell silent upon our approach and pre-
tended not to look at us. Since that time, I have been present at many
scenes of carnage. I have seen the great redoubt of the Moskowa, one
of the most celebrated horrors of war . . . Nowhere did I feel the

same emotion. The sight of torment is more poignant than that of death."

*   *   *

Lannes kept faith with most of the terms of the capitulation although there was one notable example of their breach. Shortly after the fighting had ended, both Santiago Sas and Palafox's old tutor, Don Basilio, were killed by French soldiers and probably under orders. Daudevard de Férussac stated that Basilio had been taken from a monastery at night and offered the opportunity to place his talents at the disposal of King Joseph. When he refused, he was bayoneted and flung into the Ebro from the bridge. Daudevard himself had seen a body floating by the bridge and was told that it was the priest's. Palafox was treated with great harshness. Even while it was uncertain whether he would live or die, officers threatened him with being shot if he did not sign documents governing capitulations in various small towns outside Sara-gossa. Orders arrived from Napoleon that Palafox was to be taken to France where he would be treated as a rebel. As soon as it was possible, he was taken away in a carriage to a long captivity in the fortress of Vincennes, where he remained until December 1813 when the Treaty of Valençay brought an end to the war.

On February 24, Lannes and his staff made their ceremonial entry into the city. A solemn *Te Deum* was sung in the Pilar basilica in the presence of many leading citizens who had been obliged to attend the occasion, but the inhabitants in the streets paid little or no attention to the magnificently uniformed French Marshal and his officers. Brandt related that at the moment of the Elevation of the Host, when the French drums rolled "as is customary in French military masses, the Spanish congregation started with surprise and horror. They had at first taken this sound for the signal for a massacre and were only re-assured when they saw the two Marshals [Lannes and Mortier] kneel devoutly".

According to Billon, although the ruins of the city were still smoking, the French were ready again for pleasure and amusement. A troupe of amateur actors and singers was formed and reinforced by a few pro-fessionals from the municipal theatre. Fêtes, concerts and even balls were held. No Spanish men attended but there were a number of ladies who explained that "they were there to divert themselves by order". Billon had been one of the soldiers guarding Palafox, and his unflattering impression of him was that "he seemed to me to be more capable of causing insomnia among the beautiful women of Aragon than Napoleon's generals."

The city was cleaned up, bands of peasants for miles around had to be requisitioned to bury the dead, and Lannes instructed his officers to calculate the cost of the whole operation. A total of 32,700 cannon balls, bombs and grenades had been fired into the city and 69,325 kilograms of gunpowder had been expended, not counting 9,500 kilograms used for mines. The French losses, according to official figures, were some 3,000 killed and wounded in the second but, as historians have pointed out, many more thousands must have died from typhus and other diseases. In all, the besiegers may well have lost 10,000 men.

In a letter to Napoleon's chief-of-staff, Berthier, written on March 19, Lannes gave the figures of the Spanish losses:

"I have made a count of persons dead in Saragossa since December 21 until February 21, the day of our entry into this city. Your Highness will see from the enclosed state of returns that 54,000 odd persons have died: it is inconceivable. Since our entry, a good 8,000 to 10,000 have died, so that this city is at this moment reduced to about 12,000 or 15,000 inhabitants. I also enclose a letter which Palafox wrote me before his departure, as well as one of his proclamations. Your Highness will see that this poor wretch lent only his name to the monks and intriguers. The former are nearly all dead; only very few are counted for each monastery and their appearance is absolutely cadaverous. It is impossible that Saragossa should ever recover; this city is a horror to behold." Two days later, Lannes left the city for ever.

The rest of Aragon was soon subdued as far as regular armed resistance went, but guerrilla warfare with all its atrocities continued to plague the French until the end of the war—as in the rest of Spain. Suchet became military governor of the city and administered it efficiently and humanely. The leader of Saragossa's last *Junta*, Don Pedro Maria Ric, married the beautiful Countess Bureta, and compiled a collection of letters and documents relating to the siege. The new ecclesiastical head of the city was the auxiliary bishop, who preached a sermon on resignation and submission to superior force after the *Te Deum* on February 24 and became notorious as a collaborator. Most of the heroes of both sieges sank back into oblivion though their names are in Spanish history books and have been given to some of Saragossa's streets. Agustina herself escaped in circumstances now unknown and was seen in uniform by Byron and others in Seville two years later. She was always greatly honoured, lived to a ripe old age and, with other Saragossan heroines, is buried in the Portillo church.

The surrendered garrison marched into captivity in France. Many died on the way and only a handful joined Joseph's forces. Did any of them wonder whether the resistance had been worth all the bloodshed, the suffering, the destruction and suicidal heroism of the last terrible month? The price of Saragossa's resistance was 54,000 dead and a city in ruins. Had it all been a futile gesture of bravado? Was Saragossa merely a symbol for the tenacious resistance of the whole Spanish people against Napoleon?

Saragossa's heroic stand *was* more than a symbol, more than an example of the legendary stubbornness of the Aragonese character, more than proof of local fanaticism and pride. Its effect on French morale was immense. It sickened many of France's best soldiers, it opened the modern era of total war and marked the beginning of the final phase in Napoleon's career. Other cities, such as Gerona, were to endure ferocious sieges, and the whole nation never wavered in its hostility towards the French for the rest of the war. Hundreds of thousands of soldiers, whom Napoleon badly needed elsewhere, had to be diverted to Spain and constituted a terrible drain on his diminishing resources. Together with the destruction of the Grand Army in the Russian campaign, the Spanish war weakened Napoleon fatally and lowered the confidence of his soldiers.

As the last survivors of Saragossa's garrison were marched to the French frontier, it might have comforted them to know that it was before the walls of their city that Napoleon's men had begun to tread the path which was ultimately and inexorably to lead them to Waterloo.

Epilogue

Little now remains of the old city of Saragossa. As always, the Pilar basilica is the main attraction for pilgrims and tourists. The Seo cathedral, the Archbishop's Palace, Palafox's palace and the stone bridge are still standing and several monasteries and convents which survived the two sieges have been preserved. The most famous relic of the fighting is the shot- and bullet-marked Carmen gate, a few hundred yards from the main railway station. With the exception of a few streets around the Pilar basilica and the Seo, the only district which has retained some of the aspect and atmosphere of the city of 1808 is precisely that where the fighting and destruction were greatest during the second siege—the area between the Plaza de San Miguel and the former monastery of San Agustín. The monastery is now a military barracks, but from the small, historic square in front of it the visitor can still see the battered tower of the church which saw such bitter hand-to-hand fighting.

Several of the nearby streets still have their old names and a few ancient houses: the Calle Palomar, the Calle de San Agustín, the Calle de las Arcadas, etc. The old Calle Quemada is now the Calle de Heroismo and the road running between the little Huerva stream and the old line of walls to the east of Santa Engracia now bears the names of Paseo de la Mina and Asalto. Several of the narrow streets behind retain a certain atmosphere of anguish and desolation and, in the Calle Palomar, a bullet-scarred corner house bears a plaque with the names of its heroic defenders and provides an excellent example of a typical Saragossan house of the period.

The Calle Pabostre, where the French and Spaniards fought so desperately for possession of a few small houses in the last days of January 1809, is now called after the heroine Manuela Sancho. The church of Santa Engracia has been entirely rebuilt but the ancient crypt with its martyrs' relics may still be visited. The Calle de Santa Engracia was widened later in the 19th century to make the Paseo de la Independencia which is now the main avenue in the city centre. To the west, the remains of the old cavalry barracks and the Aljaferia castle may be seen as well as a few 17th-century houses and mansions. The Portillo church contains the pantheon for the heroes of the sieges and the tomb of Agustina. There is a statue of Agustina and her cannon outside the church and a monument commemorating the sieges in the little square outside the Museo Provincial—the Plaza José Antonio. Otherwise, there is little to remind the historically-minded tourist of the sieges although bullet- and cannon-ball marks can be seen on the walls and façades of several buildings and churches including the Archbishop's Palace, the Pilar and Seo churches, San Felipe near the site of the old Torre Nueva, and other edifices.

Today, Saragossa is a booming industrial city attracting many American servicemen from the nearby air force base. Large parts of the city have been demolished to raise new hotels and office blocks. Even in the last century, many old landmarks and historical buildings of interest were destroyed for speculative reasons. It is sad to report that the modern city seems to show little interest in its past. There is no museum of the sieges and very few books on the subject in the main library of the city. This situation is not new.

In 1908, a *Junta del Centenario* was formed by a number of local historians and prominent citizens to commemorate the first centenary of the revolt and the sieges. It declared its aim of publishing an extensive collection of documents on the sieges but it only succeeded in bringing out a single volume of official reports by members of the French artillery corps. A leading local historian, Carlos Riba y Garcia, lamented the general lack of enthusiasm and support for the venture, declaring that "there is not in Saragossa one public or even a provincial or university library in which one can find even the most current histories of the sieges". After complaining of the lack of coordination and perseverance among the members of the *Junta del Centenario*, Riba added: "Many scholars, principally French, who have visited this city have rushed to its archives in the hope of finding a rich source of materials. Their disappointment was immense [*as was that of this author*] . . . Saragossa bears little love for its historic buildings and ruins. It allowed the demolition of the Torre Nueva and the Casa del Infante which were pages of its history and monuments of Aragonese art, unique in Spain. There is no hope that it will preserve relics when it is unable to preserve whole buildings . . . Less barbaric than the pick-axes wielded on behalf of sordid self-interest, the French shells respected the historic Torre Nueva."

Strangely enough, there is no large square or important street bearing the name of José Palafox—only a military barracks near the University City.

*   *   *

Palafox's subsequent career after his release from captivity in the fortress of Vincennes in 1813 illustrates the tragedy of Spain's history in the last 160 years. He followed Ferdinand VII back to Spain and was confirmed in his post of Captain-General of Aragon and made a member of a commission to reorganise the Spanish army. Palafox came out in support of the liberal Constitution adopted by Spain and which the odious Ferdinand repudiated, and published a proclamation condemning the campaign of persecution launched by the King. He was deprived of his titles and rank and retired to his estates for several years. In 1823, French troops again entered Spain after Louis XVIII had decided to support the same despicable King whom Napoleon had deposed and imprisoned fifteen years previously. This must have been one of the bitterest and most ironic moments in Palafox's life!

Palafox was later made Duke of Saragossa, became Captain General again and a senator to the Spanish parliament. He supported the rights of the infant Queen Isabella II when the first Carlist War broke out leading to a series of military dictatorships during her long reign. He died in Madrid in 1847.

In 1936, Saragossa joined General Franco's side during the Civil War but escaped fighting and serious damage.

SELECT BIBLIOGRAPHY

Alcaide Ibieca (Agustin), *Historia de los dos sitios que pusieron á Zaragoza en los años de 1808 y 1809 las tropas de Napoleon.* 3 vols. Madrid, 1830, 1831.

Daudebard (Also known as Daudevard) de Férussac (André Etienne), *Journal historique du siège de Saragosse.* Paris, 1816.

Beauchamps (Alphonse de), *Collection de mémoires relatifs aux révolutions d'Espagne.* 2 vols. Paris, 1824.

Belmas (J.), *Journaux des sièges faits ou soutenus par les Français dans la péninsule de 1807 à 1814*, Vol. II, Paris, 1836.

Billon (François), *Souvenirs d'un Vélite de la Garde sous Napoleon Ier.* Paris, 1905.

Bourgoing (Jean-François de), *Modern State of Spain.* 4 vols. London, 1808.

Brandt (Heinrich von), *Souvenirs d'un officier polonais. Scènes de la vie militaire en Espagne et en Russie, 1808–1812.* Paris, 1877.

Casamayor y Zeballos (Faustino), *Los Sitios de Zaragoza, Diario de Casamayor, etc.* Saragossa, 1908.

Cavallero (Manuel), *Défense de Saragosse ou Relation des deux sièges soutenus par cette ville en 1808 et 1809.* Paris, 1815.

Chevillard (Jean-Baptiste), *Souvenirs d'Espagne (1808)* in "Revue de Paris", July–August, 1906.

Clerc, (J. C.), *Guerre d'Espagne, Capitulation de Baylen, etc.* Paris, 1903.

Desdevises du Dézert (Georges N.), *L'Espagne de l'ancien régime.* 3 vols. Paris, 1897–1904.

Documentos del Ejercito frances, sitiador de Zaragoza (1808–1809), exhumados por G. Garcia Arista. Saragossa, 1910.

Farias (Rafael), *Memorias de la guerra de la Independencia, escritos por soldados franceses.* Madrid, 1919.

Fischer (Christian Augustus), *Travels in Spain in 1797 and 1798.* London, 1802.

Foy (Maximilien S., Count), *Histoire de la guerre de la Péninsule sous Napoleon, etc.* 4 vols. Paris, 1827.

François (Charles), *Journal du Capitaine François*, 2 vols. Paris, 1903.

Garcia Mercadal (José), *Palafox, Duque de Zaragoza, 1775–1847.* Madrid, 1948.

Geoffroy de Grandmaison (C. A.), *L'Espagne et Napoleon.* 3 vols. Paris, 1908.

Gille (Philippe, *ed.*), *Mémoires d'un conscrit de 1808.* Paris, 1892.

Gomez de Arteche y Moro (José), *Guerra de la Independencia. Historia militar de España de 1808 y á 1814.* 14 vols. Madrid, 1868–1903. (For the background to the Spanish revolt and the sieges: vols. I, II, and III).

Grasset (A.), *La Guerre d'Espagne*, 1807–1813. Vols. 1–3. Paris, 1914–1932.

Herr (Richard), *The 18th century revolution in Spain.* Princeton, U.S.A., 1958.

Laborde (A. L. J. de), *A View of Spain*. 5 vols. London, 1809.

Lejeune (Louis François, Baron), *Mémoires de général Lejeune*. 2 vols. Paris, 1895.

Lovett (Gabriel H.), *Napoleon and the Birth of Modern Spain*. 2 vols. New York, 1965.

Lucas-Dubreton (J.), *Ce qu'a vu Goya. Napoleon devant l'Espagne*. Paris, 1946.

Napier (William), *History of the War in the Peninsula and in the South of France from . . . 1807 to . . . 1814*. 6 vols. London, 1828–1840. (Vols. I and II only).

Oman (Charles), *A history of the Peninsular War*. 5 vols. Oxford, 1902–1914. (Vols. I and II only).

Palafox (José de), *Autobiografía*. Taurus Ediciones (Temas de España). Madrid, 1966.

Pano y Rueta (Mariano), *La Condesa de Bureta . . . Episodios y documentos de los sitios de Zaragoza*. Saragossa, 1908.

Peréz de Guzmán y Gallo (Juan), *El Dos de Mayo de 1808 en Madrid*. Madrid, 1908.

Riba y Garcia (Carlos), *Lo que se ha escrito sobre los sitios de Zaragoza*. Saragossa, 1911.

Rogniat (*Baron*), *Relation des sièges de Saragosse et de Tortose par les Français*. Paris, 1814.

Schepeler (Andreas), *Geschichte der Revolution Spaniens und Portugals, etc.* 2 vols. Posen and Bamberg, 1826–1827.

Tascher (Maurice de), *Journal de campagne d'un cousin de l'Impératrice, 1806–1813*. Paris, 1933.

Thiers (Louis Adolphe), *Histoire du Consulat et de l'Empire*. Paris, 1845–1862.

Torcal (Norberto), *Historia popular de los sitios de Zaragoza*. Saragossa, 1908.

Toreno, Count of (Queipo de Llano y Ruiz de Saravía), *Historia del levantamiento, guerra y revolución de España*. 4 vols. Madrid, 1848.

Townsend (Joseph), *A Journey through Spain, etc.* London, 1971.

Vaughan (Charles Richard), *Narrative of the Siege of Saragossa*. London, 1809.

Index

Abad, Don Miguel, 105, 129

Abrantès, Duc d', *see* Junot

Abrantès, Duchess d', 13, 14, 17, 44, 52, 70

Aguila, Count of, 43

Agustina, *see* Zaragoza

Alagon, 80–1, 82, 83, 87, 105, 109, 182, 183, 187, 189, 194, 195

Albalat, Count of, 43

Alcala, 49

Alcañiz, 211

Alcolea, 98

Alexander I, Czar, 169

Alfonso I (the Warrior), K. of Castile, 53

Alfranca, 61, 150

Algeciras, 47

Almeria, 58

Andalusia, 31, 40, 42, 47, 72, 77, 96–8, 100, 110, 130, 135, 136, 137, 140, 166

Andujar, 97, 132–3, 135–6

Antonio, Don (brother of Charles IV), 11, 29, 30, 34, 35, 54, 60

Aragon, 5, 42, 44, 47, 49, 50, 52–3, 57, 60, 65, 66, 67, 68, 69, 70, 72, 73, 74, 77, 78, 106, 108, 109, 123, 128, 129, 139, 170, 171, 198, 211, 220

Aranda, Count of, 14, 17–18, 49, 252, 255

Aranjuez, 12, 29, 31, 32, 33, 54, 59, 167, 169, 175

Arteche (Gomez de Arteche y Moro, José), 67, 194, 200

Asturias, 40, 72, 77

Austria, 3, 22, 109, 168, 169

Badajoz, 12, 40

Barcelona, 4, 12, 26, 47, 54, 72, 73, 79, 106

Barcelona, Count of, 58

Baylen, 97, 102, 133, 135, 136, 137, 138, 162, 166, 168, 170, 175

Bayonne, 30, 32, 33, 34, 39, 41, 55, 57, 59, 60, 62, 69, 74, 76, 96, 97, 104, 106, 111, 123, 169

Bazancourt, General, 143, 146, 147

Beauharnais, Comte de, 29

Belair, General Ligier, 100

Belchite, 83, 107, 115

Belliaud, General, 132, 162

Belmas, Jean, 116, 155, 157, 161, 193, 216, 232, 263

Belvedere, Duke of, 169

Berthier, Prince Louis Alexandre, 104, 113, 206, 266

Bessières, Marshal, 27, 71, 73, 130, 131, 168

Beurnonville (Fr. amb. to Spain), 70

Bidassoa river, 3

Billon, François, 155, 159–61, 242, 251, 258, 265–6

Blake, General, 72, 130, 169, 206

Blaze, 131

Boggiero, Basilio, 58, 59, 187, 229, 265

Bonaparte, Joseph, ix, 30, 39, 41, 55, 108, 131–2, 138, 165, 168, 169, 175, 261–2, 267

Bonaparte, Louis, 30

Bonaparte, Lucien, 21

Bonaparte, Napoleon, 21, 41, 110, 138, 183, 188; Saragossa and, *see* s.v.; Spain and, 8, 9, 10, 20, 21, 22–5, 27, 29, 31, 32, 37, 39, 41, 42, 43, 44, 47, 70–2, 131, 132; Jena victory, 22–3; Ferdinand and, 24, 26, 27, 29–31, 33, 39, 60, 63; at Bayonne, 55, 68, 74, 96, 104, 111, 123; Palafox and, 65, 68, 73, 104; encourages Joseph, 131; Dupont and,